T0340376

## Access your online resources

*Behaviour Barriers and Beyond* is accompanied by a number of printable online materials, designed to ensure this resource best supports your professional needs

Activate your online resources:

Go to www.routledge.com/9780367704292 and click 'Support Material'

# Behaviour Barriers
# and Beyond

This practical resource helps school staff to reframe behaviour as a means of communicating a need, ensuring they can sensitively and effectively support children with a range of Social, Emotional and Mental Health (SEMH) needs and Special Educational Needs and Disabilities (SEND).

With case studies and examples woven throughout, the book focuses on relational and strength-based approaches to improve mental health and wellbeing, self-esteem, sense of safety and, in turn, behaviour and educational outcomes. All advice is carefully designed to have the maximum positive impact on the child and minimum impact on teacher time and resources.

Key features include:

- Accessible explorations of a range of difficulties and their effects on school life
- A variety of supportive strategies, tips and advice, designed to be easy to implement effectively within a busy classroom
- A focus on building and maintaining positive relationships, making the classroom a safe learning environment

Small adjustments can make a huge difference to wellbeing, whether they are for those with a diagnosis, with SEND, with SEMH needs, with anxiety, or just those having a hard time. This book will be an essential tool for teachers, SENCOs and school leaders in both mainstream and specialist settings.

**Rachel Thynne** qualified as a teacher at Bath College of Higher Education (now Bath Spa University) in 1996. Since then she has taught in both mainstream and specialist settings, in the UK and Malaysia. She has taught from Nursery to Key Stage 3 and has also taught children with English as an Additional Language.

Rachel is currently the Outreach Lead in an outstanding, attachment-aware specialist provision for pupils with SEMH needs. She works with staff in local mainstream schools, from early years to Key Stage 4, specialising in providing training, advice and guidance from whole school level through to planning for individual pupils in order to provide support for the effective inclusion of pupils with SEMH needs in school.

Rachel is also a Specialist Leader in Education for Behaviour and Special Educational Needs, working with school leaders to develop inclusive practices and remove barriers to learning to help children to flourish.

Rachel lives in Dorset, UK, with her husband, two children and her little dog Milo and loves going for walks in the countryside and at the beach.

# Behaviour Barriers and Beyond

## Practical Strategies to Help All Pupils Thrive

Rachel Thynne

Routledge
Taylor & Francis Group

LONDON AND NEW YORK

First published 2022
by Routledge
2 Park Square, Milton Park, Abingdon, Oxon OX14 4RN

and by Routledge
605 Third Avenue, New York, NY 10158

*Routledge is an imprint of the Taylor & Francis Group, an informa business*

*British Library Cataloguing-in-Publication Data*
A catalogue record for this book is available from the British Library

*Library of Congress Cataloging-in-Publication Data*
Names: Thynne, Rachel, author.
Title: Behaviour barriers and beyond : practical strategies to help pupils thrive in school /
    Rachel Thynne.
Other titles: Behavior barriers & beyond
Description: First Edition. | New York : Routledge, 2022. | Includes bibliographical
    references and index.
Identifiers: LCCN 2021025123 (print) | LCCN 2021025124 (ebook) | ISBN 9780367704308
    (Hardback) | ISBN 9780367704292 (Paperback) | ISBN 9781003146292 (eBook)
Subjects: LCSH: Behavioral assessment of children. | Classroom management. |
    Communication in education. | Problem children—Behavior modification. |
    Teacher-student relationships.
Classification: LCC LB1124 .T49 2022 (print) | LCC LB1124 (ebook) | DDC 371.102/4—dc23
LC record available at https://lccn.loc.gov/2021025123
LC ebook record available at https://lccn.loc.gov/2021025124

ISBN: 978-0-367-70430-8 (hbk)
ISBN: 978-0-367-70429-2 (pbk)
ISBN: 978-1-003-14629-2 (ebk)

DOI: 10.4324/9781003146292

Typeset in DIN
by Apex CoVantage, LLC

Access the Support Material: www.routledge.com/9780367704292

*This book is dedicated in memory of my beloved mum,
Georgina Clare Watts. She was incredibly proud when she
knew it was going to be written and published and
so looking forward to having a signed copy on her shelf.
She sadly died in October 2020, before it was completed.
Endless love Mum and thank you for the memories.*

# Contents

# Foreword
## by Dr Pooky Knightsmith
*(internationally respected specialist in child and adolescent mental health, keynote speaker, lecturer, trainer and author)*

Having been aware of her work for some time, I had the pleasure of interviewing Rachel for my podcast recently when we explored the topic of how we can engage learners who lack confidence and motivation. I was inspired by Rachel's approach to the topic, a combination of gentle but persistent challenge of common viewpoints and highly practical and actionable strategies. Throughout our conversation and throughout her wider work, Rachel's depth and breadth of experience shone through; it's evident that the ideas she shares have been tried and tested at the chalkface and you need never fear that these are ideas that sound fine on paper but could never work in practice.

Having picked her brains thoroughly and finding my own practice infused with her ideas in the subsequent weeks, I could not wait to get my hands on the draft for her book. *This* book ... and now it's here. It does not disappoint. From the very first pages, I could imagine what a huge impact that this book could have on the lives of the children and young people lucky enough to be supported by a practitioner who reads it and lives it. Rachel has been so generous in her curation and sharing of ideas and has done tremendous work to translate research into practice, to test out that practice, and to refine her ideas into a wide range of simple strategies that we can all build into our day-to-day to help us better understand and respond to the behavioural needs of children, and in turn to help them better understand and respond to those needs themselves, too.

I love the checklists throughout this book; they give clear calls to action following each chapter, as well as acting as a great summary of what you've read and helping you to reflect on what might work and what might not with a particular child you have in mind. I also think that Rachel's approach of sharing general principles and ideas that are broadly applicable in her opening chapters before drilling down into the specifics of helping children with particular experiences, traits or diagnoses is a very helpful approach. Whilst many of us prefer to see the child than the label, knowing that we can quickly flick to, for example, the ADHD chapter or the FASD chapter when looking for ideas for working with a child with a specific need, is deeply reassuring.

The range of needs that Rachel addresses in this book is impressive and the care that has been taken to share information and ideas tailored to a range of scenarios and needs is remarkable. Whilst I think that every chapter in this book is merit-worthy, the chapter about supporting children who've been bereaved is especially so. This felt, to me, like a fresh perspective on grief and one that will provide adults with the guidance they need to help children navigate loss and bereavement with children in a way that is supportive without being stifling. This is vital as it will give children the space, skills and permission they need to process grief healthily. This chapter stood out for me both because it was unexpected in a book about behaviour and because it meets a huge need during these times of pandemic-induced death and separation.

Behaviour is a bit of a hot topic at the moment and, bluntly, the way that those leading on behaviour are behaving towards and about each other leaves a lot to be desired. With her approach of quiet curiosity, evidence-based, practised and tried and tested ideas that will make a difference to the adults and children who need them most, I hope that Rachel and this book will skirt around the big debates and just quietly get on with changing the worlds of many individuals. It's fantastic, I love it, I'll live it. I hope you will too.

# Acknowledgements

Huge thanks to my family and friends, who have heard very little of anything apart from this book, for the last nine months. Particular thanks to my husband Paul for his support and relentless chapter-reading, my daughters Amelia and Elena for being fabulous in every way and teaching me something new every day, and to Milo our dog; many chapters have been typed, one-handed, with him pinned to my lap. Also, thank you to my sister Emily, for always being at the end of the phone or text.

Enormous thanks need to be given to Ginny and Alisa, my colleagues and friends, for their invaluable advice and support throughout this process. Thank you also to Tina for her knowledge, insight and ideas, as well as her continued support and valued friendship. Sophie, thank you for your friendship and for such positive feedback on the bits you read. Everyone needs a Sophie to be their champion!

Thanks to Gavin, my fabulous boss, for his unwavering support, advice and infinite wisdom. It's amazing how much work can be done fuelled by coffee and chocolate.

Thanks to Jemma and Natasha for their support, right at the beginning of this process, believing in me and seeing the value in a book such as this and helping to get this project started.

It would never, ever have crossed my mind that I could undertake this task without Dorothy, who believed in me way before I believed in myself and imparted so many words of wisdom as my mentor and friend when I started working in Outreach.

Thank you to Julie at Mosaic Family Support for her time and invaluable advice and to Rachel at Barrowford School for chatting to me and proving that everything I always believed in really could happen!

A huge thank you to the fabulous Pooky for her support and for writing the most amazing foreword *ever*.

Thank you to Clare, Leah and all the staff at Taylor & Francis who have believed in me, offered advice and written the loveliest emails each step of the way.

And, last, but by no means least, thank you to all the wonderful schools I work in, to the SENDCOs, leaders, teachers and support staff who have embraced all strategies with enthusiasm and worked tirelessly to implement the advice and suggestions offered and have, over the years, fed back what works effectively and provides maximum impact for our most vulnerable pupils.

# Introduction

This book came about because I wanted to share strategies and ways of working which I wish someone had told me earlier in my career. The areas of need discussed in these chapters are not always covered in teacher training programmes or with continued professional development, meaning staff need to support pupils with a variety of needs, often without any specialist training. Furthermore, behaviour is reported to be one of the most stressful concerns for school staff. This book has the information all in one place; tried and tested advice, ideas and strategies which can quickly and easily be implemented in a busy and ever-complex classroom with very little time and few resources needed. I also signpost towards further reading and resources in the 'tool kits' at the end of each chapter. Case studies are included, to emphasise key points or provide context and encourage reflective thinking. All case studies are based on real circumstances, but names and certain information have been changed to provide anonymity.

Positive mental health and wellbeing, for adults and young people, is essential for pupils to succeed and flourish socially, emotionally and academically. The advice in this book has pupils' Social, Emotional and Mental Health (SEMH) needs at the forefront and focuses on how to support them to thrive within the school setting, by providing for their individual needs.

Approaches within this book reflect behaviour as communication and an attempt to meet a need. They are child-centred, attachment-aware and 'trauma-infused' (Treisman, undated), with relationships at the heart. I aim to reframe the language of behaviour from 'challenging' to 'stressed' or 'distressed' behaviour, encouraging staff to look beyond behaviour to see the child underneath and offer support in an empathic and nurturing way. It is essential to understand and get to know the whole child beyond any diagnosis. It is also important to understand the

DOI: 10.4324/9781003146292-1

difficulties that those pupils may encounter in order to provide support and make necessary adjustments to help all children to thrive. Changes made for individual pupils can have an enormous, positive impact on the whole class, and although I link strategies to a range of diagnoses and difficulties that pupils experience in our schools, the advice and strategies will be relevant for all pupils, not solely those with a diagnosis.

I have taught for 25 years in both mainstream and specialist settings, primarily in the UK but also for five years in Malaysia. Making the move, after 18 years of teaching in mainstream schools, to teach in a residential specialist provision for pupils with moderate and complex learning and SEMH needs was deeply rewarding and a hugely steep learning curve. Working with the amazing pupils there reinforced for me the value of relationship, the importance of positive communication and language, getting to know the person behind their behaviour and focusing on their individual strengths. I am currently the Behaviour Outreach Lead Teacher and a Specialist Lead in Education (SLE) in an outstanding, attachment-aware, specialist provision for pupils with SEMH needs, where I have worked for the last six years.

As part of my Outreach role, I work in mainstream schools, from Early Years to Key Stage 4, observing pupils and classroom interactions, advising and supporting staff to implement strategies, as well as delivering training in order to help pupils with a variety of behaviour presentations and SEMH needs. I have seen and experienced the range of difficulties faced by pupils and school staff. Within this book, I have included the main areas with which I am asked to support and advise. The suggested strategies are research- and evidence-based and are those that I have seen working effectively within mainstream classrooms. They are easy and quick to implement and have repeatedly been observed to have had the greatest impact on pupil outcomes, when used consistently.

Our classrooms are busier than ever, with an increasing number of pupils presenting with a variety of complex needs, as well as difficulties arising from trauma, adversity and SEMH needs. School staff are stretched in terms of their time. Stress and workload are ever-increasing. I aim to give staff the strategies that have the maximum positive impact on pupils whilst having the minimum impact on precious time and resources.

At the time of writing, the majority of pupils in the UK are returning to school following the global pandemic, Covid-19. Expectations, boundaries and ways of working changed significantly, with the majority of pupils spending a large proportion of time learning from home. Now, more than ever, school staff require consistent, trauma-infused strategies to ensure that pupils can attend school, with staff meeting their SEMH needs effectively, as well as ensuring that all pupils are emotionally ready for learning. The impact will continue for years to come and mental health and wellbeing needs to be a priority.

Anxiety for school staff, pupils and families is currently running high and additional pressures in terms of behaviour and results will continue. This book will support staff to put effective strategies and approaches in place to meet the needs of all the pupils within their class and the wider school as well as offer regulation strategies.

In addition, it will give a clear overview of a range of specific needs, the symptoms associated with each difficulty or diagnosis and the challenges our pupils may face in school because of different experiences or neurodiversity. Each chapter will offer a range of classroom management techniques which can be quickly and easily implemented to sensitively support each of these pupils in school.

The first two chapters are 'Behaviour is communication' and 'Self-regulation' and will support all pupils. I would strongly recommend reading these first and implementing these strategies alongside any other chapters used. Most chapters include a strength-based approach and focus on difference rather than deficit. Pupils presenting with different behaviours in school quickly get into a negative spiral which is difficult to get out of. By focusing on strengths and reframing behaviours, the situation can quickly and simply seem much more positive for the pupil, caregivers and staff members.

At the end of each chapter is a checklist, to be used as a quick reminder. It is not intended that all the strategies are implemented at once (which would be completely overwhelming for both staff and pupil!). Many strategies you will have already tried and have in place and you can just tick them off; others you may have tried and decided are not for you or the pupil, which you can cross off. Hopefully, that will leave a few that you would like to try now, some you may have tried in the past and wish to re-visit and some you may try in the near future. I would highlight two or three to put in place straight away, but, obviously, use them in the way you feel most effective. It is important to give it a good few weeks before deciding if it is working or not. It generally takes about two months for new strategies and alternative behaviours to become embedded and fully effective.

I hope you find it useful. Happy reading!

# References

Treisman, K. in Barnardo's (undated) *The A–Z of Childhood Adversity Jargon Buster* [online] Available at: https://proceduresonline.com/trixcms1/media/8082/tx330-a-z-of-childhood-adversity-jargon-buster.pdf [Accessed 13 February 2021]

# Chapter 1

# Behaviour is communication

Throughout this book, the key message is that behaviour is a form of communication. It is essential to see beyond the behaviour to its underlying function (such as anxiety, stress, tiredness, hunger, adversity, trauma, a basic need, sensory overload, communication difficulties, or a lack of understanding or skill). Be curious as to why the pupil is behaving in a certain way. A useful, popular analogy is to picture behaviour as an iceberg. The behaviours observed are just the tip of that iceberg (the symptom of the problem rather than the underlying problem); what lies beneath is a range of thoughts, emotions and triggers driving those behaviours. Once the behavioural function is understood, then support can be provided for any fear or anxiety beneath the behaviour and necessary skills can be taught.

Relationship and connection are of fundamental importance in understanding the person behind their behaviours, supporting empathically and giving pupils the skills needed to regulate their emotions and communicate their needs more effectively.

Let's look at *challenging behaviours* by *challenging* typical or traditional views of those behaviours. By reframing negative language and perceptions around behaviour, the ethos becomes more positive, enabling children to get their needs met more readily with empathy and understanding. Let's view 'challenging behaviour' as 'distressed behaviour' or a 'stress response' or as 'anxious' or 'overwhelmed behaviour' instead. The perception changes to one where a child is not

DOI: 10.4324/9781003146292-2

deliberately being 'difficult'; they are 'dysregulated' or 'stressed' and are communicating that dysregulation or stress. By changing the language used, adults often have more capacity to be compassionate and empathic, understanding that pupils are not deliberately behaving in a certain way but are communicating that something is very wrong.

Behaviour is an attempt to meet a need. As well as looking at the communicative function of behaviours, it is important to be aware of the needs the pupil is meeting by their actions, for example, are they anxious, afraid, gaining adult time and attention (positive or negative, it is still attention), avoiding a task, lacking a skill or seeking co-regulation? Can adults support pupils to ensure they get those needs met in a more appropriate way? Their behaviour will not change if that behaviour is meeting a need unless they are given an alternative means to get that need met. 'Children's behaviour is not good or bad. It's just how they show us their emotional and developmental needs' (Evans, 2018).

Below is a range of strategies that have been tried and tested and found to support pupils who communicate through different behaviours in school. There is a checklist at the end of this chapter.

## *A strength-based approach*

- Value difference and neurodiversity. Focusing on what each pupil can do, their strengths, achievements and successes, is essential in preventing pupils from getting into a negative spiral, in building self-esteem and changing the way adults view and respond to them. Encourage pupils to share, develop and build on strengths, interests and knowledge and offer roles and responsibilities around these to boost self-esteem.
- Reframing language around behaviour into positives helps adults effectively support pupils compassionately and empathically and helps pupils to view themselves much more positively. 'If we learn to focus on what's right with a person rather than what's wrong we will make leaps forward in creating thriving people and flexible environments in which everyone can bring their talents to bear and positively contribute to their classroom, family, future employer, and community' (Peters, 2015). As discussed, 'challenging behaviour' can be reframed as 'stressed' or 'distressed' behaviour, 'inappropriate behaviour' may be 'dysregulated behaviour'. 'Hard to reach' can be reframed as 'that child who I've been unable to build a relationship with yet' and 'difficult to engage' becomes 'I haven't found a way to ignite their spark yet?' (Finnis, 2021, p.66).

In further language reframes 'won't' becomes 'can't yet', 'melt-downs' are seen as 'panic-attacks' or 'crisis points', 'attention-seeking' becomes 'connection-seeking' or 'attachment-needing', 'stubborn' could be 'determined', 'always calling out' is 'enthusiastic', 'can't sit still' is 'energetic'. See Attention Deficit Hyperactivity Disorder (ADHD) chapter for more examples of specific behaviour reframes.

## *Relationships and communication*

The most important resource available in school is a nurturing, empathic relationship with a trusted adult. 'The latest neuroscience findings underscore and evidence what we've really always known: we are designed to function best in relationship' (Bombèr, 2020).

- Build genuine, understanding, trusting, engaged relationships with the pupils, attuning to their needs to develop their sense of self-worth and feelings of belonging. As Finnis (2021, p.26) advocates: 'remember their birthday ... brag about them outrageously to others ... be their biggest cheerleader ... believe in them'. Regular check-ins and positive interactions between staff and pupils support children to feel safe, learn and have their needs met appropriately, thus improving behaviour. 'When students feel liked, respected and trusted by their teachers, they find more success in school, academically and behaviourally' (Finnis, 2021, p.20). See p.65 for more information on relationships and the PACE approach.
- Relationships within the school, among school staff, are important for staff and pupil wellbeing. Through adult modelling of positive relationships and interactions, pupils learn about positive relationships and interactions. The way staff communicate to and about others is essential and can create a positive atmosphere which is reflected through the whole school. This is not only through our language, but our entire way of being. Finnis (2021, p.18) discusses how the mindset of pupils and the wider school community is affected by 'the look on our faces, the way we greet each other, our tone of voice and our body language, as much as through the things we actually say. It's about how we talk among ourselves, how we are there for each other. It's about the weather we create around us.'
- Relationships extend beyond the school. Form a positive partnership with caregivers to work collaboratively. Aim for genuine, trusting, reciprocal connections. Regularly share the pupil's successes and strengths and build rapport before discussing

concerns or strategies and open up channels of conversation for shared problem-solving.

■ Involve the pupil in the planning process and in finding solutions, where appropriate, so that they feel involved and included and can communicate their concerns and suggestions.

■ Use direct (unambiguous), positive language, focusing on moving the pupil on (rather than on the negative behaviours). State the behaviours that you would like to see, instead of those that you don't; for example, say 'put your feet on the floor' rather than 'take your feet off the chair' or 'put the ball on the floor' rather than 'don't throw the ball'.

---

**Personal case example:**

I will always remember taking my class of excited Year 1s on a school trip. As I stated, 'don't all push to the back of the bus', I could almost see light dawn as they all thought 'oh, yes, let's get a seat at the back, quick', and my lovely calm line of children rapidly descended into chaos. Ever since then, I simply state, 'fill up the seats from the front first'. I tell them what I do want, rather than what I don't want!

---

■ Pick your battles. Avoid confrontations, negotiations and power struggles. Dix (2017, p.112) advises remaining focused on the expected behaviours to avoid getting drawn into *secondary behaviours* intended to provoke a reaction. For example, if a pupil is asked to take their hat off and they do so, with grunting, groaning and moaning, they have still taken their hat off (complied with the request); aim not to get drawn into a downward spiral about the groaning, but thank them for following the instruction and move on. Secondary behaviours can always be addressed later, if necessary, but might be better tactically ignored altogether.

■ 'You will get more of the behaviour you notice the most' (Dix, 2021, p.2). Focus on positive behaviour and 'catch the pupil being good', praising the small steps towards success. For example, if a student is sitting down, shouting across the class to their friend, an appropriate response might be, 'Meera, fabulous, you are sitting in your space and ready to learn, now eyes on me and use your indoor voice, thanks'.

■ Alternatively, start with a positive, before giving an instruction, such as, 'Chris, lovely shiny shoes today, very smart, now tuck your shirt in too, thank you'. (*Thank you* suggests you expect compliance rather than *please*, which can imply that there is an element of choice.) Pupils are more likely to comply and less likely to come back with a negative or aggressive response when faced with a positive comment first.

■ Positive feedback produces dopamine in the brain, making a person feel positive and motivated to repeat the experience (Kaufman, 2020). A study at De Montfort University developed the *5 Praises a Day* initiative, finding that children praised at least five times a day by caregivers were better behaved, appeared calmer, could concentrate for longer and listen more carefully than those who did not receive the same levels of praise. From personal observation, these results appear to be reflected in the classroom situation. Be specific and tell pupils what they have done well instead of a vague 'well done'. Praise for things that they have control over, such as effort, kindness, manners and behaviours for learning, rather than test results or correct answers. Focus on the small steps towards success: 'Jade, fabulous, I can see your pencil is in your hand ready to start the first question, let's get those ideas down on paper now' rather than 'Jade, why haven't you started your writing yet?'

■ The importance of positive relationships is summarised by Treisman (2017), who states 'every interaction is an intervention'. Aim for ten positive interactions or comments for every (perceived) negative.

■ Offer two or three clear positive choices to increase a pupil's feeling of control; for example, 'what are you going to use to do your writing task, your favourite handwriting pencil, my special pen or the pencil with the yellow pencil grip?' Include choices around where they will work, who with, which equipment to use, which paper to use or how the task or learning objective will be carried out. It is within the teacher's parameters but allows flexibility and ownership for the pupil.

■ Avoid inadvertently reinforcing cycles of negative or inappropriate behaviour and support pupils to find an alternative means of getting their needs met. Explore what the pupil is gaining (sensory break, adult time, support for a task or developing a skill) and be creative in providing this for them proactively and positively before they need to escalate their behaviours. Avoid the pupil needing to escalate behaviour to gain attention. Go over to them when they are making the right choices (or taking steps towards the right choices).

**Case study:**

Kelly-Anne was a Year 2 pupil. Her class were regularly being evacuated as she was throwing equipment and turning over tables daily. Each time this happened, the SENDCO (Special Educational Needs and Disabilities Coordinator), deputy head and often the headteacher would support her. It often took well over an hour for her to calm down with the senior staff members, only for it to happen again later or the next day. The most effective calming strategy seemed to be for her to go outside on the scooter, although it was often difficult to get her back inside again.

*What needs were being met by Kelly-Anne's behaviours and how could staff support her?*

Having observed Kelly-Anne, it was necessary to establish what needs were being met by her behaviour – an awful lot of adult time and a lovely play outside on the scooter. In discussion with the senior staff, we decided we needed to flip this. Time with one of the senior leaders was planned in each morning, including 15 minutes on the scooter outside or her choice of game (from a limited selection). This was included on her personal visual timetable, along with a photo of the adult and her choice of activity.

Over time, as Kelly-Anne trusted that she would get this relational time with adults, she no longer threw the tables and chairs and was much calmer. Alongside this, the adults set up a safe space for her to go if she needed it. They modelled and used the place and she took photos of it. Instead of throwing things, she was taught to go to her safe space if she felt distressed or overwhelmed.

**Case example:**

Kai was a Year 2 pupil who quickly became heightened. Each time his behaviours escalated, he could go outside and run around the playground to calm down. This worked and he then was able to engage in his learning. Having observed him, in discussion with the teacher, we decided to flip the situation. Each morning, Kai was invited outside for a run before sitting and learning before his behaviours escalated. He no longer needed to escalate his behaviours to meet his needs.

- Help children to feel a sense of belonging and connectedness. 'Establish classroom rituals that help build connections and a sense of belonging, such as providing greetings and goodbyes, complimenting students and initiating traditions and celebrations' (Henson, 2020). Show genuine interest in what pupils have been doing and achieving or are interested in outside of school, welcome them in and ensure that they feel a valued member of the class.
- Actively listen by giving time and attention, showing an interest and asking open-ended questions. Convey that you understand what they are saying by clarifying and repeating key phrases back.

## *Supporting to repair and restore relationships*

- Apologise when things go wrong or you make a mistake. Model a sincere apology, including acknowledging the pupils' feelings and suggesting how you will aim to learn from the experience and get it right should a similar situation arise in the future.
- After an incident, encourage pupils to problem-solve alongside a trusted adult, looking at alternative responses and means of behaving next time. Teach, model and support how to repair relationships if something has gone wrong. 'Random acts of kindness', 'paying back time' (such as tidying up, sweeping the floor, helping the site manager) and visuals such as sorry cards (Bombèr, 2020, pp.253–254) can work well for pupils who need to put something right yet struggle to reflect or see the consequences of their actions.
- Support pupils to reflect after an incident, once they are calm. Dix (2017, p.126) suggests 'walking and talking', playing with Lego™ or playdough, stacking books or gardening with pupils to enable authentic conversations. Further suggestions include drawing whilst talking or playing a simple game (such as Uno, Jenga or throwing and catching a ball), or having a hot chocolate together. Any such shared activity will often enable a pupil to talk more freely and feel less pressured than when just talking with an adult. Display and model empathy when talking about incidents. ('I can see that you were very frustrated. I understand why you felt that way.')
- 'Punishment doesn't teach better behaviour, restorative conversations do' (Dix, 2017, p.125). Restorative conversations focus on relationships. They enable pupils to explore the effect of their actions on others, resolve conflict, repair, and move on with empathy, understanding and kindness in a way that is non-shaming

and helps them to make better choices, should a similar situation arise in the future. Two key questions: 'who else has been affected?' and 'what can we do to make things right?' (Dix, 2017, p.131) make an effective starting point for adults wishing to engage in restorative conversations with pupils. 'Restorative practice describes a way of being, an underpinning ethos, which enables us to build and maintain healthy relationships' (Finnis, 2021, p.10).

■ Help pupils begin to see the perspective of others. Comic Strip Conversations™ (Gray, 1994), the *Hand of Options* (Bombèr, 2011, p.186) or puppets, role play, story or video clips can be used to help pupils to explore alternative scenarios and other perspectives and to begin to understand how others have been affected by an incident.

■ Avoid asking 'why' after an incident. Even with the best of intentions, it can often sound accusatory and a pupil will often not know or be able to articulate why they have presented with certain behaviours.

## *Teaching and learning*

■ Chunk work into simple, individual steps and make tasks appear less daunting by asking pupils to complete one or two steps or questions at a time, before having a quick movement break (sharpening the pencils, having a drink of water or giving out the books). Providing a visible structure will reduce stress and encourage involvement. Provide a checklist (see p.249–50) so that pupils can tick off each step as they achieve it (use a picture/ symbol format for younger pupils). This helps focus their attention on the task and enables them to see the progress which they are making towards completion. To make it more tactile, Velcro™ each step on so the pupil can remove it as each step is achieved. Alternatively, put a lump of playdough in the tick box and the pupil presses this down like a button when they have completed the step (leaving an indentation to show it is complete) or press an actual button into the playdough to show that the stage is completed. A smiley face or word of praise from an adult as they complete each step adds positive feedback and encouragement to continue.

■ Writing is often a trigger; being faced with a blank page can be particularly daunting, and children often fear making mistakes. Alleviate anxieties around written tasks by breaking them down into smaller chunks, giving sentence starters or cloze procedures, using posters, writing captions for pictures, or writing in smaller boxes or speech bubbles or on shaped paper or sticky notes. Offer visual cues such as phonics or vocabulary mats and story maps. Be aware that anxiety can be increased by the internal pressure of having to have 'perfect' handwriting or for pupils who struggle with fine motor control. At times, offer alternative ways of recording or demonstrating knowledge, such as creating posters, diagrams, using the computer, taking pictures or recording video or sound clips.

■ Introduce legitimate movement breaks such as running errands, giving out equipment or getting a drink of water and include whole class movement breaks (see the 'Self-regulation' chapter). Where possible, include an active, multisensory element to learning.

■ Provide safe, predictable (yet flexible) routines. Visual cues support all pupils by providing consistent structure and helping to lessen anxiety. They are permanent, easier to process and reduce the load on working memory. They can focus attention towards a task or activity, help pupils to feel in control and more organised and are also non-confrontational and can reduce negotiation. Have clear expectations and present rules and routines visually by using visual timetables and photographs of pupils engaged in the 'expected behaviours' as a non-verbal reminder.

■ Model and rehearse behaviour expectations regularly, or as Finnis (2021, p.21) puts it, 'So, the behaviours you want? You've got to give them to get them.'

■ Present instructions clearly and simply and one step at a time, reinforced with visual cues (such as symbols, photographs, posters, checklists or flow charts), where possible. Allow processing time before expecting a response and repeat keywords as necessary.

■ Ensure tasks are carefully scaffolded and communication is differentiated to account for social and emotional developmental level rather than chronological age.

■ Be aware that copying (from the board or paper) can be time-consuming and challenging for many pupils, so limit this and avoid where possible. Instead, give printed notes to annotate or highlight. Print or scribe dates, learning objectives and questions so that the pupil can focus their energy and time on the learning task rather than copying text.

## *Supporting executive function*

Executive functions are the set of intrinsic mental skills needed to manage behaviours and to function effectively in many areas of life. They are required for organising and prioritising, focusing and maintaining attention, time management and transitioning between tasks, information and language processing, self-control and regulating emotions, impulse control, planning and forward-thinking, working memory and recall, information-filtering and motivation. Children need to be enabled and supported to develop these skills that may be delayed.

Executive function decreases in times of distress; therefore, difficulties become more noticeable and symptoms may increase with increased anxiety, pressure and as more demands are placed on pupils.

- By lowering anxiety levels, the behaviour improves, as the part of the brain responsible for logical thought and reasoning comes back online (see the 'Anxiety' chapter). Provide support and help alleviate stress, particularly at times when symptoms appear worse than usual. Learn to spot (and help the pupil to spot) their triggers and behaviour patterns. Plan to avoid these or provide appropriate support and strategies to lessen anxieties, particularly around transitions, unstructured times and starting a task. Look for times when things are going particularly well, as well as when the pupil is struggling, to try and establish a pattern of what works well and is supportive for the pupil.
- Support pupils with **organisational** strategies by ensuring all resources are easily accessible ahead of a task. Provide resource checklists (including pictures or photographs as appropriate), showing visually the order in which the tasks or activities need to be carried out or the sequences of events. Keep work areas clear and free of distractions.
- Help with **planning**. Teach pupils to put 'to do' lists in order of priority and model how to use them. 'Remember to keep instructions simple and short, and use the same key words or phrases for particular tasks' (NHS Ayrshire & Arran, 2019). Use mind maps and create plans together for writing tasks and projects.
- Support pupils to **prioritise**, **sequence** and **organise** their thoughts logically, for example, cutting out and sequencing stories or instructions, describing everyday events by giving step-by-step instructions (such as cleaning teeth or making a sandwich) or asking them to describe something in order, with a beginning,

middle and end (a book, sports match or favourite film), following directions or programming a robotic toy to get from one place to another or following a simple recipe together.

■ Pupils with delayed executive function may lack flexibility of thought and have very polarised thinking. A pupil may need reminding that one bad moment does not mean that they have had an awful day, but it was just a part of the day which was negative. Support **flexible thinking** by showing that there are alternative ways of doing and saying things. Use 'activities that involve multiple-meaning words, word categories and number puzzles' exploring language ambiguity through 'visualizing and discussing jokes, riddles, puns and multiple-meaning words' and exploring different approaches to problem-solving (Kusnyer & Stanberry, 2013). Kerstein (2019) shares some ideas for increasing flexibility at home and school, such as playing games and changing the rules, having a backwards day or moving the seating plan around.

■ Teach regulation strategies (see the 'Self-regulation' chapter).

■ Use movement and exercise as much as possible. 'Exercise turns on the attention system, the so-called executive functions – sequencing, working memory, prioritizing, inhibiting, and sustaining attention ... On a practical level, it causes kids to be less impulsive, which makes them more primed to learn' (Ratey, 2020).

■ Support pupils to shift attention and prepare them for **transitions and change** by giving plenty of warning and using timers. Pupils may need a bespoke *Now and Then* board in addition to the visual timetable to alleviate anxieties around transitions, for example, 'now we are doing our Maths, then it will be time for reading'. Use photographs of the activities and as Maths finishes, the card is removed, the reading picture becomes 'now' and the next activity is put on the 'then' space. Where appropriate, make transitions sensory and fun, such as by marching, striding, walking tall or spotting as many items beginning with a certain letter, or of a particular colour, as you can on the way. If a pupil struggles to move from a preferred activity to another task, giving them a photograph as a reminder that they can return to it later can be helpful (for example, when their turn on a favourite trike or with the sand has finished, swap the task for a photograph of the trike or sand).

■ A *Stop, Breathe and Think* card can be an effective visual reminder to support impulse control. Rehearse using it, playfully, when the pupil is calm.

## *Supporting working memory*

- Pupils who have difficulties with working memory may struggle to follow a series of instructions, appear not to listen, struggle to complete tasks and lose sight of goals or objectives, appear to be daydreaming, frequently forget what they were going to say and struggle to reflect on and correct their work (Kusnyer & Stanberry, 2013). Be aware of difficulties with working memory and spot signs of memory overload. Reduce demands and the amount of information that needs to be stored and processed (Gathercole & Packiam Alloway, 2007). Where possible, use visual cues to support processing.
- Pre-teaching and over-learning vocabulary and key concepts will help pupils feel confident and engage in their learning. Be prepared to repeat key concepts and vocabulary regularly.
- Scaffold and model each step of the task for the pupil to complete before moving on to the next step, thus reducing the need to remember large chunks of information.
- Shorten tasks or instructions and make each step very clear and reinforce with visual supports.
- Aim to draw on and link to previous skills, knowledge or understanding and build on existing learning. Give visual prompts alongside verbal cues and be willing to repeat as necessary. Teach strategies to help pupils connect and recall key information such as posters, visual maps, colour coding, flow charts, memory prompts, mnemonics and flashcards.
- Encourage pupils to 'read single sentences or small chunks of text, and then check for understanding'. In written work or Maths tasks, ask pupils to 'review their most common errors and, from there, create a personalized list of errors to watch out for' (Kusnyer & Stanberry, 2013).
- Ensure students know who, when and how to ask for support when key information has been forgotten (Gathercole & Packiam Alloway, 2007). Help cards with photos of key adults or a buddy card with photos of carefully chosen peers can be helpful.
- Teach pupils positive self-talk to create greater understanding and encourage 'reflection and greater awareness of one's learning and performing process' (Kusnyer & Stanberry, 2013). Pupils need this modelled to them and to have opportunities to practise. It is useful to reinforce with visual supports such as posters, sticky notes, postcards or pebbles with key phrases on them.
- Allow plenty of processing time.
- Play memory games such as matching pairs, *Kim's Game* (show a range of items then cover them up, remove one and the child has

to say which one is missing (could be topic-related), *I went to the shop and I bought...*, or put five (again, possibly topic-related) items in a sequence, pupil looks at them for a period of time, then they are covered up, and the pupil copies the sequence from memory; build a brick tower, cover it and the pupil copies the tower; and play observation games (adult leaves the circle and the others need to remember what they were wearing, or watch video clips and answer questions based on observations).

■ Repeat dance or musical sequences to support memory and sequencing.

## Environmental considerations

■ Pay careful attention to the seating plan to ensure pupils feel comfortable, safe and able to learn. Understanding what works for each child is important, and if unsure, talk to them. One pupil may do better at the front of the class in order to focus on the teacher and whiteboard with no one walking around in front of them. Some pupils may be better away from distractions such as direct sunlight, noisy projectors or fans. One pupil may be distracted looking out of the window, for another, this may be positive at times, reducing less appropriate behaviours. Some pupils may need to sit away from busy areas, such as the drawers or books, since people moving past will cause a distraction and frustrations can arise for those with sensory sensitivities if they are getting knocked or disturbed regularly. Those who are hypervigilant may need to be near a wall or at the back with a view of the whole room to increase feelings of safety. Pupils with an exit strategy may need to be near the door or their safe space. Access to a quieter work station may be a supportive option at times.

■ Offer and encourage access to a quiet, calm space for pupils to use if they feel overwhelmed (see p.42).

## Unstructured times

■ Have a predictable routine for PE, break and lunchtimes (including wet playtime routines), with clear rules and expectations presented visually.

■ Carefully manage unstructured times, ensuring pupils can access a key adult and a safe space if they are feeling overwhelmed, anxious or frustrated. Use a photograph as a visual reminder and practise when the pupil is calm. Introduce clubs and smaller, quieter zones at times.

■ Teach, model and practise structured games, team-building, turn-taking and social skills. Provide a range of interesting equipment in sufficient quantities for the pupils to enjoy and explain and model how to use it. Keep the novelty factor by introducing different themes or equipment throughout the year.

## Rewards and consequences

Unfortunately, school behaviour policies and traditional systems of sanctions, such as isolation and exclusion, tend to be least effective and can even be damaging and shaming for our most troubled or distressed pupils. De Thierry (2019, p.29) describes the 'negative impact and consequences of such a deeply painful method of encouraging conformity', explaining that 'shame will never elicit positive emotions and outcomes – it will only cause the child who experiences it to create methods of coping which are mostly counter-productive, subconscious and toxic'.

In a conversation in 2021 with Rachel Tomlinson, Headteacher at Barrowford School (Lancashire, UK), she described to me her sanction and reward-free environment, stating, 'We shape our school and our provision around the needs of our children'. It is 'child-centred, with the children at the heart of everything'. It works (and has worked and evolved over the last 12 years) by focusing on safe and trusting relationships, with repair and practical consequences as an extension of these relationships. Staff reflect on what is really important in order to avoid unnecessary conflict, asking themselves, 'are the children safe, happy and can they learn?' With exclusion not being an option, staff are creative in how they respond to the pupils' needs, with relationship always at the heart of this. It is based on trauma-informed and attachment-aware approaches and powerfully effective nurture; an ethos running through all of the classrooms. It is based on open communication and unconditional positive regard for children, staff and caregivers. In describing the reward-free element, she states, 'reward-free does not mean unvalued and unrecognised; actually, it means the opposite. It means that we value achievement for the effort it has taken at that stage in the process. It is personal recognition on a very individual level' (Tomlinson, 2020).

■ If the current system of rewards and sanctions isn't working for a particular pupil, they need an alternative or adjusted system. Reasonable adjustments need to be made for behaviours as well as for learning needs; one size does not fit all and requires a 'differentiated discipline' (Bombèr, 2020, p.63). 'When you plant lettuce, if it does not grow well, you don't blame the lettuce. You look for reasons it is not doing well. It may need fertilizer, or more water, or less sun. You never blame the lettuce' (Thich Nhat Hanh, undated). Pupils do not need blame or punishment when they get it wrong; they need to be taught skills and how to regulate and calm, taking account of their developmental age and needs, within a supportive adult–pupil relationship. They need co-regulation to calm in the moment (see p.34).

■ Pupils need compassion and 'connection' rather than 'correction'. They need adults to model and connect with understanding and kindness to help them achieve success. Siegel and Payne Bryson (2012, p.48) suggest that adults 'engage, don't enrage', calming their 'downstairs brain' and helping them to regulate before engaging the 'upstairs brain' to problem-solve and find an alternative means of behaving or reacting (see p.40). Knightsmith (2020) recommends adults 'be curious, not furious'. It is essential to understand why a pupil is behaving in a certain way, to support them in learning the skills and strategies to behave differently next time and respond with calmness and curiosity. 'When we are calm (and in turn help a child to calm), and we become curious about what the child is experiencing, we begin the process of making sustainable change for that child and helping them build the skills, understanding and neural pathways that will help them to thrive at school and in life' (Knightsmith, 2020).

■ Understand the communicative function of the behaviours and the needs that are being met by those behaviours, in order to offer effective support. Differences in behaviour could be signifying overwhelm, confusion or frustration, sensory overload, anxiety and stress, lack of understanding or a lack of skill, that the young person has experienced adversity, is not feeling well, is hungry, thirsty, tired, or has had a bad morning. Listen to and translate what the behaviour is communicating and then provide support. Pupils need boundaries but within a deeply nurturing context. 'Boundaries, structures and rules should underpin a much more relationships-based approach. If we only see the behaviour they display then we don't see the child. There is a purpose to that behaviour, if we understand what it is we can change it' (Chatterley, 2020).

■ Pupils learn best from consistent regulatory and relational approaches, with adults understanding, accepting and responding to their needs. 'If a pupil is distressed and is communicating this through their behaviour, then surely it would be more ethical to attempt to attune to and translate what they might be trying to say?' (Bombèr, 2020, p.39).

■ Pupils need logical, practical consequences, and they need to learn the effect their behaviour has on others. This needs to be achieved by problem-solving with the pupil. It needs to be within relationship, alongside trusted, caring, empathic adults, not further inducing shame by being based on punishment, isolation and exclusion. 'When punishment is replaced with therapy, mentoring, coaching and love, the children change. In short, when the adults change, everything changes' (Dix, 2017, p.114).

■ Support pupils to repair and restore relationships (see p.11). Comic Strip Conversations™ (Gray, 1994) or similar can be used creatively to explain how other people may be feeling and are useful to explore and problem-solve alternative actions visually, should a similar situation arise in the future.

■ In establishing their *School Without Sanctions*, Baker and Simpson (2020) focused on rewarding the positive behaviour they wanted to see and removing all sanctions; 'We didn't waste a second thinking about the behaviours we didn't want to see – the days of focusing on negatives were behind us'. Focus on the positives, achievements and successes. When using rewards, keep them 'fresh', fun and interesting and keep the novelty factor – a whole class dance-off, a 'bring your teddy to school' day, a hot chocolate and a game of Jenga. The possibilities are endless and just need a bit of creativity. Ensure the rewards are what the pupils actually would like, include them; they often come up with some fantastic ideas. Try to make individual rewards as immediate as possible. Failing to gain a reward may induce shame and lead to rejection of the system. Accumulative systems, where pupils have control over the rewards and collect them over time (rather than ones where rewards are taken away if not earned) are often more effective.

■ Foster intrinsic motivation by developing a love of learning, a sense of curiosity, enjoyment, satisfaction in achieving and introducing student-led learning and personal choices and autonomy, rather than relying on extrinsic motivators (rewards).

■ The focus needs to be on pupils feeling safe enough to learn and to thrive. 'Where did we get the crazy ideas that in order to make children – or indeed anyone – do better, we first have to make them feel worse?' (Finnis, 2021, p.28). Many schools are increasingly becoming more aware of the importance of relationships within their setting and adopting relationship policies, either instead of or alongside behaviour or discipline policies. 'Establish policies that ensure a safe place for learning. Real safety, however, comes from fostering and maintaining caring relationships' (Finnis, 2021, p.49). Bombèr (2020, pp.275–283) and Trauma-Informed Schools have examples of relationship policies that can be adapted or adopted in schools. 'Incentive or threat-based strategies are not powerful enough to stop deep-rooted behaviour that has served as protection in the past … Mercifully schools are beginning to replace "discipline" policies with "relationship" policies' (Miles, 2019).

■ Avoid whole class sanctions; they are ineffective, unfair and give inappropriate control to the pupil making inappropriate choices. Dix (2017, p.170) makes the point that punishing the whole class 'for the behaviour of the wobbly few is quite obviously ridiculous … The children who have been the trigger for everyone having to stay in are always at the top of the hierarchy. The mass detention for the class on their behalf is further confirmation of this.'

---

**Case example:**

Elsa didn't want to go to school in the morning and started crying. The previous day, she (and the whole class) had been kept in again because three pupils continued talking after the teacher had asked them to stop. Elsa expressed that she felt guilty even though she knew deep down that she had done nothing wrong. She kept saying how bad the whole class were, and none of them could ever do anything right. She was also struck by the unfairness that her break times were determined by three pupils when she hadn't done anything wrong. One of the three told his friends, with a smile, that it was better for him if the whole class stayed in, as then he wasn't missing out on anything; he didn't want them having fun if he couldn't.

---

■ Avoid consequences for things the pupil cannot control, such as symptoms and behaviour presentations related to anxiety, a medical condition, diagnosis or executive function delays and focus on teaching skills and strategies to support.

■ Avoid consequences being carried over to the next day, wherever possible, and start each day with a clean slate.

■ Flip the dialogue within the classroom and focus on the positive, expected behaviours and notice these with abundance. Dix (2017, p.24) suggests *recognition boards* to focus on all the great behaviour within the classroom, suggesting that adults 'routinely advertise the behaviour you do want'. Names are written on the board for all the pupils who present with fabulous behaviour, rather than names and ticks for the minority who don't.

Ultimately the only behaviour it is possible to change and have complete control over is our own. Adults can change how they communicate, react and respond. They can change the environment but they should not attempt to change the child. Teach regulation skills and offer support and understanding and the behaviour will improve.

## Activities to support with attention, concentration and executive function

- Play a range of physical games (outdoors where possible), such as catch (gradually increase the difficulty by using both hands, using differently sized and shaped balls, stand further apart) to increase focus and organisational skills, sequencing and timing as well as improve hand–eye coordination and attention. Try a range of activities to develop balance and coordination, such as wobble boards, standing on one leg, hopping, badminton or riding a bike.
- Play name games such as saying someone's name before rolling a ball to them.
- Play a range of games to teach turn-taking, winning and losing and the following of rules, such as *Uno, Operation, Hedbanz, Pictionary, Articulate for Kids, Mexican Train Dominoes, Mapominoes, Kerplunk, Dobble, Buckaroo* and *Pick Up Sticks*. Gradually build up the time spent on them (start with less complicated games to avoid frustration and ensure they are successful more often than they are not). *Labyrinth* has been found useful in teaching children that things change. Giant outdoor versions of *Snakes and Ladders, Jenga, Connect Four, Draughts* and *Chess* allow pupils to be outside and move around more, whilst playing.
- Develop impulse control by playing *Simon Says, What's the Time Mr Wolf?* or *Traffic Lights* (move around in a variety of ways and when the adult says and holds up 'green' it means go, 'amber' means go slowly and 'red' means freeze).
- Building activities using a variety of construction kits, copy each other's models or follow their instructions (visual and verbal).
- Make dens together or design and create their own safe space.
- Jigsaw puzzles and word searches, crosswords, pencil mazes, *Spot the Difference* and *Where's Wally*-type activities.

■ Listening to music can help maintain focus and activates all areas of the brain. Learning an instrument can focus attention, improve executive function (including working memory), lower stress levels, increase self-regulation, give a sense of control and build self-esteem. Drumming can help with calming and regulation. Woodwind and brass instruments help pupils focus on and control their breathing. Singing can be calming.

## Activities to develop listening skills

■ Sound walks
■ Repeating rhythms by clapping or using instruments
■ *Musical Statues*
■ Storytelling – each person says a sentence to build up a story
■ *Find the Thimble* – someone silently thinks of a place to 'hide the thimble' (e.g. on the moon, in Africa, under the desk), the rest of the group ask questions, to which the 'hider' may only answer 'yes' or 'no'
■ *What am I?* – someone silently thinks of an item or animal, the rest of the group ask questions, to which they may only answer 'yes' or 'no'
■ *Do as I Say Not as I Do* (e.g. say put your hands on your head, but put your hands on your shoulders, the pupil has to do as you say and not copy your actions)
■ *Don't Clap This One Back* (clap rhythm patterns for the pupil to copy, if you clap the rhythm pattern of the words *don't clap this one back* the pupils remain silent and don't clap)
■ Listen to a video clip or news clip and answer questions afterwards

## Activities to teach cause and effect

**Cause-and-effect play** can show pupils that their actions have an effect and increase feelings of control.

■ 'Teach cause and effect with the use of three-dimensional tactile resources, such as pop-up toys, scented bubbles, jigsaws and books with sound effects' (Blackburn et al., 2012).
■ Use toys and games in which an action produces a desired result, such as musical instruments, cause and effect cards, *Kerplunk*, *Pick Up Sticks*, marble runs and remote-control toys. Encourage computer programming activities such as *Scratch*.

### Activities to support pupils to feel a sense of control

Offer pupils a sense of control and the chance to laugh and engage in fun, playful activities within relationships by playing power reversal games where the pupil is given control and allowed to take the lead within a safe environment.

- Engage in role play, being led by the pupil's interest. Try some role reversal, such as they can be the teacher and you become the pupil.
- Give the child a 'magic wand' which they can use to transform you into an object, animal or person of their choice.
- Let them set a timer and give you a challenge to do within the time (write your name or complete as many Maths questions or star jumps as you can within the time).
- Play games where the pupil takes the lead, such as *Follow the Leader* and *Simon Says.*
- If a child can't follow an instruction, rather than reprimand, be playful. For example, say, 'OK, I will have to do it then' and do the Maths task wrong, in a funny exaggerated way (to induce laughter), such as by having your worksheet upside down or trying to write with the eraser.
- If transitions are difficult, for example, at the end of break time, suggest it is time to go back to the classroom and then turn and walk the wrong way, do a funny walk or go into the PE shed. Allow the child to laugh along with you and then help you to find the right way.
- Play opposite games such as you say stand up and they sit down.

## Resources, further information and 'tool kits'

### Books for adults

*After the Adults Change: Achievable Behaviour Nirvana* by Paul Dix

*Building Positive Behaviour: Returning to Learning Using a Sequential Approach* by Graham Chatterley

*Independent Thinking on Restorative Practice: Building Relationships, Improving Behaviour and Creating Stronger Communities* by Mark Finnis – an amazing book about building relationships and restorative practice and so much more

*Learn to Love, Love to Learn* by Rachel Tomlinson (to be published) – if the conversation with Rachel is anything to go by, this book will be amazing

*The Mentally Healthy Schools Workbook: Practical Tips, Ideas, Action Plans and Worksheets for Making Meaningful Change* by Pooky Knightsmith

*Restorative Practices at School: An Educator's Guided Workbook to Nurture Professional Wellness, Support Student Growth, and Build Engaged Classroom Communities* by Becky McCammon

*A School Without Sanctions* by Steven Baker and Mick Simpson

*When the Adults Change Everything Changes: Seismic Shifts in School Behaviour* by Paul Dix – a fabulous book which all school staff really should read

*The Whole-Brain Child – 12 Proven Strategies to Nurture Your Child's Developing Mind* by Daniel Siegel and Tina Payne Bryson

## Books to share with pupils

*Have You Filled a Bucket Today? A Guide to Daily Happiness for Kids* by Carol McCloud

*Kindness Is My Superpower: A Children's Book about Empathy, Kindness and Compassion* by Alicia Ortego

## Websites

https://www.corc.uk.net/media/1506/primary-school-measures_310317_forweb.pdf Anna Freud wellbeing framework for primary schools

https://www.corc.uk.net/media/1517/blf17_20-second-school-measuresbl-17-03-17b.pdf Anna Freud wellbeing framework for secondary schools

## Podcasts

https://www.pookyknightsmith.com/podcast
https://www.thesendcast.com/sendcast-episodes/

# References

Baker, S. & Simpson, M. (2020) *A School Without Sanctions: A New Approach to Behaviour Management* Bloomsbury Education, London

Blackburn, C., Carpenter, B. & Egerton, J. (2012) *Educating Children and Young People with Fetal Alcohol Spectrum Disorders – Constructing Personalised Pathways to Learning* Routledge, Oxon

Bombèr, L. (2011) *What about Me? Inclusive Strategies to Support Pupils with Attachment Difficulties Make It Through the School Day* Worth Publishing, London

Bombèr, L. (2020) *Know Me to Teach Me – Differentiated Discipline for Those Recovering from Adverse Childhood Experiences* Worth Publishing, London

Chatterley, G. (2020) *Building Positive Behaviour: Returning to Learning Using a Sequential Approach* Independently Published

De Thierry, B. (2019) *The Simple Guide to Understanding Shame in Children – What It Is, What Helps and How to Prevent Further Stress or Trauma* Jessica Kingsley Publishers, London

DeMontfort University (undated) *5 Praises a Day Initiative* [online] Available at: https://www.dmu.ac.uk/documents/about-dmu-documents/news/tips-for-using-praise.pdf

Dix, P. (2017) *When the Adults Change Everything Changes: Seismic Shifts in School Behaviour* Independent Thinking Press, Carmarthen

Dix, P. (2021) *After the Adults Change: Achievable Behaviour Nirvana* Independent Thinking Press, Carmarthen

Evans, J. (2018) *Children with Problems or Problem Children?* [online] Available at: https://thejaneevans.com/children-with-problems-or-problem-children/ [Accessed 24 March 2021]

Finnis, M. (2021) *Independent Thinking on Restorative Practice: Building Relationships, Improving Behaviour and Creating Stronger Communities* Independent Thinking Press, Carmarthen

Gathercole, S. & Packiam Alloway, T. (2007) *Understanding Working Memory – A Classroom Guide* [online] Available at: https://framework.thedyslexia-spldtrust.org.uk/resources/understanding-working-memory-classroom-guide [Accessed 1 December 2020]

Gray, C. (1994) *Comic Strip Conversations* Future Horizons, Arlington

Henson, W. (2020) *4 Key Pillars of a Trauma-Informed Approach During COVID-19* [online] Available at: https://www.eschoolnews.com/2020/12/17/4-key-pillars-of-a-trauma-informed-approach-during-covid-19/?all [Accessed 8 February 2020]

Kaufman, T. (2020) *Building Positive Relationships with Students: What Brain Science Says* [online] Available at: https://www.understood.org/en/school-learning/for-educators/empathy/brain-science-says-4-reasons-to-build-positive-relationships-with-students [Accessed 23 February 2021]

Kerstein, L. (2019). *Ten Ways to Increase Your Child's Ability to Be Flexible* [online] Autism Awareness Centre. Available at: https://autismawarenesscentre.com/ten-ways-to-increase-your-childs-ability-to-be-flexible/ [Accessed 10 December 2020]

Kusnyer, L. & Stanberry, K. (Eds) (2013) *Executive Function 101 e-Book* [online] Available at: https://www.edrevsf.org/resource/executive-function-101-e-book/ [Accessed 13 January 2021]

Knightsmith, P. (2020) *Behaviour: Inclusion Using a Trauma-informed Approach* [online] Available at: https://www.headteacher-update.com/best-practice-article/behaviour-inclusion-using-a-trauma-informed-approach-schools-wellbeing-students-teachers-1/231669/ [Accessed 8 February 2020]

Miles, L. (2019) *Adverse Childhood Experiences and the Implications for Schools* [online] Available at: https://www.headteacher-update.com/best-practice-article/adverse-childhood-experiences-and-the-implications-for-schools/215017/ [Accessed 8 February 2020]

NHS Ayrshire & Arran (2019) *Understanding Fetal Alcohol Spectrum Disorder (FASD) What Educators Need to Know – For Education Staff Working with Children and Young People with FASD* [online] Available at: https://www.nhsaaa.net/media/8391/fasd_whateducatorsneedtoknow.pdf [Accessed 12 January 2021]

Peters, D. (2015) *A Strength-Based Approach Helps Children Learn to Ask 'What's Right' Instead Of 'What's Wrong'* [online] Psychology Today. Available at: https://www.psychologytoday.com/us/blog/worrier-warrior/201504/strength-based-approach-helps-children [Accessed 3 February 2021]

Ratey, J. (2020) *Exercise and the ADHD Brain: The Neuroscience of Movement* [online] ADDitude Magazine. Available at: https://www.additudemag.com/exercise-and-the-adhd-brain [Accessed 18 November 2020]

Siegel, D. and Payne Bryson, T. (2012) *The Whole-Brain Child – 12 Proven Strategies to Nurture Your Child's Developing Mind* Robinson, London

Thich Nhat Hanh (undated) *Nine Life Lessons from Thich Nhat Hanh* [online] Available at: https://www.guidedmind.com/blog/9-life-lessons-from-thich-nhat-hanh [Accessed 3 February 2021]

Tomlinson, R. (2020) Twitter [online] Available at: https://twitter.com/BarrowfordHead/status/1255599474006777856 [Accessed 9 March 2021]

Treisman, K. (2017) *Working with Relational and Developmental Trauma in Children and Adolescents* Routledge, Oxon

## Checklist to support pupils who are communicating through behaviour

| STRATEGY | COMMENTS |
|---|---|
| **Please also refer to the 'Self-regulation' chapter** | |
| **A strength-based approach** | |
| Value difference and focus on strengths, achievements and successes | |
| Reframe language around behaviour into positives when talking to and about pupils | |
| **Relationships and communication** | |
| Build positive relationships based on the PACE approach (see p.65) | |
| Model positive relationships and interactions within school | |
| Work collaboratively with the caregivers and share successes as well as concerns | |
| Involve the pupil in the planning process and in finding solutions | |
| Use direct language and focus on positive behaviours and moving the pupil on | |
| Avoid confrontations, negotiations and power struggles | |
| Focus on positive behaviour and praise small steps to success | |
| Ten positives for each negative | |
| Offer positive choices | |
| Avoid inadvertently reinforcing cycles of negative or inappropriate behaviour by meeting needs proactively | |
| Help build a sense of belonging and connectedness | |
| Actively listen | |
| **Supporting to repair and restore relationships** | |
| Apologise when things go wrong or you make a mistake | |
| Support pupils to reflect after an incident | |
| Restorative conversations | |
| Help pupils begin to see the perspective of others and to repair relationships | |
| Avoid asking 'why' after an incident | |

| STRATEGY | COMMENTS |
|---|---|
| **Teaching and learning** | |
| Tasks broken down into simple steps, presented in a checklist | |
| Alleviate anxieties around written tasks | |
| Regular movement breaks and a multisensory element to learning tasks | |
| Use visual cues and model and communicate behaviour expectations | |
| Single-step instructions with visual reminders | |
| Take account of social and emotional development level | |
| Avoid copying and provide print-outs or scribe dates, learning objectives and questions | |
| **Supporting executive function** | |
| Spot triggers and patterns and provide support or alleviate anxieties | |
| Equipment checklists, resources accessible to support organisation | |
| Help with planning and teach pupils to create and use 'to do' lists | |
| Support pupils to prioritise, sequence and organise their thoughts logically | |
| Support flexible thinking | |
| Teach regulation strategies | |
| Use movement and exercise | |
| Support pupils to switch attention and prepare them for transitions and change – warnings, timers, *Now and Then* boards | |
| **Supporting working memory** | |
| Be aware of working memory difficulties, reduce demands and information, use visual cues | |
| Pre-teaching, over-learning and repetition of key vocabulary and concepts | |
| Scaffold and model each step of a task | |
| Shorten tasks or instructions and use visuals | |

*(Continued)*

## Continued

| STRATEGY | COMMENTS |
|---|---|
| Draw on existing skills and knowledge as a starting point | |
| Ensure pupils know who, when and how to ask for help | |
| Allow processing time | |
| Play a range of memory games, repeat dance or music sequences | |
| **Environmental considerations** | |
| Seating plan to ensure pupils feel comfortable, safe and able to learn | |
| Safe space to calm | |
| **Unstructured times** | |
| Predictable routine for PE, break and lunchtimes with clear rules and expectations presented visually | |
| Carefully manage unstructured times – provide quieter areas/clubs and key adult and safe space | |
| Teach structured games, team-building, turn-taking and social skills | |
| **Rewards and consequences** | |
| 'Differentiated Discipline' (Bombèr, 2020). Teach regulation skills and take account of developmental age | |
| View behaviour as communication and translate what the pupil needs with compassion and kindness | |
| Logical, practical consequences, problem-solving with the pupil | |
| Support pupils to repair relationships | |
| Focus on success, strengths and achievements rather than negative behaviours | |
| Adopt a relationship policy instead of or alongside a behaviour policy | |
| Avoid whole class sanctions | |
| Avoid consequences for symptoms and behaviour presentations related to anxiety, a medical condition or executive function delays | |

| STRATEGY | COMMENTS |
|---|---|
| Flip the dialogue and recognise all those pupils behaving beautifully | |
| **A range of activities and games to support attention, concentration, executive function, listening, understanding cause and effect and feel a sense of control** | |

# Chapter 2

# Self-regulation

Self-regulation is the ability to appropriately recognise, understand and manage feelings to cope with a range of difficult situations or changes without emotional outburst, overwhelm or shutdown. It is being able to control behaviours and actions and to cope and calm the self when experiencing a range of feelings such as frustration, sadness, fear, tiredness, surprise, happiness or excitement. It is being 'in a position of mental and physical integration where our thoughts and emotions are influencing each other to remain focused, moderate and stable' (Bombèr & Hughes, 2013, p.44). To self-regulate, a pupil needs to be able to 'regulate emotions, self-soothe, delay gratification and tolerate transitions' and must be 'neurologically "organised" – that is, able to moderate internal highs and lows' (Biel & Peske, 2018, p.208).

Indications that a pupil may be needing support to regulate in the classroom are when they are presenting with unusual or stressed behaviours such as moving around more than usual, inability to concentrate and focus, shouting, running away, hiding, sitting with their head on the desk, seeming withdrawn, dissociating, being defiant or showing increased sensory sensitivity. Pupils who need support to self-regulate may lack impulse control. They may show extremes of heightened emotions, seemingly over-reacting to everyday stressors by becoming cross or frustrated at the smallest trigger or may show pleasure with extreme, giddy excitement and uncontained glee.

Children need to be shown how to regulate and calm and it cannot be assumed that they know the strategies or have the skills. They need

DOI: 10.4324/9781003146292-3

the techniques modelled and the skills taught. Each pupil is different and different strategies will work for different pupils and at different times. 'We seem to have forgotten that differentiation, used when we're engaged in the curriculum, is necessary for learning about behaviour, as well as how to self-regulate' (Bombèr, 2020). It is effective to model and trial a range or techniques and let the pupil choose their preferred methods. Self-regulation is such an important skill, but it is so often ignored or assumed that pupils already know how.

Below is a range of strategies that have been tried and tested and found to be useful when helping pupils to co-regulate and then self-regulate. There is a checklist at the end of this chapter.

## Co-regulation before self-regulation

Pupils who are overwhelmed and struggling to regulate their emotions will need co-regulation before they can begin to regulate themselves. Treisman (2017, p.24) asks, 'Without co-regulating, how can you self-regulate?' The simple answer is that you can't. Children will not be able to self-regulate if they have not had their emotions attuned to and soothed in infancy. Adults in school need to take on the role of 'stress regulator' (Bombèr, 2020, p.84) to support pupils with regulation techniques. Co-regulation is 'the ability of one person to influence the regulatory state of the other' (Bombèr & Hughes, 2013, p.45). If the adult is able to remain calm and regulated, the pupil is likely to pick up on these emotions and calm much quicker themselves. In the classroom, the adult needs to display, teach and model regulation strategies.

- Model, teach, verbalise and practise the chosen regulation strategies alongside the pupil, regularly, when they are calm so that they become embedded and more natural. Bombèr (2020, pp.152–153) states that 'the time to lay down new neural pathways so that our pupils can begin to know what calm actually feels like, is when a crisis is not happening'. Trial a range of techniques and allow the pupil to select the ones that they prefer. Share how you are both feeling when using the techniques. Encourage the pupil to photograph the chosen strategies to keep as a visual reminder or record on a stress scale (see p.248).
- Name and label emotions for increased understanding by being empathically curious about what is happening for the pupil. Use calming and connecting commentaries, wondering aloud techniques (Bombèr, 2007, pp.88–89, pp.147–150; Bombèr, 2011, p.116) and Gottman and DeClaire's (1997) emotion coaching to

tentatively begin to name and validate the pupil's feelings 'I wonder if you are feeling … because?' or 'I understand why you are feeling …'. In this way, pupils will begin, over time, to understand, make sense of and reflect on the strong emotions that they are feeling and begin to regulate these alongside a caring adult, as well as begin to understand the actions and emotions of other people.

■ Gottman and DeClaire's (1997) emotion coaching can also be used to teach emotions within moments of dysregulation. Adults can empathise yet set limits on behaviour and put boundaries in place, as necessary. Learning some calming scripts to use in the heat of the moment may be supportive, such as 'X, I can see you are really cross right now, let's go to your safe space and talk' or 'I can see that you are really cross at the moment, but it is not OK to throw the chairs. Let's go for a walk together and you can be cross safely.' Model calm facial expression, tone and body language, as well as calming words.

■ Make a happy box together – a box of things that make the pupil feel positive. Ideas include a small soft toy or squishy, a photo of a pet or place that induces happy feelings, a sticky note with something nice that someone has written about them. Encourage the pupil to come up with their own ideas. Alternatively, make a calm book using photos of the chosen calming techniques, soft or fluffy fabric, calming mantras and other ideas from the pupil. Similarly, an alerting book or box can be made using textured material such as cutting shapes out of bubble wrap, sandpaper and Velcro™ or using vibrating or flashing toys and alerting activity flashcards.

■ Create a sensory bag with the pupil, including items for a range of the senses. Bombèr (2020) suggests using a toiletry bag or pencil case of items for older pupils. Include two of each item so the key adult can model using the tools, with the aim of the pupil mirroring (rather than instructing the pupil to 'calm down and use a calm tool'). Trial a range of sensory tools and techniques for all of the senses with the pupil and let them choose which they would like to include. Ideas include stress and fiddle tools such as tangles, marble pushes, toys that are manipulative, squeezy, squashy or stretchy, gel shapes, textured toys, making scented playdough with the pupil (peppermint or lemon tend to be alerting, whereas lavender or vanilla tend to be calming), a hand massager, lip balm, hand cream (gain permission from home and check for allergies), liquid motion timer or glitter jar, comforting smells (such as tissue sprayed with a parent's perfume or aftershave or an item of clothing washed with familiar washing powder).

■ Louise Bombèr, at an Attachment Conference (in Dorset in 2018), suggested an SOS bag ready to grab if a pupil leaves the classroom in a dysregulated state. She describes these in her recent book (Bombèr, 2020, p.178), advising that they include 'a microtowel to sit on' 'chewy sweets', 'mindful colouring book/postcards and pens' and 'sensory bits'. Adults model how to calm by sitting down, using the calm tools and slowing their breathing; by being the essence of calm. 'Rather than chasing the pupil or merely following them, you set up a base nearby... engage with the contents of the bag, and occasionally smile and wave at the pupil to come join you' (Bombèr, 2020, p.178). Pupils are not further heightened or told to calm down – they are shown.

---

**Personal case example:**

A few months after the Bombèr conference (above), I was observing Heather, a Year 5 pupil, who had left the class in visible signs of distress. One of her trusted adults was with her and suggested she played with her playdough (Heather's usual preferred calming activity). Heather paced the corridor, screaming and rejected all adult efforts to engage her in a calming activity. Remembering Louise Bombèr's suggestions, I whispered to the adult, 'What would happen if you sat on the floor and just played with the playdough yourself?' I received a look suggesting I had lost my mind, but the key adult did as I suggested. Within minutes, Heather sat down and joined her; both the adult and Heather visibly calmed. I returned a few minutes later and Heather and her key adult were laughing and making little animals together.

*Why do you think the modelling of a calming strategy was more effective than merely suggesting Heather used a calm tool?*

---

■ Drawing on Bruce Perry's *Neurosequential Model of Therapeutics* (Perry and Dobson, 2013), it is understood that the brain develops from the bottom up, starting with the brainstem or reptilian system, then the limbic or mammalian system and finally the pre-frontal cortex, responsible for logical thinking and reasoning. Therefore, in times of dysregulation, the brain needs to be soothed from the bottom up by providing sensory, repetitive, predictable activities and co-regulation to calm the brainstem and limbic system. 'Traumatised children's brains become stuck in the brainstem, and they therefore swing between their survival modes of fight/flight/freeze/collapse. One of the most helpful ways to move children from these super-high anxiety states, to their calmer 'thinking brain', is patterned, repetitive, rhythmic activity' (Beacon House Therapeutic Services and Trauma Team, undated).

*Brainstem calming activities* should be carried out regularly, alongside and modelled by a key adult. When a pupil is in emotional turmoil, they need to be provided with low-key, concrete, mechanical and predictable activities. Suggested activities include walking, dancing, drumming, tapping, singing and music (Information courtesy of Beacon House Therapeutic Services and Trauma Team). Other activities include counting, sequencing objects or pictures, colouring, sorting, building structures together or bouncing a ball to each other. Engaging in a creative activity is often effective, such as drawing or painting together.

■ Model and teach pupils **positive self-talk** such as 'I can do this' or 'I can keep calm'. Reinforce this through creative activities such as writing positive affirmations on strips of paper and making paper chains, writing on cut-out leaves and creating a tree display, posting positive notes into a box or assigning each positive affirmation to a coloured bead and creating a bracelet or keyring or decorating and painting positive messages on a smooth pebble as a tactile visual reminder.

■ Intervene early to avoid behaviour escalations and re-direct, divert and distract, where possible. Use de-escalation strategies to help pupils regulate, calm and reduce distress but not to dismiss any overwhelming feelings they may be having. Pupils need to be able to talk about and express their emotions with a safe adult. However, they will be unable to do this effectively whilst dysregulated and will need trusted adults to support this once they are calm.

■ Getting to know and understand the pupil behind their behaviours is essential. 'We can be that compassionate, safe person who is not there to judge or label but to "learn them" and their specific needs. Then they can learn about life and how to access some level of emotional and physical regulation OVER TIME' (Evans, 2018). Connect and communicate; give pupils the time and a safe space to express their feelings. Use a soothing tone of voice and express empathy. Communicate understanding of their levels of distress or anxiety and convey a sense of safety, such as 'I can see you are worried, I am here with you'.

## *Recognising and naming emotions*

Recognising a range of emotions is a crucial step towards understanding feelings and how emotions can influence behaviours. It is estimated that about 10 per cent of people have Alexithymia, which is the inability to identify or describe emotions felt by themselves or others. Other pupils may not have had the opportunities and experiences to learn to process and manage their own emotions effectively.

- Talking about emotions needs to become a regular feature of classroom life. 'The "thinking" adults play a pivotal role in verbally and non-verbally modelling, coaching and scaffolding, how to identify, express and respond to high-intensity arousal and a range of feelings. They should endeavour, where appropriate, to openly name the feelings in the child, themselves and in others' (Treisman, 2017, p.27). Treisman suggests this should be through 'everyday opportunities' such as 'day-to-day interactions, on the TV, in a book/song/comic strip, or when playing'. Talk about and name the emotions of real people, puppets or characters in stories or sports personalities in video clips, for example.
- Give pupils a rich emotional vocabulary to help them name feelings and make talking about feelings natural, rather than something taboo or scary. '... the more we support children to have words to express themselves and to make sense of their experiences, the less likely they are to come out through tricky behaviours' (Treisman, 2017, p.26). Play emotion games such as emotion charades, matching pairs games (match the word to the emotion picture), emotions Jenga (write an emotion on Jenga bricks, leaving some blank, as the brick is pulled out the pupil talks about the experiences of themselves, others or fictional characters and acts out or describes the emotion), play with Lego™ 'Build Me Emotions', play with emotion dice and emotion cards, play *Simon Says* using different emotions. Treisman (2017, p.27) also suggests a wealth of further playful and creative ideas to help pupils' emotional understanding and expression, such as decorating biscuits and pizzas with facial expressions, designing emotions masks, and playing facial expression *Follow the Leader.* Collins-Donnelly (2014, p.28) suggests various activities such as word searches and matching faces to feelings to encourage children to begin exploring emotions and start talking about and naming feelings.
- Model talking about and managing your own emotions and verbalise your own calming strategies, for example, 'I know X is coming in to watch my lesson this morning so I feel a little anxious,

even though I know it will be OK; I am just going to take three deep breaths and try some positive self-talk'.

■ It is also useful to teach pupils how they may feel various emotions in different parts of their bodies, for example by body mapping. Draw a large picture of the body and mark how a pupil may feel emotions in different parts; for example, if exploring anger or frustration they may describe clenched fists, their head going down, rapid breathing and heartbeat or their foot tapping quickly. Alternatively, use a large teddy and some sticky notes to draw and label where in the body they may feel different emotions. Trusted adults can then use this to help pupils when they begin to spot physiological clues that the pupil is becoming dysregulated: 'I can see your head has gone down and your fists are clenched, I wonder if you are getting a bit frustrated with your Maths, let's go for a walk and see if we can tackle it a different way when we get back'.

■ It may be useful to identify particular times, activities or places that cause pupils to become dysregulated by marking on the school timetable or map of the school how they feel in different areas or times of the day and put in support and strategies to help them to regulate just before or at these times.

■ Journaling is a useful method for pupils to express and label their feelings and emotions, through drawing and writing. They may then begin to spot triggers and explore what has helped (or exacerbated) the situation.

■ Use the expressive arts to explore and express emotions safely through music, painting and drama, for example.

■ Collins-Donnelly (2014) has suggestions for exploring different 'anger triggers' and behaviours with children and their effects on those around them. She gives practical ways to 'starve the anger gremlin' by talking calmly, creating an anger box, filling in an anger diary, problem-solving as well as engaging in a range of calming and relaxing activities, which can also be used with a range of other emotions which a pupil may be exploring.

■ Teach children to recognise and communicate their feelings and emotional states using visuals such as emojis, feelings charts, stress scales (see p.248) or Zones of Regulation®.

■ Pupils need to know that all feelings are valid, no emotion is 'good' or 'bad' and everyone experiences a range of emotions. However, there are positive and negative ways of dealing with these emotions. It is how pupils are taught to recognise, understand and manage those emotions appropriately that is important. 'Provide an outlet for negative emotions. Make it possible to vent pent-up feelings. Give her a ball or bucket of wet sponges to hurl against the fence. Designate a "screaming space"' (Kranowitz, 2005 p.269). Other ideas to release frustrations include stamping on bubble wrap, using a punch bag, playing the drums, drawing a picture of the feelings, going for a run or trampolining.

## *The body and brain*

The threat response is an essential survival mechanism; the involuntary reaction in the brainstem, triggered by fear and designed to keep a person safe from danger. In times of threat (perceived or actual) the brain automatically decides how to survive: to fight (battle, rage or become aggressive), flight (run away or escape) and if these are not possible, to freeze (stay totally still – incapable of moving or decision-making), flop (go floppy, play dead or dissociate) or fawn (befriend, comply or submit).

As anxiety increases and triggers the threat response, information processing and logical thought decreases and the body reacts according to its survival instincts. If the threat response is over-activated, an everyday occurrence can be perceived as a threat as it triggers survival reactions and signals danger to the brain. The body can react in a similar way as if it were cornered in a cave by a bear as it does to reading aloud in assembly or being accidentally pushed in the playground.

The pre-frontal cortex or 'upstairs brain' (Siegel & Payne Bryson, 2012) stays 'offline' so a pupil is unable to learn or access reasoning, logic or higher-level thinking. Furthermore, when the threat response is activated, the body is primed to hear danger and the human voice is tuned out, the area of the brain responsible for speech and language production and processing is also 'offline'. A pupil is not ignoring you; they genuinely may not be able to hear or process the verbal information.

Teaching pupils how their body works in times of perceived threat helps them to understand how their brains react to keep them safe and that their actions are involuntary because they are the body's in-built means of survival. The brain is malleable, so can constantly change and adapt and be taught calming strategies. If the threat response is over-active then calming, regulating techniques need to be implemented.

- ■ Teaching Daniel Siegel's hand model of the brain and what happens when someone is 'flipping their lid' (see 'tool kit') is a useful, visual method of teaching all pupils how the body reacts when stressed. By becoming part of everyday classroom language and understanding what is happening physiologically, it is easier to support each other to calm.

■ Alternatively, teach pupils about their 'upstairs' and 'downstairs' brain (Siegel & Payne Bryson, 2012). When someone is anxious, they are in their 'downstairs' (reptilian and mammalian) brain, and their 'upstairs' (thinking) brain has gone offline. Drawing pictures of what happens in our 'upstairs' and 'downstairs' brain can strengthen understanding of the threat response. Once pupils have been taught about the brain they are often more receptive to learning strategies to 'put the lid back on' or 'bring their upstairs brain back online'. The brain develops from the bottom up, so we need to regulate the 'downstairs' brain before our 'upstairs' brain functions properly.

## Sensory input (see the 'Sensory Processing Disorder (SPD)' chapter)

Physical movement can improve focus and attention and help with self-regulation.

■ **Vestibular** (balance and moving the head position) and **proprioceptive** (weight-bearing, deep pressure and heavy work) input before a pupil is expected to sit and learn or as soon as they are becoming dysregulated can aid calming, regulation and concentration. Linear movements tend to be more calming, whereas rotational activities are more alerting. Follow alerting activities (running up and down a hill, running in and out of cones and changing direction, running in large circles, bouncing on a trampette, spinning, log rolls or using scooter boards) with more calming ones (rolling backwards and forwards on a peanut ball or gym ball, commando crawls, wheelbarrow walking, using a chin-up bar or climbing wall, balance beams, wobble boards, walk with a beanbag balanced on the head, marching, wall pushes or stretching a resistance band).

■ Help build a pupil's sense of self-esteem by giving particular roles and responsibilities. If possible, include heavy work activities, which are naturally regulating, for example, stacking or putting out the chairs, watering the plants, gardening, sweeping, pushing or pulling the lunch trolley or wheelbarrow, collecting the fruit, tidying the books, tidying the PE cupboard, giving out equipment, cooking or making playdough, moving equipment, cleaning the whiteboard or changing the visual timetable.

- Allow doodling or fidgeting whilst working or listening by providing doodle pads or fidget tools (such as Blue Tack, fiddle pencil toppers, fiddle or fidget pens, manipulative, squeezy or squishy toys, velvet attached to the underside of the table to stroke or a favourite fabric sewn into a pocket).
- Make a comfortable **safe space** using beanbags and soft blankets. Include, for example, sensory tools, scented playdough and prompt cards showing rehearsed calming, relaxation or breathing techniques. A choice of place (e.g. indoor and outdoor) can be useful. Include the pupil in deciding upon, designing and decorating the space with pictures, cushions, soft toys and fairy lights to give them a sense of ownership. Regularly rehearse and model using the safe space when the pupil is calm, through role play and walkthroughs and playing games to make it somewhere that they automatically go to feel safe and calm. It needs to be used as a supportive, genuine strategy to help pupils when feeling overwhelmed, and not seen as a punitive measure. Have the pupil take a photograph to use as a visual reminder.
- A **wobble cushion** enables a pupil to move and offers both proprioceptive and vestibular input, allowing them to engage their core muscles and improving posture whilst sitting and can be alerting. They can reduce the need to fidget and help pupils to focus, engage and concentrate for longer when used intermittently throughout the day.
- A **resistance band** around the front two chair legs gives a pupil proprioceptive input whilst they are sitting and listening or working, by giving them something to kick and push their feet against. Alternatively, placing one around the top of the table legs will give them something to push their hands against.
- A **weighted lap pad** or shoulder wrap offers proprioceptive input, helping pupils to feel grounded when sitting. They can be calming and organising for pupils and can increase focus and attention.
- For pupils who chew on clothes and mouth inedible items, a chew tool or chew pencil topper can provide more appropriate oral input. **Sensory snacks** can also help pupils to regulate (see below). Cold drinks through a straw can be calming and organising (Allen, 2016). A bottle with a bite valve can offer further sensory stimulation and help self-regulation.

## Calming and alerting activities

Collaborating with caregivers to share successes and effective strategies is essential. 'Teaching families some strategies for supporting a child's emotional regulation can also provide them with important tools they can use themselves' (Knightsmith, 2020).

Sensory activities are helpful in the moment when pupils need calming or alerting. However, they should also be used regularly to help increase tolerance levels, regulate emotions and improve focus and concentration. Teach, model, rehearse, practise and role play strategies regularly, when pupils are calm, so that they become natural and embedded. The ability to reason, think straight and process verbal information decreases when a person is distressed. Avoid telling them to calm down but model, demonstrate and show pictures of the chosen strategies as a reminder in times of heightening anxiety or stress.

Certain activities, such as heavy work, can be both calming and alerting.

## Alerting activities

Alerting activities are needed when a pupil is distracted, having difficulty concentrating, withdrawing or feeling tired. Alerting activities are usually quick, strenuous and energising. The following activities tend to be alerting (although everyone is different and will have their own preferences):

- **Fiddle tools** that are hard or textured, make a noise, light up, flash or vibrate or have buttons to press, click, twist and turn
- **Puzzles and puzzle toys** that require concentration
- **Textured material** such as Velcro™, carpet squares, sandpaper and bubble wrap
- **Mint or citrus-scented** playdough
- **Vibrating pen** or **sandpaper underneath writing paper** to give sensory feedback
- **Movement and physical activity** – go for a quick walk, do star jumps, running, spinning, bouncing, skipping, trampolining or using a trampette, exercising, dancing, stamping feet or stomping on bubble wrap, clapping, clenching and unclenching the fists or tapping
- **Heavy work activities** – pushing, pulling, stretching, lifting, climbing, hanging on a bar; Brukner (2014) suggests seat-, wall- or palm-pushes, giving the self a hand or arm massage or going into 'Superman pose'
- **Wobble and balance boards, scooter boards**
- Use a **wobble cushion or ball chair**
- **Physical sensation** such as running hands or wrists under cold water

- **Cold** – eat an ice pop or frozen fruit, suck on an ice cube, drink ice-cold water through a straw or sports bottle
- **Crunchy snacks** such as carrot sticks, apples, banana chips, pretzels, breadsticks, crackers and crunchy cereal bars (gain permission from home and check for allergies)
- **Spicy** and **sour** food
- Put the **lights** on or open the blinds
- Listen to **fast, alerting music**
- **Play** – 'Play encourages the release of positive chemicals in the brain, which has positive effects on well-being, the immune system, and readiness for learning' (British Psychology Society, 2020)

## Calming activities

Calming activities are needed when a pupil is anxious, overwhelmed, frustrated or angry and needs to relax.

A calming reset time may be needed first thing in the morning and before going home. It is often useful to follow an alerting activity (such as break time or PE) with a calming activity or before pupils are expected to sit or listen for a period of time, in order to settle them for learning. Wearing a fitness watch with a heart rate monitor may be a useful visual signal that a pupil's heart rate is increasing, indicating that they should employ a calming strategy.

Reactions to sensory input, however, depend upon the individual. Trial a range of sensory tools so pupils can explore what works best for them. Calming activities are usually slow, rhythmic, predictable and soothing. The following activities tend to be calming:

- **Calming fiddle tools** are usually quiet and stretchy, squeezy or squashy
- **Doodle pads and mindful colouring**
- Apply **lip balm or hand cream**
- **Rhythmic activities** – walking, drumming or playing other musical instruments, marching, sharpening pencils, sorting, building
- **Heavy work – deep pressure** and **weighted activities** such as chair pushes, slowly clench and unclench one muscle at a time, hand massage, squeezing and stretching or pushing and pulling, Spaghetti Arms (De Thierry, 2017, p.41) tense the whole body like raw spaghetti and then relax and wobble like cooked spaghetti, seat-, wall- or palm-pushes and finger pulls (Brukner, 2014). Use a weighted lap or shoulder pad or stretch a resistance band

- **Bilateral stimulation** or **crossing the midline** such as butterfly hugs (cross your arms and pat your back) (De Thierry, 2017, pp.40–41) or arm pretzels (hold your arm out straight in front, palms back to back, cross them over and hold hands, interlinking the fingers and bend them down and towards the chest (Brukner, 2014)
- **Positive visualisation** – teach the pupils to visualise or take a photograph of their happy place, a calming image or favourite animal or pet
- **Mindfulness, meditation, yoga** or **t'ai chi**
- **Listening** to sounds outside, listening to rainsticks, relaxing music, sea or whale sounds, seashell listening (De Thierry, 2017, p.40) or make and listen to a positive, calming playlist of soothing music
- **Chewy snacks** such as bagels, raisins, dried mango or apricot, chewy cereal bars, fruit bars or chewing gum tend to be calming and organising (gain permission from home and check for allergies)
- **Read**
- **Watch a sand timer**, the clock, liquid motion timer or glitter jar
- **Go outside** and walk, do some gardening or water the plants
- **Play**
- **Dim the lights** or shut the blinds
- **Breathing techniques** – inhale deeply and roar like a lion or dinosaur (Biel & Peske, 2018), blow bubbles or pinwheels, blow a little scrap of paper or feather through a straw, make splatter pictures by blowing paint through a straw, pretend the fingers are candles on a cake and blow them out, box breathing (inhale for the count of four, hold for four and exhale for four), play a brass or woodwind instrument or sing
- **Grounding techniques** – 5, 4, 3, 2, 1 (name five things you can see, four you can touch, three you can hear, two you can smell and one you can taste), count different colours or particular items around the room, concentration activities such as puzzles, sudoku or saying a person's name for each letter of the alphabet
- Being with **pets** or animals

## *Whole class movement breaks*

Build regular, short movement breaks into each lesson for all pupils, particularly before sitting for a period of time. 'Movement always improves sensory processing' (Kranowitz, 2005, p.268). Movement will help focus, attention and concentration and help pupils regulate. Sensory breaks should include 'heavy work' or proprioceptive input such as calming, deep pressure and activities which involve resistance, stretching and pushing or pulling.

- Brukner (2014) suggests activities to help pupils to regulate, many of which can be used as a whole class sensory break, including chair pushes, giving self a hug, arm pretzels, giving self an arm or hand massage, palm pushes and finger pulls.
- Sit down/stand up (adult says a statement; if it is correct sit down, if it is false stand up)
- Squats
- Star jumps
- Dance/yoga
- Stand up and wiggle like a worm or wobble like jelly
- Balance on one leg and then the other
- Stand, march on the spot and stretch
- Use both hands to draw imaginary numbers or letters in the air
- Pat head whilst rubbing the stomach
- Close eyes and touch the nose
- Clap, sway and sing to music
- Play *Simon Says* using stretching, balancing and movement
- Pass an object or soft ball around to the person whose turn it is to speak
- Play games where pupils need to swap places such as 'fruit salad' (label the pupils with a fruit, when 'orange' is called all those labelled 'orange' swap places. If 'fruit salad' is called, all pupils swap places)
- Be creative when moving to different areas of the school – do some wall pushes on the way, march, stamp, take giant strides, tiptoe, walk sideways like a crab, waddle like a penguin

## Rewards and consequences

- Rather than sanction, model how to regulate and regularly rehearse techniques. 'Try to view your child's anger outburst as a result of a lack of skills rather than a desire to get attention. He may not have the skills for flexibility and frustration tolerance' (Chowdhury, 2004, p.89). Perhaps consequences or 'catch-ups' could be reframed as a more positive, supportive measure and include the learning of regulation strategies (once the pupil is calm) such as mindfulness, yoga or meditation. It will be important that it is not viewed as punitive, but rather a means of offering a more positive means of reacting in the future. Supporting pupils to recognise and manage their emotions is an essential step in helping them develop more appropriate, less distressed, behaviour.

■ *Stop, Breathe and Think* cards (such as a picture of a stop sign, a breathing visual and a visual of a person with a question mark inside a thought bubble) can visually support impulse control. Practise using these when the pupil is calm.

■ All staff need to understand how the brain works when dysregulated and how to support pupils to regulate. School relationship and behaviour policies should also reflect this.

## *Staff wellbeing and self-regulation*

■ There needs to be a focus on good mental health and wellbeing for all pupils and staff. Adults need to be aware of how they can regulate their own emotions before they can support those of others. 'We are not likely to be able to effectively assist our pupils in maintaining a consistently stable level of functioning, if we find ourselves frequently becoming dysregulated' (Bombèr & Hughes, 2013, p.45). Trial some of the regulating techniques and see which work personally. A calm, regulated adult is needed to help pupils to regulate. Pupils will quickly pick up on adult dysregulation. Modelling the strategies for the pupils will also have the effect of calming yourself. 'We have to be able to manage our own feelings and stress so that we don't feel "emotionally full" and we have some emotional resources available. We need to make sure that we are not going to transfer any of our stress and negative emotions to the children' (De Thierry, 2017, p.47).

■ Look after yourself and each other. A supportive environment, where staff feel listened to, understood and able to ask for support or time to calm after an incident is essential. 'There needs to be time for the adult to recover and restore too' (De Thierry, 2017, p.47).

As schools returned after the initial lockdown (March 2020), the British Psychology Society (2020) strongly urged that 'we need to emotionally regulate before we educate. Ensuring that children are emotionally ready to learn and adults are emotionally ready to teach.' The message that the focus should be on both pupil and adult wellbeing is particularly relevant following the onset of the Covid-19 pandemic. However, this is essential at all times.

# Resources, further information and 'tool kits'

## Books for adults

*Grounded: Discovering the Missing Piece in the Puzzle of Children's Behaviour* by Claire Wilson

*The Incredible 5-Point Scale: The Significantly Improved and Expanded Second Edition* by Kari Dunn Baron and Mitzi Curtis

*The Polyvagal Theory: Neurophysiological Foundations of Emotions, Attachment, Communication, and Self-Regulation* by Stephen Porges

*Raising an Emotionally Intelligent Child* by John Gottman

*Simple Stuff to Get Kids Self-Regulating in School: Awesome and In Control Lesson Plans, Worksheets, and Strategies for Learning* by Lauren Brukner and Lauren Liebstein Singer

*The Whole-Brain Child – 12 Proven Strategies to Nurture you Child's Developing Mind* by Daniel Siegel and Tina Payne Bryson

*The Zones of Registration* by Leah Kuypers

## Books and resources to share with pupils

*The Big Feelings Activity Book* by Pooky Knightsmith, Lyra Hesmondhalgh and Ellie Hesmondhalgh

*Feelings Blob Cards* by Pip Wilson and Ian Long

*Help! I've Got an Alarm Bell Going Off in My Head: How Panic, Anxiety and Stress Affect Your Body* by Louise Aspden

*How to Be a Superhero Called Self-Control! Super Powers to Help Younger Children to Regulate Their Emotions and Senses* by Lauren Brukner

*The Kids' Guide to Staying Awesome and In Control: Simple Stuff to Help Children Regulate Their Emotions and Senses* by Lauren Brukner – fantastic ideas to help children to understand and regulate their feelings

*Little Meerkat's Big Panic: A Story About Learning New Ways to Feel Calm* by Jane Evans

*Starving the Anger Gremlin* by Kate Collins-Donnelly

*TAMs Journey* (Books 1–3) by Amanda Peddle and Rowan Ellis – a boy's journey learning about the brain and emotions

*A Therapeutic Treasure Deck of Grounding, Soothing, Coping and Regulating Cards (Therapeutic Treasures Collection)* by Karen Treisman

*A Therapeutic Treasure Deck of Feelings and Sentence Completion Cards* (Therapeutic Treasures Collection) by Karen Treisman

*Train Your Angry Dragon* by Steve Herman

*The Zones of Regulation: Tools to Try Cards for Kids* by Leah Kuypers and Elizabeth Sautter

*The Zones of Regulation: Tools to Try Cards for Tweens and Teens* by Leah Kuypers and Elizabeth Sautter

## *Websites*

https://www.annafreud.org/schools-and-colleges/resources/ A range of resources for schools including supporting school staff wellbeing and a wellbeing measurement framework for primary and secondary schools and colleges

https://copingskillsforkids.com/ Breathing exercises and suggestions in the resources section on supporting pupils to calm anxiety, manage anger and handle stress

https://www.ehcap.co.uk/content/sites/ehcap/uploads/NewsDocuments/273/Powerpoint-for-Emotion-Coaching-Lesson-Plan.PDF Information on emotion coaching

https://www.elsa-support.co.uk/ A range of resources to purchase

https://www.expressiveartworkshops.com/expressive-art-resources/100-art-therapy-exercises/ Creative suggestions to explore emotions, relaxation and happiness

https://www.kiddiematters.com/9-ways-to-teach-children-about-feelings/ Ideas for teaching emotions to children and an adaption of the song 'If You're Happy and You Know It' to include a range of feelings and actions

https://lemonlimeadventures.com/sensory-hacks-calm-an-angry-child/ Some sensory activities to make with the pupil including worry stones and Lego™ glitter jars and squishies

https://www.themindfulword.org/2012/guided-imagery-scripts-children-anxiety-stress/ Guided imagery scripts to help children cope with stress and anxiety

http://www.unseenfootprints.com/feelings-book/ Ideas for making a feelings book

www.relaxkids.com A range of relaxation resources

https://www.5pointscale.com/ Information and resources on the five-point stress scale

https://www.youtube.com/watch?v=9XyxqWiqLk0 Ideas from Karen Treisman for making a sensory box

https://www.zonesofregulation.com/index.html Information on Zones of Regulation

Dan Siegel **hand model of the brain** flipping our lids – YouTube videos (check for suitability before using with pupils):

https://www.youtube.com/watch?v=f-m2YcdMdFw Dan Siegel explaining for adults/older pupils

https://www.youtube.com/watch?v=2xeDcPBD5Fk
https://www.ehcap.co.uk/handmodel
https://www.youtube.com/watch?v=a_hPelcPRTg (Diane Gehart)
https://www.youtube.com/watch?v=V0BYs-LN5bY (Sproutable)
https://www.youtube.com/watch?v=FTnCMxEnnv8&vl=en (Mo Mindful)
https://www.youtube.com/watch?v=H_dxnYhdyuY (Jeanette Yoffe)

# References

Allen, S. (2016) *Can I Tell You about Sensory Processing Difficulties? A Guide for Friends, Family and Professionals* Jessica Kingsley Publishers, London

Beacon House Therapeutic Services and Trauma Team (undated) *Brainstem Calmers* [online] Available at: https://beaconhouse.org.uk/wp-content/uploads/2019/09/Brainstem-Calmer-Activities.pdf [Accessed 10 October 2019]

Biel, L. & Peske, N. (2018) *Raising a Sensory Smart Child: The Definitive Handbook for Helping Your Child with Sensory Processing Issues* Penguin, New York

Bombèr, L. (2007) *Inside I'm Hurting – Practical Strategies for Supporting Children with Attachment Difficulties in Schools* Worth Publishing, London

Bombèr, L. (2011) *What about Me? Inclusive Strategies to Support Pupils with Attachment Difficulties Make It Through the School Day* Worth Publishing, London

Bombèr, L. (2020) *Know Me to Teach Me – Differentiated Discipline for Those Recovering from Adverse Childhood Experiences* Worth Publishing, London

Bombèr, L. & Hughes, D. (2013) *Settling to Learn – Settling Troubled Pupils to Learn: Why Relationships Matter in School* Worth Publishing, London

Bowler, A. in Reber, D. (2020) [podcast] Available at: https://tiltparenting.com/2020/09/22/episode-227-amelia-bowler-talks-about-her-new-book-the-parents-guide-to-oppositional-defiant-disorder/ [Accessed 4 February 2021]

Brukner, L. (2014) *The Kid's Guide to Staying Awesome and in Control – Simple Stuff to Help Children Regulate their Emotions and Senses* Jessica Kingsley Publishers, London

Chowdhury, U. (2004) *Tics and Tourette Syndrome: A Handbook for Parents and Professionals* Jessica Kingsley Publishers, London

Collins-Donnelly, K. (2014) *Starving the Anger Gremlin – A Cognitive Behaviour Therapy Workbook on Anger Management for Children Aged 5–9* Jessica Kingsley Publishers, London

De Thierry, B. (2017) *The Simple Guide to Child Trauma – What It Is and How to Help* Jessica Kingsley Publishers, London

Evans, J. (2018) *Children with Problems or Problem Children?* [online] Available at: https://thejaneevans.com/children-with-problems-or-problem-children/ [Accessed 24 March 2021]

Finnis, M. (2021) *Independent Thinking on Restorative Practice: Building Relationships, Improving Behaviour and Creating Stronger Communities* Independent Thinking Press, Carmarthen

Gottman, J. and DeClaire, J. (1997) *Raising an Emotionally Intelligent Child* Simon and Schuster, New York

Knightsmith, P. (2020) *Behaviour: Inclusion Using a Trauma-Informed Approach* [online] Available at: https://www.headteacher-update.com/best-practice-article/behaviour-inclusion-using-a-trauma-informed-approach-schools-wellbeing-students-teachers-1/231669/ [Accessed 8 February 2020]

Kranowitz, C. (2005) *The Out-of-Sync Child. Recognizing and Coping with Sensory Processing Disorder* Tarcher Perigee Books, New York

Perry, B. & Dobson, C. (2013) *The Neurosequential Model of Therapeutics* in J. D. Ford & C. A. Courtois (Eds), *Treating Complex Traumatic Stress Disorders in Children and Adolescents: Scientific Foundations and Therapeutic Models* (pp. 249–260) The Guilford Press, New York

Siegel, D. and Payne Bryson, T. (2012) *The Whole-Brain Child – 12 Proven Strategies to Nurture Your Child's Developing Mind* Robinson, London

The British Psychology Society (2020) *Emotionally Regulate Before We Educate: Focusing on Psychological Wellbeing in the Approach to a New School Day* [online] Available at: https://www.bps.org.uk/news-and-policy/%E2%80%98emotionally-regulate-you-educate%E2%80%99-urges-bps [Accessed 2 March 2021]

Treisman, K. (2017) *Working with Relational and Developmental Trauma in Children and Adolescents* Routledge, Oxon

## Checklist to support pupils to regulate

| STRATEGY | COMMENTS |
|---|---|
| **Co-regulation before self-regulation** | |
| Model, teach, verbalise and practise the chosen regulation strategies regularly when the pupil is calm | |
| Name and label emotions, empathise yet set limits on behaviour | |
| Make a happy/positive/alerting box or book | |
| Set up a sensory bag and an SOS bag, including items for a range of senses | |
| Brainstem calmers – predictable, repetitive, rhythmic activities | |
| Positive self-talk | |
| Intervene early to de-escalate and help pupils to regulate | |
| Connect and communicate and give pupils a safe space to express their feelings | |
| **Recognising and naming emotions** | |
| Name feelings of the pupil, other people, characters in stories, video clips, sports personalities | |
| Teach emotions through a range of games and activities | |
| Model talking about and managing emotions | |
| Explore where they feel various emotions in different parts of their bodies through body mapping | |
| Explore key times or activities that pupils become dysregulated and put in support at these times | |
| Express and explore emotions through journaling, the expressive arts or practical activities | |
| Communicate emotional states using visuals | |
| Provide an outlet for negative emotions | |
| **The body and brain** | |
| Teach the 'hand model of the brain' (Siegel) or the 'upstairs' and 'downstairs' brain and what happens when we 'flip our lids' | |

| STRATEGY | COMMENTS |
|---|---|
| **Sensory input** | |
| **Vestibular** (balance and moving the head) and **proprioceptive** (weight-bearing, deep pressure and heavy work) input | |
| Responsibilities which involve movement or heavy work – carrying boxes, stacking chairs, sweeping, pushing or pulling | |
| Allow fidgeting or doodling whilst listening | |
| Create and use a safe space | |
| Trial a wobble cushion, resistance band on the chair legs or a weighted lap pad (not all at the same time) | |
| Chew tool or chew pencil topper, sensory snacks or drink from a water bottle | |
| **Alerting activities** | |
| Fiddle tools, puzzles, textured material, minty or lemon-scented playdough, vibrating pen | |
| Movement and heavy work, balance boards, wobble or balance boards, scooter boards | |
| Physical sensation | |
| Sensory snacks – cold or frozen, crunchy, spicy or sour | |
| Turn the lights on or open the blinds | |
| Listen to fast music | |
| Play | |
| **Calming activities** | |
| Fiddle tools, doodle pads, mindful colouring, use lip balm or hand cream | |
| Rhythmic activities, deep pressure, weighted activities, bilateral stimulation | |
| Positive visualisation Mindfulness, meditation, yoga, t'ai chi | |
| Listening to relaxing sounds or music, play an instrument, sing | |
| Chewy snacks or a warm drink | |
| Read, watch a timer, go outside, play, dim the lights | |
| Breathing or grounding techniques | |

*(Continued)*

## Continued

| STRATEGY | COMMENTS |
|---|---|
| **Whole class movement breaks** | |
| Build a range of whole class movement breaks into each lesson | |
| **Rewards and consequences** | |
| Rather than sanction, teach and rehearse regulation strategies | |
| Whole staff understanding of how the brain works, co-regulation and self-regulation strategies | |
| **Staff wellbeing and self-regulation** | |
| Staff trial a range of strategies and establish preferences and model using these to calm | |
| Look after yourself and each other | |

*Chapter 3*

# Adverse Childhood Experiences (ACEs), trauma and attachment-aware approaches

## Adverse Childhood Experiences (ACEs)

Felitti et al. (1998) conducted a study in the United States to understand the lifelong effects of Adverse Childhood Experiences (ACEs) on adult lives. ACEs include neglect, abuse, maltreatment and family turmoil (for example, a parent with mental illness or substance abuse, parental death or imprisonment, divorce or witnessing domestic violence). The study linked ACEs to disrupted neurological development, social, emotional and cognitive difficulties, increased harmful or risk-taking behaviours and a range of physical and mental health difficulties lasting a lifetime (Wavetrust.org, undated). At least five of the top ten leading causes of death are associated with ACEs (CDC, undated). The study found increased risk correlated with an increased number of ACEs experienced. 'Toxic stress from ACEs can change brain development and affect how the body responds to stress. ACEs are linked to chronic health problems, mental illness and substance misuse in adulthood' (CDC, undated).

DOI: 10.4324/9781003146292-4

Research has been ongoing since the original study, which has been replicated internationally, finding very similar results globally. In the United Kingdom, Bellis et al. (2018) found a 'prevalence of each common childhood condition, poor childhood health and school absenteeism increased with the number of ACEs reported'.

However, there are key factors, particularly in childhood, that were found to prevent this negative trajectory, increase resilience and improve education and health outcomes. 'Childhood community resilience assets (being treated fairly, supportive childhood friends, being given opportunities to use your abilities, access to a trusted adult and having someone to look up to) were independently linked to better outcomes' (Bellis et al., 2018). Therefore, 'school is well placed to make a significant impact and change the trajectories of struggling children's lives' (Miles, 2019).

'Negative impacts of ACEs are significantly mitigated by having an Always Available (trusted) Adult (AAA)' (Wavetrust.org, undated). One of the most important resilience assets which school can provide is a team of caring, empathic adults. Consistent, nurturing environments and positive, trusting relationships support children to feel safe and develop effective social and emotional skills and the resilience required to thrive.

## Trauma

De Thierry cites the Institute of Recovery from Childhood Trauma (IRCT), which gives the definition: 'Trauma is an event or a series of events such as abuse, maltreatment, neglect or tragedy that causes a profound experience of helplessness leading to terror' (IRCT, 2015 in De Thierry, 2017, p.14). She goes on to state that trauma 'shatters our sense of safety, stability, trust and innocence'.

Developmental trauma differs from a one-off traumatic event or crisis and stems from an overriding sense of fear and powerlessness. It can develop when a child is exposed to overwhelming stress over a sustained period, caused by, or not reduced by, their caregiver and can occur as a response to certain ACEs. 'Trauma is one of the possible outcomes of exposure to adversity. It occurs when a person perceives an event or set of circumstances as extremely frightening, harmful or threatening – either physically, emotionally or both' (Miles, 2019).

Treisman (2017, p.6) uses metaphor to explain relational and developmental trauma: the image of a child in 'shark-infested waters' to describe, for example, the experience of 'abusive or frightening parenting', where a child is 'waiting, anticipating, expecting and/or fearing being attacked' and a 'desolate island' to describe the experience of 'neglect and relational poverty' as 'a place where one feels discon-nected, disengaged and invisible'. The images can be useful for adults to imagine the distress experienced by pupils, developing increased empathy and compassion.

'Trauma impacts a person's behaviour, emotions, relationships and future' (De Thierry, 2017, p.33). It causes differences in brain devel-opment, affecting self-regulation, self-control, ability to learn, to feel safe and to trust. Pupils who have experienced developmental trauma may have a social, emotional and developmental age significantly lower than their chronological age. This impacts their engagement academically, socially and emotionally since 'some key skills such as problem-solving or sharing' may be under-developed, meaning that pupils 'might not have had the opportunities and care they needed to fully develop' (Treisman, 2017, p.10).

## Attachment difficulties and relational trauma

'The term relational trauma or attachment-related trauma refers to children who have experienced trauma within the context of their relationship; often interfamilial, or within their caregiver relationship' (Treisman, 2017, p.14). Children may develop attachment difficulties and struggle to develop and maintain appropriate relationships if their early attachments 'have been characterised by neglect, abuse, trauma and loss, rather than love and attunement ... they will have a distorted interpretation of themselves, others and the world around them' (Bom-bèr, 2007, p.7).

When infants form a **secure attachment** and have experienced 'good enough' care (Winnicott, 1988) they develop feelings of safety within the world and in relationships. They learn to trust, to self-regulate and develop a positive sense of wellbeing. If a child has experienced a wealth of 'relational treasures' (Treisman, 2017) such as empathy, compassion, unconditional love, protection and kindness, they will have a 'secure base' (Ainsworth, 1982) from which to develop relation-ships, explore the world and feel safe enough to engage and to learn.

Conversely, if a child's needs are not met, both emotionally and physically, and they have had little or inconsistent access to such 'relational treasures', if they have lived in a world of neglect, abuse or violence and have experienced a caregiver who was terrifying or aggressive or one who was living in a constant state of fear and anxi-ety, then they may develop an **insecure attachment** style. Rather than experiencing unconditional love, understanding and attunement, they may have learnt that adults do not meet their emotional needs and are unreliable, inconsistent and frightening. Their view of the world is as an unpredictable and frightening place. Their 'internal working model' (Bowlby, 1969) is fundamentally of being bad, worthless and unlovable.

Pupils may fear further rejection and can come across as fiercely independent, fearless, isolated or withdrawn. The pupils who aim to draw as little attention to themselves as possible 'can be easily over-looked' or 'forgotten' (Bombèr, 2007, p.30). They may be 'people pleas-ers' or overly compliant and can 'sometimes be observed engaging in perfectionist-type behaviours' (Bombèr, 2007, p.32).

Pupils may present with behaviour and learning responses led by **separation anxiety,** seeming to need adult attention continually. They may constantly call out or interrupt and become agitated if attention is focused elsewhere. They appear 'preoccupied with relationship' (Bom-bèr, 2007, p.35), possibly stemming from a fear that if they lose your attention, they won't get it back. It can feel like they are drawing you in one minute, only to reject you the next, which possibly could mimic inconsistent and unpredictable caregiving experienced previously.

Relationships, to some pupils, are dangerous and they are likely to reject and hurt you as they fear that you will do the same to them. They appear oppositional but 'behind the façade of defiance, there can be a profound sense of fear, panic and helplessness. These children are so preoccupied with trying to survive that they find it very hard to relax into relationships, or the learning process' (Bombèr, 2007, p.37).

Disorganised early experiences can lead to unpredictable, chaotic, 'bizarre or distressingly extreme behaviours' (Bombèr, 2007, p.35). Pupils may have experienced an enormous sense of powerlessness, and need to remain in control to feel safe and 'cannot bear the risk of being dependent or vulnerable in any way' (Bombèr, 2007, p.37).

Pupils with an insecure attachment style are likely to be highly anxious and have a strong need to control. They may present with hyperactivity or restlessness. Pupils tend to be hypervigilant and feel unsafe since they haven't previously experienced a sense of safety. Their emotions are strong, uncontrolled and overwhelming and they have difficulties expressing and understanding these. They may have a heightened sense of shame or anger and often have sudden reactions to unseen triggers. Focus, concentration and attention, memory and creativity and capacity for learning, empathy and compassion can be affected.

These early relational experiences form the foundations when building new relationships and affect their engagement in learning and their behaviour. Pupils may struggle with social relationships, interac-tions and to understand and interpret social cues. They often distrust adults, particularly those in authority. Their primary focus is on keeping safe, rather than learning.

## The threat response (see p.40)

Pupils who have experienced prolonged adversity or trauma often have heightened reactions to seemingly small triggers, which may be learnt, involuntary reactions adapted from previous experiences. As McCory (2020) puts it, 'children – and their brains – adapt to survive'. Pupils may respond to certain situations similarly to how they previously kept themselves safe, for example, shouting or raised voices (even if not directed at the pupil) may trigger the survival response of flight, so a pupil may hide under a table or run out of the room, since shouting may have previously meant that they or someone they loved was going to get hurt. Hiding or running away has become embedded as a means of keeping safe. Their default setting is fear and a sense of overwhelm with little or 'no capacity for reflection or making good choices; only the capacity for reactivity – to defend and attack' (Bombèr, 2020). Such pupils spend most of the time in survival mode or the 'downstairs' part of their brain (Siegel & Payne Bryson, 2012) to keep them safe. 'Some experiences can be so overwhelming for children and young people that it creates a sense of terror and helplessness in the short term, which can be triggered without warning later in life' (Miles, 2019).

If the threat response is regularly triggered and is not 'soothed' and 'calmed', the brain becomes 'wired on hyper alert because the world seems so scary' (De Thierry, 2017 p.24). 'Words can be difficult to use when someone is traumatised because the part of the brain that is responsible for speech and language goes "offline" when there are high levels of stress' (De Thierry, 2017 p.19).

For pupils who have lived through (or are living through) a prolonged or recurrent state of threat, the continual activation of the threat response will impact emotional regulation, behaviour and relationships as well as the ability to engage and learn. 'Their trauma will come out in their behaviour as they are constantly in survival mode' (Evans, 2018).

'One of the most significant developmental vulnerabilities that traumatised children and young people have to contend with is faulty neuroception. Basically, their neuroception has been altered in such a way that they now see threat everywhere, even when there isn't a threat' (Bombèr, 2020, p.111). These pupils are functioning even though their survival response has developed so that everything and everyone is seen as a threat and the world is perceived as unsafe.

## Toxic stress

If a child has experienced prolonged, repeated, stressful or traumatic experiences or extreme adversity in childhood, with a low number of resilience assets, it can over-activate the child's stress response system and regularly release stress hormones into the body leading to toxic levels of stress. As De Thierry (2017) writes

> Toxic stress is created when the trauma is prolonged and where the child is powerless and can't change the continually frightening experience. It can impact a child immediately in the short term and in the long term unless there is an appropriate response given.
>
> (De Thierry, 2017)

Toxic stress is how adversity and trauma damage a child's development and wellbeing. 'Toxic stress impacts human biology. Toxic stress results in a disruption to the stress response' (Bombèr, 2020, p.1) resulting in 'dysregulation and distrust'.

## Toxic shame

Shame is an 'intensely painful feeling or experience of believing that we are flawed and therefore unworthy of love and belonging' (Brown, 2012, p.69). If a child is 'exposed to regular experiences of shame, they can develop negative coping mechanisms which can cause significant toxic stress and have a lasting impact on their relationships, emotions, behaviour and learning' (De Thierry, 2019, p.16).

Criticism or perceived negative feedback and the fear of making mistakes may all be indicators of shame. Brown (2019) uses the visual concept of *Shame Shields*; barriers unconsciously used by people to disconnect from the 'pain of shame' and from relationships, connection and engagement.

## Understanding pupils in the classroom

In the classroom, pupils may communicate distress through a range of behaviours. 'Teachers' perspectives begin to change when they realise that these kids' disturbing behaviours started out as frustrated attempts to communicate distress, and as misguided attempts to survive' (Van der Kolk, 2015, p.352). Pupils may present as hypervigilant, hyperactive and have sensory sensitivities. Toxic stress can change brain development and affect attention, decision-making, learning and response to stressful situations (CDC, undated) as well as executive function (see p.14–15). Pupils may appear to be in their own world, struggle with transition and change, and lack a sense of joy, awe and wonder in the world.

Troubled pupils usually have difficulties regulating their behaviour and emotions because they have not had access to consistent, regulating, trusted adults. 'If we can try and understand that the children who are traumatised are essentially "stuck" internally in a period of time where they didn't have their needs met, it can make their behaviour less strange or disconcerting' (De Thierry, 2017, p.49).

'The good news is that brains are plastic and every single time a child has a positive experience or interaction a little bit more work is being done to move towards a brain whose default wiring is not a fear response' (Knightsmith, 2020). Essentially, positive relationships and interaction re-build brains!

Schools can be challenging for traumatised pupils who arrive with fear and mistrust and are then required to 'relinquish control and to instinctively trust that teachers are safe adults. For children who have experienced relational trauma, often at the hands of trusted adults, this can be extremely difficult, almost like facing a phobia' (Treisman, 2017, p.147). Alongside this, pupils need to 'share adult support/attention with multiple others' as well as 'spending long periods away from their attachment figure' (Treisman, 2017, p.148). It isn't surprising that their distress is manifested through their behaviour.

## Adversity-, trauma- and attachment-aware strategies to help pupils thrive

All strategies need to be implemented within a trusting relationship, focusing on building and maintaining connections and a sense of emotional safety within a supportive, nurturing and consistent environment.

All children are different and not all pupils who have experienced ACEs, trauma or insecure attachments will present with difficulties in school. However, trauma- and attachment-aware strategies are effective with all pupils and are essential for those who struggle with making and maintaining relationships and engaging in learning. 'Some of the children who may struggle to engage in class or whose behaviour presents us with challenge are exhibiting a learned trauma response. Using a trauma-informed approach will support these children (and their peers as well)' (Knightsmith, 2020). Following the onset of Covid-19, now more than ever, we need trauma-infused approaches for all pupils.

The main focus must be ensuring that pupils feel physically and emotionally safe; the most effective way to do that is through trusting, consistent, predictable and positive relationships with key adults. Pupils need adults to take the time to connect with them, understand them and support them, teach them strategies to manage their emotions and provide necessary skills with empathy and nurture.

Miles (2019) sums up the importance of supportive and understanding school staff when discussing her own school experiences:

> These teachers just got me. I could never sit still and could not relax because I needed to release my anxiety regularly. I was permanently hypervigilant, so every new room I walked into I scanned for safety and needed to choose where I sat – it was exhausting, for them and me, but they made the necessary accommodations. School was my safe place – it was the few hours of joy I experienced every day.

Below is a range of strategies that have been tried and tested and found to support pupils who have experienced ACEs, trauma or attachment difficulties. There is a checklist at the end of this chapter.

## A strength-based approach

- Reframe language into positives when talking about and to pupils. Interpret 'challenging' behaviour as a communication of distress or anxiety. Pupils' behaviours are probably what has previously been keeping them safe and enabling them to survive. 'Positive reframes can be beneficial in re-storying and reframing behaviours. For example, instead of saying "he's lazy and doesn't try" one might say "he must be exhausted with trying", or instead of "she refuses to sit still" one might say "she seems to be overstimulated".' Rather than 'attention-seeking' pupils are seen and described as 'attention-needing' or 'attachment-seeking' (Treisman, 2017, p.69), as they are aiming to make or maintain a connection. Reframing language can change the perception of adults and the pupils' understanding of themselves. It changes the atmosphere in the classroom and the whole school. It increases the capacity for empathy and compassion.
- 'In some people, adversity can foster perseverance, deepen empathy, strengthen the resolve to protect, and spark mini-superpowers'

(Burke Harris, 2018, p.218). Focus on the pupil's strengths, successes and achievements and help them to find and develop their 'superpowers'.

## Sense of safety

All pupils, but particularly traumatised pupils, need to be and feel safe in school. 'Safety is at the core of healing trauma' (Tucci, 2019). Children can only explore and learn when they feel safe and calm. 'In essence, fear restricts and safety expands learning and relationships' (Treisman, 2017, p.10).

- Repeated experiences of safety in relationships are essential; 'Physical safety first, but we also need to create social, emotional and cognitive safety' (Knightsmith, 2020). Explicitly communicate safety to pupils through relationship and consistent and predictable language, actions and routines at all times during the school day. 'The only way to enable a child to recover is to help them feel calm and safe by being a safe person who can support and help them' (De Thierry, 2017, p.27).
- Communication of safety also needs to be through non-verbal behaviour: 'Prosodic voices, positive facial expressions, and welcoming gestures trigger through neuroception feelings of safety and trust that spontaneously emerge when the social engagement system is activated' (Porges, 2017, p.2). The Covid-19 pandemic and the wearing of masks has made this difficult and people have had to make a real effort to smile with the eyes; let's continue to convey genuine warmth and safety through our whole demeanour. Treisman (2017, p.25) draws on the work of Perlman et al. (2008), suggesting that pupils who have experienced relational and developmental trauma may find it difficult to interpret still faces which may therefore be a trigger, as they 'struggle with differentiating facial expressions, and are more likely to interpret events and faces as being negative, angry, threatening; and subsequently have stronger emotional reactions to them'.
- Pupils will need access to a small team of trusted key adults and a safe space to go to, with a range of calming activities. 'Note spaces and faces that make a child feel safe. Can these be accessed in times of need?' (Knightsmith, 2020). Adults need to take time to build relationships and understand the pupil. 'Safety is a relational experience' (Tucci, 2019).

## *Relationships and communication*

The most important thing adults in schools can do is build positive, trusting relationships with pupils. 'When a person has been hurt in a relationship, they can only be healed in a relationship' (De Thierry, 2017, p.27).

- 'When trauma is processed in the context of a warm and genuine relationship, the impact is minimalised if not altogether transformed into greater resilience and so can totally change the degree of the impact on the child and their future' (Knightsmith, 2020). Everyday interactions between adults and pupils have an essential relational role in developing a pupil's sense of safety, self-worth and how they view the world and the people within it. 'The skills of empathy, kindness, patience, attunement, listening and valuing each child can change the lives of traumatised children forever and stop the traumatic experience leading to significant problems later on in life' (De Thierry, 2017, p.36).

- One of their team of key adults will need to regularly check in with the pupil throughout the day, particularly at trigger points. (Key adults refers to a team of adults who have built a strong, positive, trusting relationship with the pupil, rather than a full-time 1:1 adult, leading to fewer difficulties if a key member of staff is absent, as the pupil has a key team in place.) 'What's most needed for such deep change for children and young people who have experienced developmental trauma is – us! The adults. The very tool that many of us in education have underestimated – ourselves!' (Bombèr, 2020, p.7).

- Work collaboratively and develop a relationship with caregivers and outside agencies as well as the pupil. Help them feel part of the process so that they feel decisions are not 'done to them' but 'with them'. Give choices and involve them in discussions, where appropriate. Outcomes tend to be improved when families and schools have a shared, consistent approach. Knightsmith (2020) recommends that schools 'work with families for long-term change', stating that 'when we work in partnership with families, signposting support as needed, sharing advice and ideas and building trust and safety in the relationship between the school and the family, the child always wins.'

- Genuine relationships between adults and pupils take time but are essential. Treisman (2017, p.152) describes them as 'the anchor on which children learn, flourish and make behavioural changes'. Spending quality, regular time with a pupil can build trust and resilience, help pupils to feel understood and emotionally connected and have a lifelong impact. Build relationships based on Dan Hughes' PACE approach (Playfulness, Acceptance, Curiosity and Empathy) – a way of thinking, feeling, communicating and behaving that aims to help pupils feel safe and secure, develop trust and form emotional connections (Bombèr, 2020, pp.200–210; Bombèr & Hughes, 2013, pp.79–141).

- **Playfulness:** Build connections, have fun and play together. Laughing and interacting with others produces oxytocin which can reduce stress, regulate emotions and create a sense of psychological safety, thus increasing the capacity to engage, learn and, over time, calm an over-active threat response (Kaufman, 2020). Relationship-building ideas include 'make something with them, cook with them or play a game with them' (De Thierry, 2017, p.22). Try doing some 'heavy work' activities together (see p.43–4), for example, go outside and do some sport or bounce a ball together, do some gardening, play giant Jenga or get creative and crafty, play musical instruments together or dance. Any activities to promote shared joy and pleasure will help build positive relationships.
- **Acceptance:** Accept the pupil for who they are and provide *unconditional positive regard* (Rogers, 1957). Acceptance is communicated by verbal and non-verbal communication. Acknowledge and attune to a pupil's emotions, needs and perceptions (whilst setting limits on behaviours, if necessary), rather than dismissing them, even if they differ from your own.
- **Curiosity:** Understand behaviour as communication and be 'in a place of compassionate curiosity to "learn the child" and their needs' (Evans, 2018). Use calming and connecting commentaries and *wondering aloud* techniques (Bombèr, 2007, pp.88–89, 147–150; Bombèr, 2011, p.116) to tentatively begin to name and explain the pupil's feelings: 'I wonder if you are feeling ... because?' In this way pupils will begin, over time, to understand, make sense of, express and reflect on the strong emotions that they are feeling and begin to regulate these alongside a caring adult, as well as begin to understand the actions and emotions of others. Knightsmith (2020) explains how curiosity can be used to help adults reflect and develop: 'Be curious about yourself: "I wonder why this is making me feel so agitated?" Be curious about the situation: "I wonder what we can learn from this?" Be curious about the future: "I wonder what we can do differently next time?"'
- **Empathy:** The importance of conveying empathy (rather than sympathy) to traumatised pupils cannot be stressed enough and

is essential in understanding and connecting with them. Children cannot show empathy if they have never received empathy and need this shown and modelled to them. Brown (2012) states, 'empathy is the antidote to shame', explaining that shame cannot survive being spoken about and shared with an empathic listener.

■ Show the pupil that they are 'kept in mind' (Bombèr, 2007, p.34) even when they are apart from you; for example, 'I thought about you at the weekend because I saw the train go across the bridge and I remembered how much you love trains'. Or 'I missed you every day as I watered the plants when you were away, because that is normally your job'. Just knowing that you care enough to have thought about them is incredibly powerful. Aim to maintain a relationship to help pupils remain connected during periods of absence; for example, use phone calls and video conferencing to show you are keeping them in mind. During school holidays, send pre-written postcards or emails home periodically, or give the pupil a transitional object to take home such as the class mascot or a plant to look after.

■ Try to understand the reason for the behaviours. Spot triggers and patterns, and then help reduce stress and teach skills to manage at these times. 'When things are really kicking off our pupils need us close by'. (Bombèr, 2020, p.114). Ensure a key adult checks in at times of increased stress and helps the pupil to cope, for example, moving around school a few minutes earlier to avoid busy corridors, a special job to do in assembly, smaller zones or a club at lunchtimes, transitional objects and visual cues at change-over times, being at the front or back of the line (or not in the line at all). Think of creative ways to reduce anxiety and help pupils be successful.

■ A *meet and greet* in the mornings can alleviate stress. The adult and pupil can engage in sensory-calming activities, talk through the day, the pupil can talk about any worries and the adult can check that the pupil is settled before going to class. Something similar may be needed after lunchtime and before going home.

■ 'Powerlessness is at the very essence of trauma' (Bombèr, 2020, p.190). Offer positive choices to increase a pupil's sense of control, within safe, limited parameters; for example, 'Where are you going to do your writing, here with me, with your group or with a clipboard in the book corner?' Avoid offering a negative choice (for example, 'you can either finish your work now or at break time'), since a pupil who has a low sense of self-worth may take the negative option, as that is what they feel is expected of them (or, in the example given, may prefer to stay inside with an adult).

■ Traumatised pupils often have difficulty making and maintaining friendships and may misread or misinterpret social and emotional cues. They need support in building positive relationships with their peers. Start in a pair or small group, playing games and teaching turn-taking. Support pupils to repair and restore relationships after an incident (see p.11–12).

**Case study:**

Lincoln lived in foster care and had previously experienced neglect and physical abuse and had witnessed domestic violence. He had recently moved into Year 4 and his behaviour had escalated. He was described as 'unmanageable' and was at risk of permanent exclusion.

Lincoln left the classroom without permission, crawled under tables, ran away from staff and 'refused' to engage in his learning. On one particular occasion, he grabbed a roll of masking tape and wrapped himself up in it, from foot to head, before diving into a cardboard box, covering his head with his hands and screaming at the top of his voice.

*How could adults support Lincoln in school?*

Let's look carefully at Lincoln. His behaviours weren't 'unmanageable'; they were incredibly 'distressed'. The first thing to do was reframe the way staff were seeing and communicating with and about Lincoln. In a meeting with key staff, the idea of distressed behaviour was introduced. Without going into the details, staff were made aware of his past trauma and asked what his behaviours may have been communicating. Once words like 'fear', 'unsafe', 'anxiety', 'stress' and 'trauma' were linked to his behaviours, staff began to display much more compassion and empathy. All adults were then asked to state something they liked about Lincoln, something he was good at and a strategy that worked for him. They were asked to remember these at the beginning of each session and refer to as many as they could to build self-esteem. It turned out that he loved basketball.

The next time Lincoln was distressed, and left the classroom, instead of rushing after him and trying to get him back, his key adult grabbed the basketballs he had previously left on a shelf by the exit. He started bouncing a ball (modelling) and invited Lincoln, when he was ready, to join him (mirroring). The next day, before English (which was often a trigger), his key adult quietly suggested they popped outside for ten minutes to play basketball before the lesson. Over time, during these planned basketball sessions, the relationship and trust gradually started to build and Lincoln was able to spend a longer time in lessons.

The next time Lincoln got in the cardboard box and tried to hide, his key adult used *noticing* and *wondering aloud* techniques and empathy to name his emotions – 'I notice that sometimes you just want to hide away from everything. I understand that. I wonder if we could work together to turn this big box into a bit of a safe den for you? We could paint or decorate it and put some nice cushions in there and choose some nice calming things you might like. What do you think?'

Lincoln had a safe adult to co-regulate with him and a safe place to go to when he needed to. His behaviours became more 'manageable', but more importantly, staff understood him more and were much more empathic.

- Pupils may struggle to understand, manage and communicate their emotions and to regulate these. They may not have had an adult modelling and regulating with them in infancy. 'A trauma/fear response can take many forms – it is as likely to look like anger as fear. When we are in a state of high alert, higher thinking and language is shut down. This is not the time for reasoning – in this moment calming is the number one priority' (Knightsmith, 2020). Pupils will need co-regulation before they can self-regulate (see p.34). Trusted adults will need to model and teach calming strategies and trial these with the pupil.

## Teaching and learning

- Teach a broad and balanced curriculum, using the pupil's interests as a starting point, where possible and help them to find their strengths. 'They need music, art, drama, dance, sport and technology – subjects that are practical with therapeutic qualities that help children regulate, allow them to feel a sense of success, let them express themselves and their creativity, and help to repair some of the damage done to the brain through early adversity' (Miles, 2019).
- Be aware of, and teach to, the pupil's developmental social and emotional age rather than their chronological age 'particularly

in times of perceived threat or dysregulation' (Treisman, 2017, p.149) and especially when teaching self-regulation, behaviour expectations, relational and interaction skills and at unstructured times. 'We can be more forgiving when we view a child's responses as if they were those of a younger child (due to a brain development delay caused by trauma)' (Knightsmith, 2020).

■ Support pupils in managing change and transitions. Carefully plan for the start of the day (and the start of each lesson), changes of adult or space and the end of the day. Plan goodbyes and ways to save memories if the child, friend or a key adult is moving on. Transitional objects can support separation anxiety (see p.91).

■ A deep sense of shame can mean that making mistakes is a trigger. Provide erasers and have spare copies of work. Be aware that correcting and editing work may cause a negative reaction, as can receiving perceived negative feedback. Model making and learning from mistakes. Asking pupils to mark and feedback on the teacher's work or 'spot the deliberate mistake' activities are often more effective than correcting their own work.

■ Notice the pupil specifically and give specific positive feedback for small steps to success. Some pupils find it difficult to cope with direct praise and may respond by sabotaging relationships or successes. If their 'internal working model' (Bowlby, 1969) is negative and one of low self-worth, praise may be difficult to accept. Build up gradually and consider private or non-verbal praise, initially, for pupils who find it difficult to accept public or direct praise. Ideas include a sticky note telling the pupil what they have done well or collecting blocks to add to a tower or jigsaw or chess pieces to collect or give a quiet gesture such as a smile or a thumbs-up, rather than verbal praise. Be sure to give rewards if they have been promised or earned. Pupils may have been let down in the past by adults who were unable to fulfil their promises so will be wary of rewards and take time to build trust.

---

**Case example:**

Marcelo was in Reception. Although seemingly desperate for adult attention, Marcelo became incredibly violent whenever he was praised. As soon as he was told something positive, he would shout, use obscene language, kick, hit, throw equipment and run out of the room.

Staff within the Early Years Foundation Stage (EYFS) agreed that, if Marcelo had done something well or made a positive choice, they would silently and privately show him a little construction brick and put this on a tower for him. Marcelo gradually began to smile to himself when he gained another brick on his tower.

A few weeks later, Marcelo was able to receive private verbal praise and later, more public praise. Now he is in Year 2 and he can stand up in celebration assemblies and receive a certificate with visible pleasure.

## Environmental considerations

- When creating a seating plan a hypervigilant pupil may need to have a view of the whole room with their back to the wall in order to feel safe. Another pupil may feel secure near to an adult or chosen peer or a pupil may need to be near the door to use their exit strategy more easily. Speak to pupils and explore their preferences.
- Provide an exit strategy and access to a safe place with calm tools and key adult to model calming strategies (see p.44–5).
- Traumatised pupils or those with attachment difficulties may have increased sensory sensitivities (see the 'Sensory Processing Disorder (SPD)' chapter). Subconscious memories are stored by the senses and the body is largely in survival mode; 'the body keeps the score' (Van der Kolk, 2015). The more stressed the pupil feels, the more difficulty they will have processing sensory information. 'Sensory processing is very much linked to our early experiences in that having inappropriate sensory input may result, for example, in hypervigilance. A child may seek out sensory experiences which they lacked as an infant. Or a child, for example, who heard a lot of distressing shouting may be auditory defensive' (Stephens, 2018, information courtesy of Beacon House Therapeutic Services and Trauma Team, www.beaconhouse.org.uk).

## Rewards and consequences

Traditional behaviour systems, such as isolation, exclusion, shouting, cross faces or 'relational withdrawal' (Hughes, 2009, p.82), tend to be ineffective, shaming and damaging for pupils who have experienced developmental and relational trauma. They increase stress and anxiety, convey messages of rejection and can re-traumatise pupils, re-triggering the threat response. 'We need programmes and resources that acknowledge that punishment, deprivation and force merely retraumatize these children and exacerbate their problems' (Perry & Szalavitz, 2017).

Traumatised (and all) pupils learn best by consistently being taught regulation skills and through predictable, positive relationships and connections.

■ Pupils need 'relational proximity' (Bombèr, 2020). They need 'time in' and co-regulation alongside a trusted adult, rather than 'time out', which induces shame, increases stress and dysregulation and fails to teach alternative, more appropriate behaviours. 'Ironically, when behaviour gets really tricky and most difficult for us, this is the precise time these pupils need us most' (Bombèr, 2020, p.67). They need to learn boundaries and behaviour expectations within safe relationships, with empathy, compassion and co-regulation.
■ Adults need to be 'stress-regulators' and 'shame-regulators' rather than 'behaviour managers' (Bombèr, 2020). They need to support pupils to access the higher-thinking, logical parts of their brain and spend less time in their survival brain. They need to help them to feel safe, moving them from distress to de-stress.

## Resources, further information and 'tool kits'
### Books for adults

*Attachment in the Classroom: A Practical Guide for Schools* by Heather Geddes

*Attachment Play: How to Solve Children's Behavior Problems with Play, Laughter, and Connection* by Aletha Jauch Solter – fantastic ideas for home and school for building attachments through play

*Conversations that Make a Difference for Children and Young People: Relationship-Focused Practice from the Frontline* by Lisa Cherry (to be published)

*Conversations that Matter* by Margot Sunderland

*The Developing Mind: How Relationships and the Brain Interact to Shape Who We Are* by Daniel Siegel

*Know Me to Teach Me* by Louise Michelle Bombèr – every single person working with children and young people needs to read this book

*Inside I'm Hurting* by Louise Michelle Bombèr

*The Pocket Guide to the Polyvagal Theory: The Transformative Power of Feeling Safe* by Stephen Porges

*Settling to Learn* by Louise Michelle Bombèr and Daniel A. Hughes

*The Simple Guide to Child Trauma* by Betsy De Thierry

*The Simple Guide to Understanding Shame in Children* by Betsy De Thierry

*The Trauma and Attachment-Aware Classroom: A Practical Guide to Supporting Children Who Have Encountered Trauma and Adverse Childhood Experiences* by Rebecca Brooks

*Toxic Childhood Stress* by Nadine Burke Harris

*Using Story Telling as a Therapeutic Tool with Children* by Margot Sunderland

*What About Me?* by Louise Michelle Bombèr

*When the Body Says No* by Gabor Mate

*The Whole-Brain Child* by Daniel Siegel and Tina Payne Bryson

*The Whole-Brain Child Workbook: Practical Exercises, Worksheets and Activities to Nurture Developing Minds* by Daniel Siegel and Tina Payne Bryson

*Working with Relational and Developmental Trauma in Children and Adolescents* by Karen Treisman – a must-read book

*Working with Relational Trauma in Schools: An Educator's Guide to Using Dyadic Developmental Practice* by Louise Michelle Bombèr, Kim Golding and Sian Phillips

### Books and resources to share with pupils

*How Are You Feeling Today Baby Bear? Exploring Big Feelings After Living in a Stormy Home* by Jane Evans

*A Treasure Box for Creating Trauma-Informed Organizations: A Ready-to-Use Resource for Trauma, Adversity, and Culturally Informed, Infused and Responsive Systems* (Therapeutic Treasures Collection) by Karen Treisman

*A Therapeutic Treasure Box for Working with Children and Adolescents with Developmental Trauma: Creative Techniques and Activities* by Karen Treisman

### Websites

www.beaconhouse.org.uk/ Advice, fabulous resources, training and more

www.bravehearteducation.co.uk Advice, fabulous resources, training and more www.creativeeducation.co.uk/ Fantastic on-demand courses and resources from Pooky Knightsmith and her team

www.isst-d.org/resources/faqs-for-teachers/ – International Society for the Study of Trauma and Dissociation – FAQs and answers for teachers, particularly on dissociation and lots of useful ideas on how to support

www.kca.training Kate Cairn's Associates offer information and training including Attachment Aware Schools status

https://static1.squarespace.com/static/5c1d025fb27e390a78569537/t/5cc e03089b747a3598c57947/1557005065155/porges_nicabm_treat ing_trauma.pdf Further information on neuroception and polyvagal theory

https://www.ted.com/talks/karen_treisman_good_relationships_are_ the_key_to_healing_trauma Karen Treisman talking about the importance of relationships

www.touchbase.org.uk Advice, information, resources and training (including AATR training)

www.traumainformedschools.co.uk Advice, information, resources and training (including the trauma-informed practitioner diploma)

https://traumainformededucation.org.uk/ Training, resources and support on trauma-informed and attachment-aware approaches, for education staff

https://uktraumacouncil.org/resources Useful resources, including the booklet *Childhood Trauma and the Brain* by Eamon McCory and links to the videos *How the Brain Adapts to Adversity* and *Linking Childhood Trauma to Mental Health*

## Podcasts

https://www.thesendcast.com/supporting-anxiety-and-trauma/
https://www.lisacherry.co.uk/8-top-podcasts/
https://howtoacademy.com/podcasts/when-the-body-says-no-the-costs-of-hidden-stress/ Gabor Mate

# References

Ainsworth, D. (1982) *Object Relations, Dependency and Attachment: A Theoretical Review of the Infant-Mother Relationship* Child Development, 40, 969–1025 [online] Available at: http://www.psychology.sunysb.edu/attachment/ courses/620/pdf_files/attach_depend.pdf [Accessed 15 February 2021]

Beacon House Therapeutic Services and Trauma Team (undated) *Brainstem Calmers* [online] Available at: https://beaconhouse.org.uk/wp-content/

uploads/2019/09/Brainstem-Calmer-Activities.pdf [Accessed 10 October 2019]

Bellis, M., Hughes, K., Ford, K., Hardcastle, K., Sharp, C., Wood, S., Homolova, L. & Davies, A. (2018) *Adverse Childhood Experiences and Sources of Childhood Resilience: A Retrospective Study of Their Combined Relationships with Child Health and Educational Attendance* BMC Public Health, 18, 792 [online] Available at: https://doi.org/10.1186/s12889-018-5699-8 [Accessed 11 February 2021]

Bombèr, L. (2007) *Inside I'm Hurting – Practical Strategies for Supporting Children with Attachment Difficulties in Schools* Worth Publishing, London

Bombèr, L. (2011) *What about Me? Inclusive Strategies to Support Pupils with Attachment Difficulties Make It Through the School Day* Worth Publishing, London

Bombèr, L. (2020) *Know Me to Teach Me – Differentiated Discipline for Those Recovering from Adverse Childhood Experiences* Worth Publishing, London

Bombèr, L. & Hughes, D. (2013) *Settling to Learn – Settling Troubled Pupils to Learn: Why Relationships Matter in School* Worth Publishing, London

Bowlby, J. (1969) *Attachment. Attachment and Loss: Volume 1* Basic Books, New York

Brown, B. (2012) *TED Talk: Listening to Shame* [online] Available at: https://www.youtube.com/watch?v=psN1DORYYV0 [Accessed 16 February 2021]

Brown, B. (2013) *Daring Greatly: How Courage to be Vulnerable Transforms the Way We Live, Love, Parent and Lead* Penguin, New York

Brown, B. (2019) *Rumbling with Vulnerability: Shame Shields* [online] Available at: https://brenebrown.com/daringclassrooms/ [Accessed 16 February 2021]

Burke Harris, N. (2018) *The Deepest Well – Healing the Long-term Effects of Childhood Adversity* Bluebird, London

CDC (Centers for Disease Control and Prevention) (undated) *Adverse Childhood Experiences (ACEs) – Preventing Early Trauma to Improve Adult Health* [online] Available at: https://www.cdc.gov/vitalsigns/aces/index.html#:~:text=ACEs%20can%20include%20violence%2C%20abuse,and%20substance%20misuse%20in%20adulthood [Accessed 11 February 2021]

De Thierry, B. (2017) *The Simple Guide to Child Trauma – What It Is and How to Help* Jessica Kingsley Publishers, London

De Thierry, B. (2019) *The Simple Guide to Understanding Shame in Children – What It Is, What Helps and How to Prevent Further Stress or Trauma* Jessica Kingsley Publishers, London

Evans, J. (2018) *Children with Problems or Problem Children?* [online] Available at: https://thejaneevans.com/children-with-problems-or-problem-children/ [Accessed 24 March 2021]

Felitti, V., Anda, R., Nordenberg, D., Williamson, D., Spitz, A., Edwards, V., Koss, M. & Marks, J., (1998) *Relationship of Childhood Abuse and Household Dysfunction to Many of the Leading Causes of Death in Adults: The Adverse Childhood Experiences (ACE) Study* [online] Available at: https://www.ajpmonline.org/issue/S0749-3797(00)X0004-9 [Accessed 16 May 2018]

Henson, W. (2020) *4 Key Pillars of a Trauma-Informed Approach During COVID-19* [online] Available at: https://www.eschoolnews.com/2020/12/17/4-key-pillars-of-a-trauma-informed-approach-during-covid-19/?all [Accessed 8 February 2020]

Hughes, D., Heinz Brisch, K., Bombèr, L., Batmanghelidjh, C., Delaney, M., Heyno, A., Earl, B., Amey, S., (2009) *Teenagers and Attachment: Helping Adolescents Engage with Life and Learning* Worth Publishing, London

Kaufman, T. (2020) *Building Positive Relationships with Students: What Brain Science Says* [online] Available at: https://www.understood.org/en/school-learning/for-educators/empathy/brain-science-says-4-reasons-to-build-positive-relationships-with-students [Accessed 23 February 2021]

Knightsmith, P. (2020) *Behaviour: Inclusion Using a Trauma-informed Approach* [online] Available at: https://www.headteacher-update.com/best-practice-article/behaviour-inclusion-using-a-trauma-informed-approach-schools-wellbeing-students-teachers-1/231669/ [Accessed 8 February 2020]

McCory, E. (2020) *A Guidebook to Childhood Trauma and the Brain* UK Trauma Council [online] Available at: https://uktraumacouncil.org/wp-content/uploads/2020/09/CHILDHOOD-TRAUMA-AND-THE-BRAIN-Single Pages.pdf

Miles, L. (2019) *Adverse Childhood Experiences and the Implications for Schools* [online] Available at: https://www.headteacher-update.com/best-practice-article/adverse-childhood-experiences-and-the-implications-for-schools/215017/ [Accessed 8 February 2020]

Perlman, S Kalish, C. & Pollak, S (2008) *The Role of Maltreatment Experience in Children's Understanding of the Antecedents of Emotion* Cognition and Emotion, 22(4), 651–670

Perry, B. & Szalavitz, M. (2017) *The Boy Who Was Raised as a Dog: And Other Stories from a Child Psychiatrist's Notebook – What Traumatized Children Can Teach Us About Loss, Love, and Healing* Basic Books, New York

Porges, S. (2017) *The Pocket Guide to the Polyvagal Theory: The Transformative Power of Feeling Safe* W.W. Norton & Company, New York

Rogers, C. (1957) *The Necessary and Sufficient Conditions of Therapeutic Personality Change* Journal of Consulting Psychology, 21(2), 95–103 [online] Available at: https://psycnet.apa.org/doiLanding?doi=10.1037%2Fh0045357 [Accessed 24 March 2021]

Siegel, D. and Payne Bryson, T. (2012) *The Whole-Brain Child – 12 Proven Strategies to Nurture Your Child's Developing Mind* Robinson, London

Stephens, R. (2018) *Sensory Processing, Coordination and Attachment* [online] Available at: https://beaconhouse.org.uk/wp-content/uploads/2019/09/Sensory-processing-coordination-and-attachment-Article-min.pdf [Accessed 31 October 2018] (information courtesy of Beacon House Therapeutic Services and Trauma Team | 2021 | www.beaconhouse.org.uk)

Treisman, K. (2017) *Working with Relational and Developmental Trauma in Children and Adolescents* Routledge, Oxon

Tucci, J. (2019) *What Really Is Safety for Traumatised Children and Young People?* [online] Available at: https://professionals.childhood.org.au/prosody/2019/01/what-really-is-safety-for-traumatised-children-and-young-people/ [Accessed 14 February 2020]

Van der Kolk, B. (2015) *The Body Keeps the Score: Mind, Brain and Body in the Transformation of Trauma* Penguin, New York

Wavetrust.org (undated) *70/30 Campaign Empowering Communities to Protect Our Children* [online] Available at: https://www.wavetrust.org/ adverse-childhood-experiences-infographics [Accessed 9 October 2018]

Winnicott, D. (1988) *Babies and Their Mothers* Free Association Books, London

## Checklist of adversity-, trauma- and attachment-aware strategies

| STRATEGY | COMMENTS |
|---|---|
| **Please also refer to the 'Behaviour is communication' and 'Self-regulation' chapters** | |
| **A strength-based approach** | |
| Reframe language about behaviour into positives. Focus on strengths, achievements and successes | |
| Focus on strengths and interests, help them find their 'superpowers' | |
| **Sense of safety** | |
| Create and communicate emotional safety, verbally and non-verbally | |
| Small team of trusted key adults who have built up a relationship with the pupil | |
| **Relationships and communication** | |
| Take time to build positive, trusting relationships and provide regular check-ins | |
| Work collaboratively with caregivers, pupil and other staff and agencies | |
| Use the PACE approach (p.65–6) | |
| Communicate that the pupil is 'held in mind' | |
| Spot triggers and reduce stress | |
| Meet and greets | |
| Positive choices | |
| Support in building positive relationships with their peers and support pupils to repair and restore relationships | |
| Co-regulation before self-regulation is essential (see p.34) | |
| **Teaching and learning** | |
| Broad and balanced curriculum, using the pupil's interests as a starting point | |
| Awareness of social and emotional age | |
| Support in managing change and transitions | |
| Awareness that mistakes can trigger shame. Provide erasers and spares. Model making mistakes and receiving feedback | |

*(Continued)*

## Continued

| STRATEGY | COMMENTS |
|---|---|
| Give specific praise, indirect if necessary and give attention for making the right choices and steps to success | |
| **Environmental considerations** | |
| Careful seating plan to enhance sense of safety | |
| Offer an exit strategy and access to a key adult and safe space where the pupil can go when feeling overwhelmed | |
| Be aware of sensory sensitivities | |
| **Rewards and consequences** | |
| Avoid exclusions, isolation, cross faces, shouting and relational withdrawal, which are shaming and re-traumatising | |
| Provide 'relational proximity' – 'time in' and co-regulation, rather than 'time out' | |
| Help regulate stress to reduce time in survival brain. Move from distress to de-stress | |

# Chapter 4

---

# Anxiety

---

Anxiety is a natural human reaction that helps people prepare for challenging, new, exciting or stressful situations (run away from danger or prepare for an exam or interview, for example). The body releases adrenaline, triggering the trauma response (fight, flight, freeze, fawn, flop, see p.40) so that it is ready to react to challenge or danger. Everyone experiences emotions linked to anxiety at some point in time and it is natural to feel nervous, worried or scared as different situations or circumstances arise in life.

The **threat response** is essential when faced with genuine danger and usually calms once that danger has passed. However, for people suffering from heightened anxiety, this response can become similar to a faulty smoke alarm system, triggering at the tiniest amount of burnt toast and refusing to switch off again. It means the body responds to everyday mild triggers or stressors as if it is in danger. When a person is highly anxious, over a period of time, the higher levels of adrenaline and cortisol produced can build up and result in unpredictable or explosive responses. The reaction is beyond the individual's control as anxiety has triggered the body's survival response.

Anxiety becomes problematic when it is heightened and has a sustained negative impact on a pupil's attainment, relationships, social, emotional or physical participation.

The Covid-19 pandemic has seen heightened anxiety across the globe. It is increasingly important that we recognise, understand and talk about anxiety to support our pupils and, more importantly, give them approaches to manage it successfully. The brain is malleable and children can increase self-awareness and learn calming and regulating strategies with adult support.

Symptoms of high anxiety can include:

## Behavioural:

- Absconding and avoidance
- Opposition or defiance
- Compliance, people-pleasing, perfectionism
- Engaging in rituals or rigid routines
- Obsessive thoughts, behaviours or compulsions
- Seeking reassurance or attention
- Risk-taking or self-harm
- Stuttering, stammering or mutism
- Increased movement or fidgeting
- Withdrawal or dissociation

## Cognitive:

- Difficulties concentrating and maintaining focus
- Negative, unrealistic or distracting thoughts or expectations
- Polarised or catastrophic thought patterns
- Difficulties making decisions or trying new things
- Forgetfulness
- Lack of organisation
- Confusion

## Physical:

- Poor sleep patterns, bad dreams or bed-wetting
- Dry mouth or difficulty swallowing
- Feeling unwell (nausea, stomach pains, headaches, muscle aches and pains)
- Rushing feeling or pins and needles in hands or feet
- Dizziness or feeling faint
- Clenched jaw or grinding teeth
- Increased need to go to the toilet
- Twitches or tics
- Heart palpitations
- Difficulty breathing or shallow breathing
- Shaking
- Poor eating habits, weight loss or gain

- Sudden increase or decrease in temperature
- Ringing in the ears
- Chest tightness or pain
- Hair loss

**Psychological or emotional:**

- Intense emotions
- Feeling fretful and worried
- Panic or dread
- Phobias
- Feeling on edge or out of control
- Tearfulness and distress
- Low self-confidence and self-esteem
- Feeling people are staring or judging
- Overwhelm
- Guilt
- Insecurity
- Frustration

Anxiety can impact academic performance, attendance, memory, language comprehension and executive function, quality of life, relationships and the ability to socially engage.

# Types of anxiety or anxiety disorders

**Separation anxiety:** Many infants struggle to separate from their caregivers. However, if children experience extreme anxiety when separating, they may need further support to manage this, particularly if it impacts their participation, wellbeing, relationships or attendance.

**Anxiety-Based School Avoidance (ABSA):** ABSA is an anxiety-driven fear of attending school. A pupil may become overwhelmed with anxious feelings when thinking about, preparing for, or entering school or with the pressure of academic work, social times or relationships within school. ABSA can affect attendance, progress, relationships and self-esteem.

**Generalised anxiety disorder (GAD):** If a pupil is excessively anxious for a high proportion of time, over a long period, and it affects their everyday lives, they may have a generalised anxiety disorder. Pupils may feel 'on edge' and tense most of the time and be hypervigilant. They may find it difficult to relax and may feel emotionally out of control.

**Phobias:** Young children may go through phases of being scared of different things. If a child does not grow out of these fears, they become overwhelming, induce panic attacks or begin to affect their daily routine or everyday life, they may require specific support.

**Social anxiety disorder or social phobia:** Pupils may feel anxious in particular social scenarios, struggle in groups or find it difficult to talk to new people or adults. They may be overly aware of physical anxiety symptoms (blushing, stammering, sweating or shaking) or feel that people are judging them. They may feel very self-conscious about aspects of themselves or feel that they don't fit in with their peers or in particular social situations. They may dwell on social incidents, worrying if people like them or are thinking negatively of them. It may lead to avoidance of certain social situations, prevent them from going to new places or trying new things and negatively impact relationships and wellbeing. People with a social anxiety disorder may be sensitive to criticism, making mistakes, rejection and speaking or eating in front of others.

**Selective mutism:** Where a child understands language and is capable of speaking comfortably in some settings, but extreme social anxiety renders them unable to speak in certain social situations, they may have selective mutism. The label 'selective' implies that this is a personal choice and Hipoliti (2020) suggests 'situational mutism' may be a more appropriate description. Mutism caused by anxiety is triggered by extreme fear. Many people with selective mutism desperately want to speak; they just physically can't at that moment in time as the body's freeze response has taken over this capacity.

**Health anxiety:** Pupils with health anxiety worry excessively about their health for no medical reason. They may predict the worst or worry about death and seek reassurance. This is particularly relevant during and following the Covid-19 pandemic, where health concerns are increased for many.

**Panic attacks:** During panic attacks, people may have difficulty breathing, feel unwell, out of control and have overwhelming feelings of extreme anxiety, the onset of which is usually sudden. Feelings gradually pass, leaving individuals feeling anxious or frightened. They can affect confidence, attendance, relationships and participation in a variety of activities. Individuals may experience anxiety after or between panic attacks, which may lead to avoidance of certain situations for fear of a further panic attack.

**If symptoms persist or begin to negatively impact a pupil's academic, social or everyday life or are causing distress, it is essential to seek professional advice.**

# Strategies to support pupils to manage anxiety

Knightsmith (2020) suggests any adaptions we make in the classroom to reduce anxieties will benefit everyone. Adults can either reinforce or break the anxiety cycle, depending on their reactions. 'Teachers can take proactive steps to check for stress and anxiety and head off negative thoughts before they begin to spiral out of control' (Minahan, 2019).

A range of behaviours, such as emotional outbursts, task avoidance, lack of concentration and running away, can be caused by anxiety. As anxiety increases, the brain cannot effectively regulate behaviour and emotions because the ability to think logically and process information decreases. Therefore, by understanding that the behaviours are communicating a state of heightened distress or overwhelming anxiety, the negative behaviours will be reduced by reducing the stress.

Below is a range of strategies that have been tried and tested and found to support pupils to manage anxiety within school. There is a checklist at the end of this chapter.

## *A strength-based approach*

- Focus on achievements and what the pupil is able and already does to manage and overcome anxiety in different situations, and build on these.
- Build self-confidence and self-esteem; for example, offer roles and responsibilities based on individual strengths and interests. Create a success scrapbook or an 'I can ... can' (where positives from the day are written and stuck in a scrapbook or posted in a can or jar) or send a positive card home. Focus on strengths and positives, reinforcing statements with evidence, telling them what they have done well and why.

## *Relationships and communication*

- Building up positive, trusting relationships is essential in alleviating anxiety and supporting wellbeing. Use Dan Hughes's PACE approach (see p.65–6). Being playful reduces feelings of anxiety and stress as pupils are more relaxed and feel safe in relationship.
- Work collaboratively with caregivers, build a relationship and listen empathically to their concerns and experiences. Share what the pupil is good at and their positive coping strategies and what works well both inside and outside of school.
- Support pupils to ask for help. Putting up a hand in front of the class can induce anxiety or embarrassment. Instead, develop a

pre-agreed, non-verbal system such as a gesture, a help card, or place a building block on the corner of the table. By giving all pupils a set of red (*I need help*), amber (*I am a bit confused*) and green (*I've got this*) cards or coloured cubes to use, it becomes routine and key pupils do not feel singled out.

■ Ensure the pupil has access to a safe space and a trusted adult when they are feeling overwhelmed. Use sticky notes, photographs or other visual prompts as a reminder to use a safe area or calming strategy (see p.42) when a pupil's anxiety is heightening.

■ It can be helpful to offer a cognitive break, rather than sending the pupil for a walk or to a safe space on their own (as this may give more time for negative thinking). Ideas include pencil mazes, construction kits, sudoku, crosswords, word searches, Rubik's Cube grounding techniques (see p.45), re-telling their favourite story, reading a book out loud, singing, answering quiz questions – any calming activity to distract from internal thought patterns.

■ Regular check-ins from a trusted adult can help calm and settle a pupil and focus their attention.

■ Support pupils to identify and change negative or catastrophic thinking patterns into more positive or realistic ones by teaching positive self-talk (see p.37). 'It is how we think about a situation that affects how we then feel both emotionally and physically and how we then choose to behave' (Collins-Donnelly, 2013, p.64). Convey confidence in the pupil with messages such as, 'I know you can do this'.

■ Keep praise quiet, factual and specific when a pupil overcomes anxiety or makes little steps towards success. Use phrases such as, 'I know it was difficult for you to step into the classroom with me today, well done for giving it a go' or 'I noticed that you did your breathing before trying that question, well done'. Praise things within the pupil's control, such as effort, persistence, attitude or behaviours for learning, rather than correct answers or amount of work produced.

■ Talk about and label feelings but avoid asking 'why' or asking leading questions such as 'are you anxious about ...'. Instead, ask open-ended questions such as 'how are you feeling about ...'.

### *Teaching and learning*

■ Model and teach how to manage stressful situations and how to cope with anxiety in healthy ways to improve mental health, well-being and resilience (see 'Self-regulation' chapter).

- Alleviate anxieties over learning tasks (see p.12–13). Allow pupils to preview work. Provide adult support to start an activity and ensure the pupil understands the instructions before moving away. Show pupils what the end product will look like and model how to complete each step of the task before asking pupils to work independently. Break tasks down into small, achievable chunks presented in a checklist (see p.249–50), and where possible, present questions one at a time. Partially completed worksheets for the pupil to complete, or having the first sentence half-written, stopping mid-word or mid-sentence, or true and false questions can often encourage engagement.
- Increase the pupil's sense of control by involving them in discussions and offering choices.
- Convey, model and reinforce the message that it is OK to make mistakes. Often it is easier for an anxious pupil to feed back and highlight mistakes on an adult's work, rather than self-assess or respond to negative feedback on their own work. Show how to learn from mistakes and model how to receive feedback.
- Provide whiteboards and erasers for those who fear making mistakes and have a second copy of any worksheets in case a mistake is made. Teach what to do when a mistake is made, such as rub out gently or cross out neatly. Share inspirational stories or quotes from celebrities about how they overcame mistakes or setbacks to achieve success.
- Speaking in front of the class can cause heightened anxiety and a fear of making a mistake. Reduce pressure on anxious pupils to speak and encourage non-verbal methods of participating and interacting, for example, give all pupils sticky notes or whiteboards to jot answers on or allow drawing or symbols. Build up gradually and encourage peer discussions, recordings and computer presentations for those anxious to present in front of the class. Pre-teach key vocabulary or new skills and give students questions in advance to allow them time to prepare and increase confidence when participating and to help engagement.
- Avoid calling out and displaying grades or test results. Not only is it disheartening (and humiliating) for those who struggle, but it also induces anxiety for the perfectionists and high-achievers who may become distressed and angry at themselves for getting an answer incorrect.
- Homework can induce high anxiety. Set homework that is achievable independently and break it down into small chunks, which include brain or movement breaks. Homework clubs at school

can reduce pressures at home. Be aware of those pupils who may spend hours on their homework to get it right and avoid mistakes or failure. Avoid collecting homework at the start of the lesson, as it will increase anxiety for those who have struggled. Collect it at the end or have it submitted virtually.

## Understanding anxiety

- Help the pupil to understand that anxiety is a normal, physical reaction. Research anxiety and its effect on the brain. Dan Siegel's hand model of the brain is a useful visual representation to aid pupils' understanding (see p.40).
- Normalise anxiety by talking about it openly and honestly. Understanding anxiety and how it presents for the individual is key to managing it. Once pupils know what they are feeling, they can employ strategies to cope. Identify and name the emotions associated with anxiety – 'name it to tame it' (Siegel & Payne Bryson, 2012, p.27). Naming and drawing their feelings and describing the anxiety helps a pupil feel that they have a sense of control over their emotions. Pupils need support to 'use their left brain to make sense of what's going on – to put things in order and to name these big and scary right-brain feelings so they can deal with them effectively ... Research shows that merely assigning a name or label to what we feel literally calms down the activity of the emotional circuitry in the right hemisphere' (Siegel & Payne Bryson, 2012, p.29).
- When calm, teach pupils to recognise the physical presentation of rising anxiety levels in themselves (headache, stomach cramps, faster breathing, clenched fists). Use a teddy or draw an outline of a person on a piece of paper. Use colours, pictures or words to represent different feelings. For example, 'when I feel anxious I feel butterflies in my tummy' and draw some butterflies on the tummy area of the body outline or stick a sticky note on the teddy, or 'before I speak to the class, I feel like my chest is going to explode' and scribble explosions in the chest area. Once we know how anxiety presents and occurs and what triggers it, we can then begin to implement calming strategies (see 'Self-regulation' chapter).
- An effective way to cope with overwhelming emotions is to find a healthy way to express them. Some young people may find it useful to express their feelings by keeping a journal. Collins-Donnelly (2013, pp.54–54) suggests exploring what anxiety looks like for an individual and supporting them to express this creatively by

drawing a picture, writing a song, rap, poem, story or blog about their anxiety, representing their anxiety through a series of photographs or writing ideas for a film or dance about their anxiety.

**Personal case study:**

At the age of 15, I was physically sick most mornings before getting on the school bus. At the time, we didn't know what it was. The physical sickness subsided after a few years but the feelings of nausea continued (and still continue) well into adulthood.

I now know that it was the beginnings of an ongoing battle with social anxiety. A lack of understanding meant a lack of support. During my A Levels and into university, I was selectively mute. I was classed as shy and quiet, but it was so much more than that. It was a crippling fear to speak in certain situations (lectures, seminars, groups of people). I wanted to speak, I would try to form the words in my head, but I couldn't. I would feel hot, start shaking, get palpitations, go red, panic. By the time I had words in my head which I felt I could say, the conversation had moved on. I was terrified of saying the wrong thing, being judged, being wrong, being laughed at, being disliked and being thought of as stupid.

I am sure that avoiding and not recognising the problem exacerbated and prolonged it. I would have the same fear at job interviews, talking to people in authority and talking socially in groups.

So, what helped?

- Recognising and naming the feelings for what they were: anxiety
- Implementing calming strategies when I felt the physical sensations linked to anxiety, (for me – deep breathing, positive self-talk, hand massage, a cup of tea, some chocolate)
- Breaking it down into smaller, achievable steps to success, rather than the final outcome (e.g. tackle a five-minute presentation, just to my husband initially, then to a trusted friend, then a small group, gradually building up, over time, as my confidence grew)
- Being overly prepared, particularly initially – reading everything I could, knowing the subject inside out
- Visual prompts

- ■ Confidence and support conveyed by friends, colleagues and bosses and being told what I was good at
- ■ Increased self-confidence
- ■ Another thing that helped me personally was stepping out of my comfort zone in a totally different area; I was terrified of putting my face in the water and learning to scuba-dive helped me to recognise how anxiety presented for me and boosted my confidence, showing me that I could overcome fear. Over time diving became something that I loved.

Don't get me wrong, I still get anxious, particularly going somewhere new, meeting new people and presenting to colleagues. In fact, just last year, I was due to present at a conference. With about ten minutes to go, I turned to my colleague and told her I thought she would need to take over, as I was unwell, I felt so sick. She told me it was probably nerves, but I was convinced I was ill. She gave me a knowing look and told me she would take over if needed. The nausea inevitably subsided as I got started (proving my colleague right as usual).

## *The stress bucket*

**The stress bucket** analogy shows different stressors which go into filling a person's stress bucket and strategies which can be used throughout the day to 'empty' that bucket, or coping strategies to relax and reset. Pupils need to be taught that they can control their stress bucket and their reactions to stress by implementing calming strategies throughout the day and particularly at times of high anxiety.

- ■ Teach pupils to begin to recognise what fills their stress bucket (stressors or triggers).
- ■ Teach and rehearse a range of calming techniques (see p.44) (ways to empty the stress bucket) when the pupil is calm. Trial a selection and ask the pupil to choose the ones that they feel will be effective for them. Create a sensory bag, take photographs or create other visual reminders.
- ■ Model using the techniques to demonstrate how you deal with anxiety and convey calm. Knightsmith (2020) suggests that adults present as a swan when working with anxious pupils, acting serene and calm (regardless of the legs furiously flapping under

the water to keep afloat). Children will soon pick up on an adult's emotional dysregulation (see p.47).

## *Breaking the anxiety cycle – scaffolding and step-by-step approaches to manage anxiety*

■ Help the pupil to manage their anxiety alongside a trusted adult. Completely avoiding the person, place or thing that is causing the anxiety will reinforce it. Support pupils to spot triggers (walking into school, speaking in front of the class, assembly, lunchtimes), offer support and scaffold how the pupil accesses that which is making them anxious by breaking it down into achievable steps.

■ Use a stepladder approach (Raisingchildren.net.au, 2019) to create a **step-by-step plan** (see pp.245, 246) to support the pupil with specific anxieties. Set a goal with small steps to achieve this with the easiest (least overwhelming) steps first, gradually increasing each step as it is mastered until the final goal is reached. It is sometimes useful to list, with the pupil, the things which cause anxiety and then cut them up or number them, to establish what is most overwhelming for the pupil.

■ Use a plan of the school or a timetable and rate it using a traffic light system (RAG rate). Colour green the areas or lessons which cause the least anxiety, amber those that cause some anxiety, and red those areas that cause heightened or overwhelming anxiety. Discuss how to make the red and amber areas gradually feel safer or more manageable. Morgan-Rose (2015) suggests using Lego™ to create an 'ideal' or 'dream' classroom with the pupils to explore what they value in the classroom and create 'non-ideal' or 'worst' classroom scenes to enable them to express fears or areas of concern within the classroom. This is useful to help pupils explore and express worries about school.

■ Support children to understand that their negative thoughts are exactly that – thoughts, not facts. Encourage pupils to jot down or draw two or three things to represent their biggest worries. Label them 'fact' or 'negative thought' or 'likely' and 'unlikely'. Come up with more positive or realistic thoughts. For example, for a pupil who fears talking to the class, identify the biggest worries (such as 'people won't like me if I say the wrong answer'), look at the worry objectively together, is it true? ('Well, it might be true, but it is very unlikely, everyone makes mistakes, we learn from them. Do you dislike people if they make a mistake? Would you want to be friends with someone who doesn't like you because of a wrong answer in class?')

## *Creative activities to support pupils to recognise and discuss anxiety*

■ Explain what is meant by *butterflies in our tummy* – when someone is feeling anxious they may have a funny feeling in their tummy as if butterflies are fluttering in there. Engage children in a **butterflies activity** where the pupil draws and cuts out butterflies and writes their worries on these. Use different sized butterflies to represent the size of their worries (big butterflies for big worries and little butterflies for smaller worries). Discuss each worry and strategies to calm down or feel better if they feel the butterflies fluttering or people they could turn to for support.

■ Pop **worry bubbles** to help children to label and let go of a worry. Encourage and model thinking about a worry and blowing this into a bubble. Picture the worry inside the bubble and floating away or chase after them and pop them. Blowing bubbles promotes deep breathing, helping pupils naturally calm and relax.

■ Use **worry monsters** or **worry boxes** (see p.251) to write and keep their worries in, to avoid having to think about them all the time or all at once. Make sure the pupil knows when they will be shared if they would like to. Alternatively, make worry dolls to tell worries to, or use toys or puppets.

■ Write or draw worries on a piece of paper, and once they have been discussed or resolved, rip them up and throw them in the bin.

■ **Make calm jars** (water, glitter glue and glitter in a plastic jar), children shake them and watch the glitter float to the bottom.

■ **Make stress tools** such as lavender playdough, slime, stress balls (using eco balloons and cornflour) or make a self-soothe box (see 'tool kit').

### *Supporting children with separation anxiety*

■ Prepare the pupil in advance so they know what to expect (who will be meeting them, which door they will go in, what they will do).

■ Encourage caregivers to arrive at the agreed time each day and **create a quick 'goodbye' ritual** when leaving, such as a silly handshake or a kiss on the nose and each cheek and then leave. It is also important for caregivers to be on time and stand in the same space each day when they return, to provide routine and predictability.

- **Have a fun job to do on arrival,** such as sensory circuits, walking the wellbeing dog, feeding the fish, collecting the fruit, watering the plants or putting the chairs out.
- **Transitional objects from home** such as notes in the pencil case or lunch box, a photo of caregivers or a pet, a special pebble, gemstone, shell or little toy are often enough to maintain connections during periods of absence.
- **Transitional objects from or in school** such as the class teddy, teacher's special pen, a note or a book can support pupils returning to school or when moving classroom or changing adult, to keep a sense of connection. If a pupil seeks adult attachment during work tasks, leaving an item belonging to the adult can help them focus for longer – 'look after my special pen and I will be back to you in just a moment'. Pupils will feel safer as they know the adult needs to return to them to collect their item. Start with leaving the pupil for a short time and build up very gradually.

---

**Case example:**

Josie used to refuse to leave the classroom to go to Maths. One day her teacher suggested that Josie take her teacher's scarf with her. She went off happily to Maths. It seems that just having a special item of the teacher's was enough to maintain the attachment during the separation and Josie was secure that she would return to the adult, as she had to give her scarf back.

---

- Playing **peek-a-boo** and **hide-and-seek** helps pupils to understand permanence (when someone goes away they will come back).

## *Supporting children with Anxiety-Based School Avoidance (ABSA)*

- Try to spot warning signs and intervene early to prevent behaviours from becoming embedded. Possible indicators of ABSA could include separation anxiety, reduced attendance or increased lateness, a change in behaviours, a negative view of school, increased anxiety observed in school or at home, social or friendship difficulties, withdrawal or isolation and reduced engagement or progress.

- Work with the pupil and the family to explore and understand the triggers, establish reasons for reluctance or barriers to attendance and what the pupil is finding particularly difficult.
- Make a step-by-step plan (see p.245).
- Focus on relationships. Support during periods of absence and maintain a connection with the pupil through daily friendly telephone calls or video conferences and occasional positive postcards home.
- Encourage pupils to access learning remotely either from home or from a safe, quiet area of the school with a key adult.
- 'Meet and greet' to support the pupil to feel welcome and increase their sense of belonging and connectedness. Provide a small team of key adults and have a safe space to share low-key fun activities, have a drink and share breakfast. Allow them to talk while playing or drawing and express any worries they may have.
- Pre-teach keywords, skills and concepts to increase confidence before they enter a lesson.
- Welcome the pupil in and avoid drawing attention to punctuality issues as this will heighten anxiety and could reinforce the avoidance.
- Enable contact home initially and during times of overwhelm or heightened anxiety.
- Plan reset times and activities to help bring down arousal levels. Help the pupil to relax and feel less anxious (see 'Self-regulation' chapter).

## *Supporting children with selective (situational) mutism*

- Take the pressure away from speaking. Use non-verbal as well as verbal means of communication – play instruments, take turns clapping rhythms, communicate through music, song, drama and art, take photographs, play with puppets, use gesture and pictures or symbols.
- Play games, initially those which do not need a verbal response. Have fun building up to simple games which have a single word response such as picture lotto, matching pairs or snap.
- Encourage pair work with a buddy. Rehearse answers with a trusted peer or adult. Use whiteboards to encourage participation in group work and allow written and video presentations.
- Use the pupil's strengths and interests as a starting point.
- Plan little steps towards success and create a step-by-step plan (see p.246).

## Environmental and organisational adaptations

- Anxieties are alleviated by clear routines, predictability and consistency and feeling prepared. Visual cues can reduce feelings of anxiety. Use a visual timetable so that the pupil knows what to expect and when. Anxious pupils may seek reassurance and ask lots of questions to alleviate these anxieties. 'Children with anxiety disorders often don't like not knowing, or don't like uncertainty, so their questioning or their reassurance seeking can at times represent their effort to try and stop being in that position of being unsure ... just tuning into that is probably one of the first steps for teachers ... just holding in mind that for students with anxiety it might represent their effort to cope' (Conroy, 2019).
- Support pupils to prepare for and manage transitions and change (see p.15). Time limits and countdowns may induce further anxiety. Some pupils feel compelled to complete all tasks and struggle to leave work unfinished; asking them to stop may cause stress. Loud noises such as school bells can trigger anxiety, particularly for auditory sensitive pupils.
- Allow students to move around earlier or later if the busy corridor or cloakroom is a trigger. Give a pupil the responsibility of tidying the equipment, give a job to do in the classroom after break times or play a short piece of music or a quick fun video clip or engage in a 'heavy work' activity (see p.43–4) when the class return from break time to settle them.

## Unstructured times

- Give support at unstructured times. Access to quiet areas or clubs can be supportive. Teach pupils where and who they go to at break and lunchtimes when they are feeling overwhelmed or anxious (and rehearse and walk through this regularly when they are calm). Allowing pupils to set up clubs based on their strengths and interests can be a confidence boost and helps them avoid a busy playground or dining hall, at times.

## Rewards and consequences

- Avoid sanctions for behaviours stemming from anxiety as these are out of the pupil's control, seldom effective and unlikely to improve anxiety-driven behaviours. Instead, teach pupils appropriate coping skills and strategies in order to manage their anxieties (and therefore their behaviours) more appropriately and effectively.

# Resources, further information and 'tool kits'

## Books for adults

*Helping Children Manage Anxiety at School: A Guide for Parents and Educators in Supporting the Positive Mental Health of Children in Schools* by Colleen Wildenhaus

*Selective Mutism in Our Own Words* by Carl Sutton and Cheryl Forrester

*The Selective Mutism Resource Manual* by Maggie Johnson

## Books to share with pupils

*All Birds Have Anxiety* by Kathy Hoopmann

*Can I Tell You about Anxiety?* by Lucy Willetts and Polly Waite

*Can I Tell You about Selective Mutism?* by Maggie Johnson and Alison Wintgens

*Cards Against Anxiety: A Guidebook and Cards to Help You Stress Less* by Pooky Knightsmith

*Don't Worry, Be Happy: A Child's Guide to Overcoming Anxiety* by Poppy O'Neill

*Help Your Dragon Overcome Separation Anxiety* by Steve Herman

*Starving the Anxiety Gremlin* by Kate Collins-Donnelly

*The Panicosaurus* by K. I. Al-Ghani

*There's a Bully in My Brain* by Kristin O'Rourke

## Websites

https://www.anxietyuk.org.uk/get-help/free-anxiety-resources/ Links to advice, support and a range of useful resources

https://charliewaller.org/information/anxiety www.charliewaller.org/resources/wellbeing-action-plan-child Mental health charity with lots of useful information and links

https://copingskillsforkids.com/calming-anxiety Ideas for supporting children with anxiety and helping them to calm

https://www.creativeeducation.co.uk/courses/anxiety-10-things-you-need-to-know/ Fabulous on-demand video course which introduces practitioners to anxiety and how to support in schools

https://www.elsa-support.co.uk/elsachat-separation-anxiety/ Practical ideas to help pupils with separation anxiety

www.handinhandparenting.org/2016/01/20-plaayful-ways-heal-separation-anxiety/ Playful activities to support parents with children with separation anxiety http://www.ispeak.org.uk/ Information on selective mutism

https://www.kooth.com/ Online support for young people

https://mentalhealth-uk.org/help-and-information/conditions/anxi
ety-disorders/what-is-anxiety/ Mental health support

notfineinschool.co.uk Support and awareness of school attendance
barriers

www.nhs.uk/conditions/social-anxiety/ Information on social anxiety

https://schools.westsussex.gov.uk/Page/10483 Information and resources
on school avoidance, including a booklet to explore anxieties with
pupil

https://selectivemutismcenter.org/dos-donts-for-interacting-with-
those-with-selective-mutism/ Guidance for supporting pupils
with selective mutism

www.southglos.gov.uk/documents/Classroom-Resources.pdf A range
of classroom resources to teach children about anxiety, worries
and feelings

https://strivingtospeak.com/; www.youngminds.org.uk Information on
selective mutism

https://raisingchildren.net.au/toddlers/health-daily-care/mental-
health/anxiety-stepladder-approach Information on the stepladder
approach

https://youngminds.org.uk/blog/how-to-make-a-self-soothe-box/
Suggestions to make a self-soothe box

https://youngminds.org.uk/find-help/conditions/anxiety/ Useful advice,
information and support

## Podcasts

Sendcast – https://www.thesendcast.com/understanding-and-manag
ing-anxiety-in-children-and-young-people/

Sendcast – https://www.thesendcast.com/emotionally-based-school-
refusal/?utm_source=Email&utm_medium=SENDcast&utm_cam
paign=EmotionalSchoolAvoidance&utm_source=ActiveCampaign&
utm_medium=email&utm_content=School+avoidance+or+refus
al+-+do+the+terms+really+matter%3F&utm_campaign=SEND
cast+-+Emotionally+based+school+avoidance

Pooky Ponders Podcasts – https://pookyh.buzzsprout.com/1183931/
5819794-what-is-selective-mutism-and-how-can-we-help-gino-
hipolito

TeacherMagazine–https://www.teachermagazine.com/au_en/articles/
podcast-special-identifying-and-managing-student-anxiety

# References

Collins-Donnelly, K. (2013) *Starving the Anxiety Gremlin – A Cognitive Behavioural Therapy Workbook on Anxiety Management for Young People* Jessica Kingsley Publishers, London

Conroy, R. (2019) *Identifying and Managing Student Anxiety* [online] Available at: https://www.teachermagazine.com/au_en/articles/podcast-special-identifying-and-managing-student-anxiety [Accessed 7 January 2021]

Hipoliti, G. (2020) *What is Selective Mutism and How Can We Help?* [online] Available at: https://pookyh.buzzsprout.com/1183931/5819794-what-is-selective-mutism-and-how-can-we-help-gino-hipolito [Accessed 14 December 2020]

Knightsmith, P. (2020) *Understand Anxiety: 10 Things You Need to Know – Creative Education* [online] Available at: https://www.creativeeducation.co.uk/courses/anxiety-10-things-you-need-to-know/ [Accessed 8 June 2020]

Minahan, J. (2019) *Tackling Negative Thinking in the Classroom* [online] Available at: https://www.kappanonline.org [Accessed 5 January 2020]

Morgan-Rose, F. (2015) *The Ideal Classroom with Lego Prompt Sheet* [online] Available at: https://theidealclassroomcouk.files.wordpress.com/2017/04/building-the-ideal-classroom-with-lego-prompt-sheet-june-2014-updated-2015.pdf [Accessed 10 March 2021]

Raisingchildren.net.au (2019) *Anxiety: The Stepladder Approach* [online] Available at: https://raisingchildren.net.au/toddlers/health-daily-care/mental-health/anxiety-stepladder-approach [Accessed 27 February 2020]

Siegel, D. & Payne Bryson, T. (2012) *The Whole-Brain Child – 12 Proven Strategies to Nurture you Child's Developing Mind* Robinson, London

## Checklist to support pupils with anxiety

| STRATEGY | COMMENTS |
| --- | --- |
| **Please also refer to the 'Behaviour is communication' and Self-regulation' chapters** | |
| **A strength-based approach** | |
| Focus on achievements and what the pupil can do, and build on these | |
| Build self-esteem | |
| **Relationships and communication** | |
| Use Dan Hughes' PACE approach to build trusting relationships (see p.65–6) | |
| Work collaboratively with caregivers | |
| Support asking for help (reduce hands up) using help cards, gestures or coloured cubes | |
| Safe space and trusted adult | |
| Cognitive breaks (word searches, crosswords, singing, reading aloud, sudoku, quizzes) | |
| Regular check-ins from _____ (trusted adult) | |
| Identify and help change negative or polarised thinking patterns. Convey confidence | |
| Praise – quiet, factual and specific. Consider non-verbal praise. Praise for things the pupil has control over | |
| Validate and label feelings | |
| **Teaching and learning** | |
| Model and teach how to manage and cope with stress and anxiety (see 'Self-regulation' chapter) | |
| Alleviate anxiety over learning tasks – preview work, break tasks down, present one question at a time and support with starting tasks | |
| Increase sense of control by offering choices | |
| Model making mistakes and receiving feedback | |

*(Continued)*

## Continued

| STRATEGY | COMMENTS |
|---|---|
| Provide whiteboards, erasers and second copies and teach what to do if a mistake is made | |
| Take the pressure off of verbal communication, offer whiteboards, pre-teach vocabulary and forewarn of key questions | |
| Avoid public sharing of grades | |
| Alleviate anxieties around homework | |
| **Understanding anxiety** | |
| Teach effect of anxiety on the brain – hand model of the brain (Dan Siegel) (see p.40) | |
| Talk openly and normalise anxiety, name and label feelings. Recognise how anxiety presents for the pupil | |
| Find ways of expressing feelings | |
| **The stress bucket** | |
| Teach pupils to recognise triggers | |
| Teach and trial a range of calming techniques (see 'Self-regulation' chapter) | |
| Model managing anxiety and convey calm | |
| **Breaking the anxiety cycle – scaffolding and step-by-step approaches to manage anxiety** | |
| Support pupils to understand and face anxieties by scaffolding and supporting (rather than avoiding) | |
| Create a step-by-step plan | |
| RAG rate timetable or school plan to find which areas cause most anxiety and work on making these feel safer | |
| Support and replace negative thoughts and polarised thinking | |
| **Creative activities to support pupils to recognise and discuss anxiety** | |
| Butterflies, worry bubbles, worry monsters, make calm jars and stress tools | |
| Specific activities to support separation anxiety, Anxiety-Based School Avoidance and selective mutism | |

| STRATEGY | COMMENTS |
|---|---|
| **Environmental and organisational adaptations** | |
| Clear routines, predictability and consistency and use visual cues | |
| Support and prepare for change and transitions | |
| Stagger times to avoid busy corridors and cloakrooms | |
| **Unstructured times** | |
| Support for unstructured times – teach social skills, use smaller zoned areas/quiet area/clubs, key adult and safe space | |
| **Rewards and consequences** | |
| Avoid sanctions for behaviours stemming from anxiety and teach coping skills | |

# Chapter 5

# Attention Deficit Hyperactivity Disorder (ADHD)

Attention Deficit Hyperactivity Disorder (ADHD) is a neurodevelopmental condition and is currently one of the most commonly diagnosed conditions in children, affecting more than 5 per cent of the population (Hallowell & Ratey, 2021). Hallowell and Ratey (2021, p.4) describe ADHD as 'a way of being in the world' which is 'neither entirely a disorder nor entirely an asset. It is an array of traits specific to a unique kind of mind. It can become a distinct advantage or an abiding curse, depending on how a person manages it'. For children, this is also dependent upon how adults support them to manage and view it.

## Presentations of ADHD

ADHD is a behavioural diagnosis and there is currently no biological test; however, recent neuroscientific research has found (and is continuing to discover) significant brain differences between children with ADHD and those without the condition. According to Radboud University Nijmegen Medical Centre (2017) 'delays in the development of several brain regions are characteristic of ADHD'. Connections have been found between ADHD and reduced neurotransmitter activity within different areas of the brain. 'The science is proving that we aren't just trying to be difficult; we're really having a difficult time inside' (Hallowell & Ratey, 2021, p.128). The symptoms of ADHD are categorised into two sub-types: *inattentiveness*, and *hyperactivity and impulsiveness* (NHS Choices, 2019). Pupils may present as predominantly inattentive, predominantly hyperactive/impulsive or have symptoms that span both categories. For specific information on diagnosis, please refer to the DSM-5 of the American Psychiatric Association (2013).

ADHD presents differently in each individual; however, a pupil with ADHD tends to have particular difficulties around attention, concentration, focus, impulsivity, self-control and emotional regulation. Hallowell & Ratey (2021, p.7) describe the complexity and somewhat inconsistent presentations of ADHD as:

> a lack of focus combined with the ability to superfocus; a lack of direction combined with a highly directed entrepreneurialism; a tendency to procrastinate combined with a knack for getting a week's worth of work done in two hours; impulsive, wrongheaded decision-making combined with inventive, out-of-the-blue problem-solving; interpersonal cluelessness combined with uncanny intuition and empathy.

Pupils with ADHD may:

- Be impulsive and struggle with self-control
- Have difficulty maintaining concentration on tasks that are perceived as tedious
- Have difficulty switching tasks
- Have many ideas or thoughts at once and have difficulty prioritising these
- Be very curious
- Make errors in written work
- Underachieve or experience inconsistent achievement
- Experience delayed executive function (see p.14–15)
- Be energetic, lively and always on the go
- Need support to make and maintain friendships, struggle to interpret social interactions and social cues
- Be talkative and eager to put their point across (and may struggle with taking turns in conversation or call out in the classroom)
- Find it difficult to wait for a turn
- Fear making mistakes and struggle to receive negative feedback or criticism
- Speak or act without thinking
- Struggle to ask for or accept help

- Be risk-takers and struggle to understand safety and danger
- Feel intense emotions and need support regulating these
- Appear easily distracted or to be day-dreaming
- Have sensory sensitivities (see the 'Sensory Processing Disorder (SPD)' chapter)
- Be highly original and inventive

Approximately 50 per cent of people with ADHD also have one or more additional condition, referred to as comorbidity, including Oppositional Defiant Disorder (ODD), anxiety, autism, attachment difficulties, Tourette Syndrome, depression, Obsessive-Compulsive Disorder (OCD), dyslexia, language delay or Developmental Co-ordination Disorder (DCD). ADHD has also been linked to eating disorders.

# ADHD and girls

Boys are currently about three times more likely to be diagnosed with ADHD than girls, with girls tending to be diagnosed at a later age than boys, if at all. However, it is increasingly becoming apparent that ADHD presents differently in females. Recent research indicates that symptoms tend to be more subtle in girls so can easily be missed. 'ADHD symptoms in girls are often thought of as characters of a girl's personality rather than ADHD, which is why they are often overlooked or explained away' (Low, 2020).

Girls with ADHD often have more symptoms associated with inattentive ADHD, with fewer presentations of hyperactivity, impulsivity and risk-taking. Displaying less disruptive and aggressive behaviours, their symptoms tend to be internalised and can therefore be more difficult to spot and are often more tolerable in the classroom. Girls are thought to mask (see p.121–3) and cope better socially and academically and are therefore harder to identify. Furthermore, girls have tendencies towards perfectionism and often hyper-focus on the things that they enjoy and are successful at, further masking challenges they may have in other areas.

Girls with ADHD may:

- Be talkative and eager to put their point across (and may struggle with taking turns in conversation or call out in the classroom)
- Struggle in paying attention to detail
- Feel emotions intensely and need support to regulate these
- Have difficulties with concentration or attention, be easily distracted and may flit from one task or conversation to another

- Appear to daydream or be in their own world
- Need support with organisation
- Need support with working memory (see p.16–17)
- Need support to start and finish tasks or assignments
- Be people pleasers
- Have difficulties maintaining social relationships and reading social cues
- Be perfectionists and fear making mistakes
- Be withdrawn
- Have sensory sensitivities
- Be highly imaginative in their thinking

Awareness and understanding of the presentation of ADHD in girls are crucial in providing appropriate support. Girls with ADHD, who are not given the support, treatment and understanding that they need, are likely to struggle with low self-esteem and anxiety and may also be more prone to substance abuse, eating disorders, self-harm and depression as they get older.

**Case study:**

Leah was in Year 5 and academically very able. She always con- tributed to class discussions. However, she spent a lot of time being sent out of class for disruptive behaviour. She particu- larly struggled around relationships, often falling out with her peers. She had one special friend to whom she was incredibly loyal, becoming heightened if her friend pursued other rela- tionships, often shouting, storming off, or breaking her friend's equipment.

Leah played the piano and practised for hours each day, pass- ing her Grade 1 and 2 exams very quickly. If she made a mistake she would scream, slam down the lid and shut herself in her bed- room, crying uncontrollably and shouting that she was 'rubbish'.

Leah loved gymnastics and was determined to do a backbend. She watched YouTube videos and practised every day. Her gym- nastics teacher was astounded at how quickly she mastered everything she put her mind to.

Four years on, Leah has passed her Grade 7 piano exam and holds several gold and silver gymnastics medals. She has received two fixed-term exclusions and had numerous detentions in secondary school. Leah was diagnosed with ADHD last year.

Since putting in supportive strategies (movement breaks, safe space, and focusing on her strengths but also teaching her when and how to seek help), Leah is managing to regulate and accept guidance, and staff are more supportive and understanding of her needs. They are supporting her to build skills rather than imposing lots of sanctions. The number of 'negative behaviour points' on the system has dramatically reduced and Leah is feeling more successful. Her self-esteem is improving.

## ADHD in the classroom

Within the classroom, pupils may appear distracted by everyone and everything going on around them. 'Researchers recognize that ADHD doesn't impair the ability to pay attention, but rather the ability to control what one pays attention to' (ADDitude Editors, 2020). Pupils may find it difficult to filter out their own thoughts and anxieties or look as though they are daydreaming. However, the child could be processing huge amounts of thoughts and information and be unable to focus on what is happening at that moment. They may have difficulties controlling their attention and focus and be seen to be flitting between tasks or excessively fidgeting and moving.

Writing has often been observed as a trigger, possibly due to the mechanics of handwriting and motor control, difficulty with spelling or anxiety around the enormity of the task. Pupils may find it difficult to cope after making mistakes or when receiving negative feedback. They may appear disorganised (the child whose drawer is constantly bulging open with all sorts of things crammed in and spilling out of it, or the pupil who has never got all the equipment they need for the lesson despite endless reminders). They may also call out excessively, act before thinking and doing and be described as risk-takers (the child who is scaling the fence and over the road, or who has disappeared up the tree in the blink of an eye).

Hallowell (2015) described his ADHD (talking very quickly as he spoke):

> It's like being super-charged all of the time. You get one idea and you have to act upon it, and then, what do you know, but you've got another idea before you've finished up with the first one, and so you go for that one, but of course a third idea intercepts the second, and you just have to follow that

one, and pretty soon people are calling you disorganised and impulsive and all sorts of impolite words and miss the point completely.

Pupils with ADHD are often very able, yet tend to under-perform, frequently described in school as *not reaching their full potential*. They may recurrently get into trouble in the classroom or playground which becomes a negative downward spiral. Pupils may appear unaware of the effect of their actions or struggle to see things from the perspective of others. Group work or unstructured times may be particularly difficult for them to manage successfully. Pupils with ADHD often have a lower emotional and developmental age than their peers. They may have heightened emotions (both positive and negative) and may display intense reactions to seemingly small triggers and take a longer time to calm or regulate.

Pupils may have low self-esteem or high anxiety (often masked by, or presented through, a range of inappropriate or challenging behaviours). To support pupils effectively, it is necessary to understand the difficulties that they are facing as well as the communicative function of their behaviours. If they could focus and concentrate better they would, and with appropriate support they can!

## Hyper-focus

Individuals with ADHD can also often hyper-focus on an activity in which they are particularly interested. This can be a huge advantage within their learning and later in working life and pupils need to be made aware of this strength.

Becoming engrossed in a task can also explain why an individual may struggle to transition from one task to another, particularly from one that they are enjoying (staying in the playground after the bell or continuing colouring in, long after the others are sitting on the carpet). Pupils may need extra support regulating attention or moving from one activity to another.

## Strategies to support pupils with ADHD to thrive

Below is a range of strategies that have been tried and tested and found to support pupils with ADHD within school. There is a checklist at the end of this chapter.

## A strength-based approach

ADHD has symptoms that cause challenges, yet it also has numerous positive features. It is important to teach children (and adults) to understand the condition and view it as a 'difference' rather than a 'deficit'. 'No brain is the best, and each of us has the magnificent, lifelong chance to find our own brain's special way' (Hallowell & Ratey, 2021, p.131). Adult responses strongly influence pupils' behaviour and attitudes towards difference. Therefore, it is essential that adults in school model tolerance, acceptance and patience and celebrate differences.

■ Reframe communication around ADHD and focus on each individual's strengths and achievements. Refer to the positives associated with the condition, rather than the negative traits:

**Language reframes**

| Negative wording | Positive wording |
|---|---|
| Hyperactive, restless | Energetic, lively, active |
| Distractible | Observant, thinking outside the box, |
| Talkative | Friendly, welcoming, enthusiastic, eager |
| Forgetful | Engrossed, pre-occupied |
| Disorganised | Spontaneous, extemporaneous |
| Stubborn | Persistent, absorbed, channelled, hyper-focused |
| Inconsistent | Shows flashes of genius, original, innovative |
| Impulsive | Creative, passionate, spontaneous, inventive, courageous |

■ Pupils will need support to explore, acknowledge and harness these positives and develop their individual strengths. Pupils with ADHD often have very low self-esteem; what better way to boost this than show them and tell them what they are amazing at? ADHD 'is often the life blood of creativity and artistic talents. It is a driver of ingenuity and iterative thinking. It can be your special strength ... even a bona fide superpower. If you really understand it and make it your own, ADHD can become the springboard to success beyond what you ever imagined and can be the key that unlocks your potential' (Hallowell & Ratey, 2021, p.xvii). ADHD needs to be viewed positively and understood by adults so they can help pupils to see and reach their full potential.

■ Low self-confidence is often associated with ADHD. Give roles and responsibilities to increase their sense of self-worth and feelings of belonging. Boost self-esteem by using a positive home-school book, send positive postcards home or create a scrapbook of successes or a success jar. In communication, aim for ten positive comments for every (perceived) negative.

■ Work with pupils to research successful, famous people with ADHD. Many extraordinary entrepreneurs, comedians, sports personalities, actors, artists and scientists have an ADHD diagnosis. Many of them associate their successes with their symptoms such as the ability to hyper-focus on a task, a tendency to be uninhibited and less risk-averse, their passion and creativity or their wish to be in control and be their own boss.

## Relationships and communication

■ Ensure all adults are aware of the pupil's strengths, yet also understand the difficulties that they have, so they are better placed to support them within a 'low-fear, high trust atmosphere' (Hallowell & Ratey, 2021, p.81).

■ Form a positive partnership with caregivers to work collaboratively, share strategies and concerns and listen to them and the pupil about what works well for them. Actively listen and problem-solve together. Be sure to focus on the pupil's strengths as well as concerns during these interactions.

■ Model the behaviour that you expect and would like to see, paying particular attention to those the pupils may struggle with, for example, using a calm voice, taking turns in conversation and thinking before acting.

■ 'Catch pupils being good' and praise any small steps towards success. 'As much as we can get down in the dumps over a minute criticism, we can fly high and put to great uses even small bits of encouragement and recognition' (Hallowell & Ratey, 2021, p.11).

■ Present rules and routines visually and support pupils with transitions (see p.15). Be sure to give plenty of notice of upcoming changes using countdowns or timers. Use an 'oops' card on the visual timetable to warn of any unexpected changes and model how these can be managed and tolerated, start with small changes that the pupil will manage successfully. An 'ooh' card can also be used to show that surprises can be positive (yet also warned about and managed and tolerated), start with small 'ooh's such as an extra five minutes of break time.

- Lengthy verbal directions are often confusing and hard to remember. Use visual cues alongside verbal explanations or instructions. Using behaviour visuals (photographs of the pupil engaging in the expected behaviours work well) or an agreed gesture can reinforce the message without the need for verbal negotiations. Presenting instructions visually (such as in flow charts, bullet points, pictures and symbols) can help pupils to focus on the task at hand.
- Cue the pupil in to significant material by using their name first and then a phrase such as 'important info coming' or 'eyes on me'. One observed teacher dims the lights before imparting important information. Ask pupils to repeat instructions to check for understanding.
- Allow extra processing time to absorb information, instructions and to respond to questions. Count to ten in your head before expecting a response, and then calmly repeat keywords; for example, if James has been asked to go and get his coat and his lunch box and gets distracted along the way by playing with the cars, calmly repeat, 'James, coat, lunchbox'.

---

**Case example:**

Zander was a Year 3 pupil with diagnoses of ADHD and ODD. He had recently moved from infant to junior school. Zander had settled well into his new school. Successful strategies had been shared and reasonable adjustments made to support his transition.

However, Zander's behaviours used to escalate each time the class had to move around the school so quickly that he would end up needing physical intervention to keep himself and others safe. This had never been an issue at his previous school. Zander was given warnings around transitions, support in visiting other areas of the school and transitional objects to take between classes. Nothing seemed to be effective.

Through a series of observations, it was ascertained that a possible trigger was the class lining up alphabetically and he was always last. Just by changing the order in which the children lined up so that Zander had turns at the front and in the middle as well as the back, or by sending him on an errand to avoid the line altogether, these crises were eliminated.

## Teaching and learning

Teachers must become informed about the difficulties that pupils may have and gain an understanding of how the condition may impact learning and behaviour and hone in on their strengths. Accept that the pupil is not behaving in this way deliberately. 'Most teachers and adults could benefit from pretending that all kids in their class have ADHD – what is good for kids with ADHD is good for all kids' (Hallowell, 2015). Adapting teaching and learning strategies to support students with ADHD can positively impact all pupils.

Pupils respond best in a well-structured, predictable environment where expectations, boundaries and rules are clear, consistent and presented visually. An encouraging, positive and nurturing environment is the most effective and supportive approach.

- Gain and maintain interest by using the student's areas of interest as a starting point; for example, encourage the history fan to research French history in Modern Foreign Languages (MFL), historic novels or those based on a particular era when choosing books in English lessons or find out about historical figures or inventions in Science or Maths or make them the 'class expert' for a key topic or area. Hallowell & Ratey (2021, p.7) state: 'Boredom is our kryptonite'. Pupils need to be challenged, interested, inspired and enthused by their learning experiences and then they will flourish.
- Use the novelty factor to 'hook' attention, including as many practical or multi-sensory learning activities into the curriculum as possible. Ensure learning is 'authentic, relevant and contextual' (Baum et al., 2017). Ideas include giving artefacts to hold and examine whilst introducing a topic, using actions or gestures as an aide-memoire when learning new topic vocabulary, using key-word cards and pictures, using a torch or laser light to cue them into key information, giving key questions in an envelope or teaching verbs through performing the actions.
- Introduce movement into lessons, by playing games where pupils move around to match sentences or information with another pupil, going on topic/number/vocabulary/'find the clue' treasure hunts, finding hidden clues or items, letters, numbers or clues in the sand, jumping on chalk numbers or writing outside with chunky chalk and paintbrushes with water.
- Additionally, find creative ways that learning can be reinforced through toys, games, dancing, music or using materials like play-dough or clay – to spark interest, curiosity, creativity, movement and foster a love of learning.

- Writing is often a trigger and being faced with a blank page can be particularly daunting. Alleviate anxieties around written tasks by breaking them down into smaller chunks, offer shaped paper or Post-it® notes, give sentence starters, use cloze procedures or multiple-choice questions, use posters, write captions for pictures or write in boxes, shapes or speech bubbles. Be aware that anxiety can be increased by the need for 'perfect' handwriting. At times, offer alternative ways of recording or demonstrating knowledge, such as typing on the computer, taking photographs or recording a sound or video clip.
- Break tasks down into simple, single steps, presented visually as a checklist (see p.249–50), use a timer and include movement breaks.
- Ensure success criteria are presented clearly, step by step and visually.
- Many pupils are unable to keep still and to listen at the same time, and if asked to remain still, this may take all of their energy or attention. Allow doodling whilst listening or give notes to annotate or highlight. Fiddle tools can help with excessive movement, as can a wobble cushion, weighted lap or shoulder pad or a resistance band around the chair legs to allow the pupil to kick against something, giving proprioceptive input whilst sitting (see p.42).
- Where worksheets are used, make them clear and simple, removing excess information and unnecessary pictures or distractions. Alternatively, cut them up and give one piece of information or question at a time. Teach pupils to note-take (using frameworks to support them to organise the information as it is given) or provide a copy of the teacher's notes for them to highlight key information.
- Be aware that copying (from the board or paper) can be time-consuming and challenging for a pupil with ADHD. Limit this and avoid where possible. Instead, give printed notes to annotate or highlight. Print or scribe dates, learning objectives and questions, where possible, so that the pupil can focus their energy and time on the learning task rather than copying text.
- Try to work within the student's attention span. Short sharp bursts of work followed by a planned movement break are effective, such as ten minutes of work followed by sharpening two pencils, giving out the books, watering the plants, taking a box of books to another class or having a drink of water.
- Moving around the class whilst delivering information will help pupils to maintain interest and allow you to focus the attention of those who need it with a quiet visual prompt or gesture. Varying the lesson pace and using visual cues will increase attention and help maintain concentration.

- If a pupil calling out excessively is disruptive, the use of 'talk tokens' or 'call-out cards' can be effective. Pupils are given a number of tokens, five for example, at the beginning of each session. Each time they call out, they give the teacher a token. If they have any left at the end of the session, they get a small reward. Use discretion, ensuring that pupils are successful the majority of the time. If they are not being successful, increase the number of tokens, or only focus on off-task talk, regarding on-task calling out as enthusiasm to contribute their ideas and therefore to be encouraged.
- Make reasonable adjustments in terms of homework expectations. Ensure homework is written down for the pupil (not copied from the board by them, but could be photographed on their 'phone). Ideally, email it home or put it on a virtual platform so that they cannot lose it, and ensure the student has a spare set of books and equipment at home. Break assignments down into small steps, presented visually, and set less work. Where possible set fun activities that encourage movement. Allow and encourage different ways of recording, including taking photographs or videos, typing or having an adult scribe some responses. Provide a homework club so it can be supported within school. Avoid sanctions around incomplete homework and offer incentives for that which is completed instead.

## Environmental considerations

- Be sensitive to smells, sounds and visual distractions that a pupil may be unable to filter out (the clock ticking, the overhead projector humming, the school dinner cooking, the display with bright, shiny items dangling down). Reduce any unnecessary distractions and remove excess equipment from desks (see the 'Sensory Processing Disorder (SPD)' chapter).
- Allow pupils to stand to work, pace whilst listening, sit on a beanbag or lie on the floor to read or use a clipboard to take notes. Some pupils benefit from standing desks or easels. Specially designed seating, such as a wobble stool or balance ball chair, can be useful for short, regular periods throughout the day, to support pupils who need a lot of movement.
- Offer the choice of using an individual work station at times when the pupil may get distracted or overwhelmed (as a supportive, rather than punitive measure).
- Provide access to a key adult and a safe space with calming tools when a pupil is feeling overwhelmed.

## *Unstructured times*

▪ Pupils may need additional support to engage successfully at unstructured times, such as being taught specific social skills, as well as access to more structured zoned areas, activities or clubs. Safe spaces and key adults need to be available at break times as well.

## *Rewards and consequences*

Traditional behaviour policies and rewards and sanctions may be ineffective with pupils who repeat negative behaviours or seem to disregard consequences.

▪ 'A person with ADHD has the power of a Ferrari engine but with bicycle strength brakes. It's the mismatch of engine power to braking capability that causes the problem. Strengthening one's brakes is the name of the game' (Hallowell & Ratey, 2021, p.xvii). Adults need to give the pupils the skills to 'strengthen the brakes'. They need to be taught regulation skills, how to make, maintain, repair and restore relationships, and necessary environmental adjustments need to be made to help pupils succeed.

▪ 'What we need – especially as children – is not punishment or ridicule; what we need is free and easy to supply – Vitamin Connect' (Hallowell & Ratey, 2021, p.56). 'Vitamin Connect' is described as 'the unsurpassed power of positive connection' (Hallowell & Ratey, 2021, p.55). The focus needs to be on building positive, trusting relationships, understanding the pupil and attuning to their needs with empathy, whilst guiding them towards success.

▪ 'Rewards work much better for the ADHD mind than do consequences' (Hallowell & Ratey, 2021, p.81) Smaller, more immediate rewards are more effective than larger, longer-term ones (pupils with ADHD often have difficulty waiting). If using rewards, aim for a small reward at the end of each day or session, rather than saving them all up for a Friday afternoon. Similarly, consequences need to be fair, logical and practical. Try to avoid consequences being carried over to the next day (which heightens anxiety) and start each day with a clean slate.

▪ 'Pick your battles' and avoid reprimands or consequences for behaviours associated with their condition (calling out, excessive movement, fiddling, lack of equipment, disorganisation, gazing out of the window) and address these in a different way (teach skills, tactically ignore, praise them when they are making positive choices, praise people nearby, use a gesture or visual prompt as a reminder).

■ Avoid the removal of break times, or keeping pupils indoors as a consequence. All pupils, but particularly those with ADHD, need break times to help them develop social skills, to self-regulate and expel some of their pent-up, excess energy. University of Illinois at Urbana-Champaign (2011) has indicated that regular time spent in a natural outdoor environment can improve mental wellbeing, have a calming effect and improve behaviours. Furthermore, exercise has been found to have a positive impact on pupils with ADHD, with research indicating that it can decrease symptoms and improve cognitive and executive function. 'One of the most fascinating and beneficial effects of exercise is that it prepares the brain to expand, learn and change better than any other human activity. It improves mood and motivation, reduces anxiety, regulates emotion and maintains focus' (Hallowell & Ratey, 2021, p.94).

## Resources, further information and 'tool kits'

### Books for adults

*ADHD 2.0: New Science and Essential Strategies for Thriving with Distraction – from Childhood Through Adulthood* by Edward Hallowell and John Ratey – a must-read for those wishing to find out more about ADHD

*Little-Known Secrets of ADHD: The Surprising Upside You Haven't Been Told* by Rachel Knight

*To Be Gifted and Learning Disabled: Strength-Based Strategies for Helping Twice-Exceptional Students With LD, ADHD, ASD and More* by Susan Baum, Steven Owen and Robin Schader

### Books to share with pupils

*All Dogs Have ADHD* by Kathy Hoopmann

*Can I Tell You about ADHD? A Guide for Friends, Family and Professionals* by Susan Yarney – child-friendly resource for talking to children about ADHD

*Thriving with ADHD Workbook for Kids: 60 Fun Activities to Help Children Self-Regulate, Focus, and Succeed* by Kelli Miller

### Websites

https://adhdfoundation.org.uk A whole host of information and support for parents/carers, young people, adults and schools https://www.additudemag.com/ Medical magazine (published, or subscribe for free online versions) that offers a wealth of information, advice, strategies and webinars on anything ADHD. Try https://www.additudemag.com/wp-content/uploads/2017/08/The-Ultimate-ADHD-Toolkit-1.pdf as a starting point

https://drhallowell.com/watch/ned-talks/ Easy access informative short talks by the amazing and inspiring ADHD expert Dr Edward M. Hallowell. There are also lots of YouTube videos and podcasts

www.weareteachers.com/active-math-games/ Ideas to get the children moving during Maths

www.weareteachers.com/kinesthetic-reading-activities/ Ideas for getting children moving and reading

## Podcasts

Additudemag.com:
https://www.additudemag.com/podcast-teaching-students-with-adhd-jerome-schultz/
https://www.additudemag.com/podcast-teaching-students-with-adhd-zeigler-dendy/
Teachermagazine.com:
https://www.teachermagazine.com/au_en/articles/the-research-files-episode-46-practical-strategies-to-assist-children-with-ADHDintheclassroom
Reasonable adjustments:
https://www.nccd.edu.au/professional-learning/classroom-adjustments-adhd

# References

ADDitude Editors (2020) *Increase Focus: Techniques for Distracted Students with ADHD* [online] ADDitude Magazine. Available at: https://www.additudemag.com/focus-techniques-for-distracted-children/ [Accessed 16 November 2020]

Baum, S., Owen, S. & Schader, R. (2017) *To Be Gifted and Learning Disabled: Strength-Based Strategies for Helping Twice-Exceptional Students With LD, ADHD, ASD and More* Prufrock Press, Waco

DSM-5 of the American Psychiatric Association (2013) *Diagnostic and Statistical Manual of Mental Disorders* Fifth Edition. Arlington

Hallowell, E. [online] Available at: https://drhallowell.com [Accessed 16 November 2020]

Hallowell, E. (2015) *What's It Like to Have ADHD?* addspark.co.uk London Workshops

Hallowell, E. & Ratey, J. (2021) *ADHD 2.0: New Science and Essential Strategies for Thriving with Distraction-From Childhood Through Adulthood* Penguin Random House, New York

Low, K. (2020) *Hidden ADHD Symptoms in Girls – 20 Signs to Look For* [online] Verywellmind.com. Available at: https://www.verywellmind.com/adhd-in-girls-symptoms-of-adhd-in-girls-20547 [Accessed 30 November 2020]

NHS Choices (2019) *Symptoms – Attention Deficit Hyperactivity Disorder (ADHD)* [online] NHS.uk. Available at: https://www.nhs.uk/conditions/attention-deficit-hyperactivity-disorder-adhd/symptoms/ [Accessed 11 September 2019]

Radboud University Nijmegen Medical Centre (2017) *Brain Differences in ADHD* [online] ScienceDaily. Available at: https://www.sciencedaily.com/releases/2017/02/170216105919.htm [Accessed 16 November 2020]

University of Illinois at Urbana-Champaign (2011) *For Kids with ADHD, regular 'green time' is linked to milder symptoms* [online] ScienceDaily. Available at: https://www.sciencedaily.com/releases/2011/09/110915113749.htm [Accessed 6 August 2018]

## Checklist to support pupils with ADHD

| STRATEGY | COMMENTS |
|---|---|
| **Please also refer to the 'Behaviour is communication' and 'Self-regulation' chapters** | |
| **A strength-based approach** | |
| Reframe communication around ADHD and develop individual strengths | |
| Build self-esteem by giving roles and responsibilities, based on strengths and interests | |
| Boost self-esteem – roles/responsibilities, positive scrapbook or postcards home | |
| **Relationships and communication** | |
| Ensure adult awareness of symptoms and understanding of difficulties; build positive relationships | |
| Work collaboratively with caregivers, pupil, other staff and agencies | |
| Model expected behaviours | |
| 'Oops' card and 'Ooh' card on visual timetable to help tolerate change | |
| Short verbal directions, reinforced with visual cues | |
| Cue pupil in when giving important information | |
| Allow extra processing time | |
| **Teaching and learning** | |
| Use pupil's areas of interest, multi-sensory learning activities, novelty factor and movement | |
| Alleviate anxieties around written tasks | |
| Clear visual success criteria | |
| Fiddle tool – fidget toy/doodle book/copy of notes to highlight. Wobble cushion/weighted lap-pad/ resistance band on chair legs | |
| Clear, simple worksheets or cut up to give one question at a time | |

*(Continued)*

## Continued

| STRATEGY | COMMENTS |
|---|---|
| Provide print-outs or scribe dates, learning objectives and questions to avoid copying text | |
| Work within pupil's attention span (e.g. ten minutes followed by a sensory break) | |
| Move around whilst teaching, vary lesson pace and use visual prompts | |
| Talk tokens | |
| Flexibility and reasonable adjustments around homework expectations | |
| **Environmental considerations** | |
| Be aware of sensory sensitivities and distractions | |
| Offer movement whilst working – standing, resistance band, sitting or lying with clip-board, wobble cushion | |
| The choice to use a work station (at times) | |
| Offer an exit strategy and access to a key adult and safe space | |
| **Unstructured times** | |
| Support for unstructured times – teach social skills, use smaller zoned areas/quiet area/clubs and key adult and safe space | |
| **Rewards and consequences** | |
| Teach regulation, repair relationships and make environmental adjustments | |
| Immediate rewards | |
| Pick battles and avoid reprimands for behaviours associated with their condition | |
| Avoid removal of break times | |

# *Chapter 6*

# Autism

Autism is a 'neurological difference which provides ... unique strengths as well as differences' (Hebron & Bond, 2019, p.9). It affects the way in which people experience, communicate, connect and interact with others and the world around them. There has been much discussion within the autism community around the language used, with the general preference seeming to be identity-first language of 'autistic person', which has been used within this book. Other people prefer the person-first language of 'person with autism'. Check with the individual or caregivers regarding personal preferences.

For specific information on diagnosis, it will be necessary to refer to the DSM-5 of the American Psychiatric Association (2013). Each individual's experience will be different, reflecting the uniqueness of ability for each person. However, autistic people tend to experience differences in the following key areas:

## Social understanding, communication and interaction

- Communicating, interacting and interpreting the actions, thoughts and emotions of others
- Interpreting and responding to social cues
- May need support to make and maintain friendships
- Information processing

DOI: 10.4324/9781003146292-7

- Generalising and transferring skills and knowledge from one situation to another
- Literal interpretation of language
- Visual, logical and analytical thinking

## Sensory sensitivities

- Differences in processing sensory information, not only 'sensory overload, but often wonderful, enhanced sensory perception' (Bridges, 2018)
- Certain sensory stimuli can, at times, be uncomfortable, overwhelming or even painful (see the 'Sensory Processing Disorder (SPD)' chapter)

## Anxiety

- May experience high levels of anxiety, stemming from sensory, societal or environmental issues
- Differences in communicating and social understanding, sensory overload, changes in routine and repressing or masking certain emotions and behaviours can increase anxiety

## Overwhelm

- May feel emotions intensely
- May experience an emotional crisis resulting in a meltdown in the form of a panic attack or shutdown (withdrawal) when overwhelmed

## Specific interests, repetitive movements and hyper-focus

- May prefer predictable, consistent routines
- May engage in repetitive, self-stimulating vocal or motor actions (stims) such as rocking, hand flapping, or flicking switches to calm and regulate, process information or for enjoyment
- May have a passionate interest in which they can hyper-focus
- May be determined and have good levels of perseverance

Traditionally, it was thought that autistic people may struggle to empathise; however, research shows that this varies between individuals. Some individuals may experience hyper-empathy, which 'can result in physically feeling someone else's distress and pain' (Smitten, 2021).

## Masking

Masking or social camouflage is when individuals (often subconsciously) learn to behave and act like their peers, a celebrity or other familiar personality to make friends, cope and fit in socially. Pupils may suppress behaviours, emotional reactions and stims whilst at school because society has taught them that it is not safe to be themselves. 'Examples of camouflaging include making eye contact during conversation, using learned phrases or pre-prepared jokes in conversation, mimicking other's social behaviour, imitating facial expressions or gestures, and learning and following social scripts' (Lai & Baron-Cohen, 2015, in Lai et al., 2017).

Masking can be difficult to identify and can also present as extreme compliance within the school setting. Caregiver concerns must be listened to, as must the experiences of the pupil. Caregivers often report behaviours at home which differ significantly from those observed in school. Pupils who mask may be described as 'fine at school' yet, at home (often their place of safety), frequently reach a crisis point of meltdown or shutdown (sometimes referred to as 'after-school restraint collapse'). Anxiety-reducing measures implemented at school can significantly reduce feelings of overwhelm, which later manifest themselves at home.

---

**Case example:**

Freddie was in Year 4. He had a cornet lesson and a bee entered the room. He was very concerned with environmental issues and knew the value of bees. His teacher (wrongly) assumed he would be frightened, so tried to get the bee out and ended up stamping on it and killing it. Freddie was traumatised and internalised the episode. He kept quiet, but later in the day, when a class monitor tried to collect his whiteboard, he refused to hand it in and reached crisis point.

His teacher understood that something must have upset him and reported this to his mother at the end of the day, but he would not share what was troubling him. It was only later that evening, after hours of further meltdowns, aggressive behaviour and shutdowns, that, when asked how his cornet lesson was, it all came out. He was utterly distressed.

His mother emailed a key adult, who spent time with him the next day, creating a picture of a bee and burying it in the school garden to give him closure. The parent truly appreciated the school's response and it supported Freddie to move on. The class teacher did not put any sanctions in place for Freddie's behaviour because she had taken the time to understand autism and Freddie specifically. The key adult made time for him, which was vital to re-engage him and meant that he was calm that evening at home.

Pupils who are masking often feel confused in social situations and fear making a mistake, causing social anxiety which may manifest as shyness, withdrawal or selective mutism resulting in an inability to communicate needs. A pupil who is masking may be anxious and quiet, avoid confrontation and be desperate to please and fit in. They may be the class clown or repeat phrases or jokes, copy the particular style of another pupil or celebrity or suddenly adopt the same interest as their peers.

Masking is traumatic and is physically and mentally exhausting. It hinders diagnosis and understanding and therefore access to appropriate support. It prevents pupils from developing self-awareness and from understanding and expressing their individual identity. Furthermore, masking can lead to school attendance difficulties, school phobia, autistic burnout and mental health difficulties.

**Case study:**

Camille was an autistic pupil in Year 7. Her parents reported that she was very anxious at home and lacked understanding in social situations. Camille would return from school, go to her room and refuse to talk to anyone. If she did interact at home, it was with verbal and physical aggression and violent outbursts. Her caregiver was concerned that school did not understand her or her needs and felt criticised.

School did not see these reported behaviours. Generally, Camille did well in class and she was very able, although it was felt that she was not reaching her full potential, except in Maths, where she excelled. She could, at times, show some low-level disruptive behaviours. She made friends but struggled to maintain friendships, liked things on her terms and to be in control. Staff were following the school behaviour policy and Camille generally appeared fine and successful. She had some strong sensory sensitivities and found noise particularly difficult to tolerate, especially at unstructured times.

*How could staff support Camille when many of her difficulties were manifesting at home?*

Staff listened to the concerns from home and began working closely with the caregiver to increase whole staff awareness and understanding of Camille's needs. To lower her anxieties in school, Camille was given regular sensory breaks. She was offered a choice of two safe spaces with calm tools, the use of which was rehearsed each morning when she was calm. Time was given to staff so that a positive, trusting relationship was built up with a team of key adults. Work was put in around social skills, supporting her in building and managing relationships with peers. An element of flexibility to the behaviour policy was introduced and Camille had access to a safe indoor space at break times.

Consequently, after several weeks, incidents of explosive behaviour at home reduced significantly. The relationships at home improved immensely, as did that between parents and staff.

# Autistic burnout

Autistic burnout is where an autistic person experiences periods of low energy, physical or mental exhaustion, loss of motivation, increased sensory sensitivity, reduced tolerance to triggers, and increased and prolonged periods of meltdown or shutdown. It can look like depression or regression and can include the loss of communication skills. Autistic burnout can be caused by being environmentally and socially overwhelmed as well as suppression and masking.

# Autism and girls

Boys are currently around four times more likely to be diagnosed with autism than girls (Healthylondon.org, 2017). Although developing, there remains limited research, knowledge and understanding around girls with autism. Current screening and referral processes, diagnostic criteria and tools tend to overlook girls' difficulties and favour more male brain traits of 'systemising' rather than female traits of 'empathising' (Baron-Cohen, 2003). Autistic females appear to present differently to the traditional understanding of autism: 'girls tend to have a quieter presentation, with not necessarily as much of the repetitive and restricted behavior, or it shows up in a different way' (Epstein, in Arky, undated).

Recent research seems to point towards fundamental differences in the presentation of autism in girls and boys. Females may have characteristics that do not match the traditional autism profile. Autistic females 'are more inclined towards sociability, emotionality and friendship ... Their strategies may include rote-learning conversational phrases, imitating social behaviours (for example, from TV soap operas), following social scripts, and "masking" or "camouflaging"' (Egerton & Carpenter, 2016).

Autistic girls tend to portray more seemingly appropriate social skills and desire to fit in than autistic boys, mimicking others to blend in socially with their peers. Autistic girls may mask and hide difficulties in social understanding. Wild (2016) describes 'social formatting: copying and pasting someone else's behaviour and trying to make it your own'. Girls may have a 'social anchor' – one other child who appears to be a best friend to whom they may become incredibly attached and copy their behaviours, attitudes, beliefs and mannerisms. However, they may struggle to build and maintain appropriate friendships, lack social understanding and find collaborative, social times particularly confusing and difficult.

Autistic girls tend to be imaginative. Their interests, although often intense, tend to be more accepted socially and shared with those of their peers (such as celebrities, music, animals or the environment) so do not tend to stand out, whereas boys' interests are often more restricted or less age-appropriate, flagging them up for a referral. Girls' difficulties tend to be internalised rather than communicated by outward behaviours so are often more tolerable to adults. Autistic girls tend to experience sensory sensitivities, struggle with changes in routine, need to feel in control and have very strong emotions.

Autistic girls are frequently misunderstood and described as 'shy' or 'quiet' or diagnosed with anxiety, Attention Deficit Hyperactivity Disorder (ADHD), Obsessive-Compulsive Disorder (OCD), eating disorders or depression before being given an autism diagnosis, which in part may be due to their adept masking.

> I was told categorically by an adult at my daughter's school that she couldn't be autistic because she has a sense of

humour and shows empathy. This kind of misunderstanding is literally preventing families from accessing help and diagnosis.

(Parent)

Not being appropriately diagnosed can mean that many girls are not reaching their full potential, lack self-awareness and miss out on appropriate support in school. More understanding and research in this area is currently developing but still needed. 'It relies much more on getting under the surface and listening to the experiences they're having rather than how they present themselves to the world' (Baron-Cohen, in Szalavitz, 2016).

# Autism in the classroom

It is essential to understand behaviour as a form of communication often stemming from societal and environmental factors and a lack of necessary adjustments. Autistic pupils may have difficulties recognising and communicating feelings, needs and anxieties or interpreting emotions (their own and those of others). Behaviours such as increased rigidity, withdrawal, stimming, defiance, rudeness or aggression for an autistic pupil are likely to indicate anxiety, a lack of understanding, communication difficulties, sensory sensitivities or could be a reaction to a change of routine or environment.

# Suggestions to support autistic pupils to thrive

Schools are social environments, relying heavily on communication and interaction. Without understanding and support, autistic pupils are at risk of being confused, frustrated, isolated, misunderstood, under-achieving and developing mental health difficulties. However, with appropriate provision, they can thrive.

Below is a range of strategies that have been tried and tested and found to support autistic pupils within school. There is a checklist at the end of this chapter.

## *A strength-based approach*

- Value and celebrate neurodiversity. View and communicate autism as a 'neurological difference' which provides many strengths, rather than a 'deficit' or 'disorder' (Hebron & Bond, 2019, p.9). 'Reframing autism is about celebrating diversity. It is tapping into the innate intelligence, brilliance and creativity of enhanced perception – a field that people on the spectrum often inhabit – and then helping people to make the most of their gifts' (Bridges, 2018).

All pupils have strengths, interests and skills which need to be recognised and encouraged to foster success and promote self-esteem. Focus and build on these and convey positives when communicating with and about young people. Autistic people 'feel and see things differently, often with exquisite empathy and sensitivity' (Bridges, 2018). Particular positive traits that have been used to describe autistic pupils may include (but are not limited to):

- Visual, logical and analytical thinking
- Seeing connections others don't
- Good observation skills
- Keen attention to detail
- Intrinsic motivation
- Good memory for detail and ability to recall information
- Understanding of structure
- Honesty
- Original and innovative approaches to problem-solving
- Perseverance
- Good concentration and focus
- Imagination
- Non-judgemental

Pupils, staff and parents will come up with many, many more.

- Research and celebrate positive and successful autistic role models and look at how their autistic traits and strengths have contributed to their success.
- Encourage pupils to share, develop and build on interests, achievements and knowledge and offer roles and responsibilities around these. Build self-esteem by offering jobs and responsibilities around their interests and strengths, for example, computer expert, register monitor, paint monitor, librarian or music maestro.

## Reduce anxieties

During the day, stress levels rise and fall, depending on certain triggers. For autistic people, stress and anxiety levels may already be high when they enter school, so seemingly minor issues may trigger heightened emotions.

- Support the pupil to recognise and be aware of what triggers their anxiety (change, homework, making mistakes, sensory overload, social situations, to name a few) and help them to learn coping mechanisms to reduce stress levels at these times. Once triggers are identified, staff can support pupils to either manage or avoid these, such as going to the cloakroom slightly earlier or later to avoid crowds, eating somewhere quieter to avoid noise, using ear defenders or giving a job in the hall before everyone else arrives for assembly (see the 'Anxiety' chapter).
- Help pupils to recognise and label their emotions, and then regulate these alongside a trusted adult. Filling in a stress scale and including visual strategies can be supportive (see p.248).
- Autistic pupils often find change difficult to manage (even good change). Provide predictable structure and routine and support pupils to manage transitions and prepare for changes. Explain changes in advance by using visual timetables and 'oops' cards, *Now and Then* boards, sand timers and countdowns. An 'ooh' card can also be used to show that change can be positive. Start with small 'ooh's such as an extra five minutes of computer time. Highlight the beginning and end of tasks and use timers and countdowns to forewarn about the end of an activity. Give plenty of warning when moving from one task to another. Reminder cards or taking photographs of activities can be helpful if a pupil is engrossed in a task, to prompt them that they can continue later, at a mutually convenient time.
- Sensory sensitivities can trigger anxiety. It might be useful to complete a sensory checklist or request an Occupational Therapist assessment to enable the implementation of strategies to calm the sensory system. Sensory resources such as wobble cushions, ball chairs, weighted lap pads or resistance bands on the chair legs can be highly effective. Providing calm tools such as fiddle toys, foot fidgets, doodle books or mindful colouring can provide an appropriate outlet for stress (see the 'Sensory Processing Disorder (SPD)' chapter).

## *Social learning and relationships*

- Time needs to be taken to build trusting relationships to understand, accept and listen to the pupil. Use the pupil's strengths and likes and encourage them to share their interests (if they feel comfortable) to build a rapport. Take time to get to know them as a person.

- Work collaboratively with caregivers. Listen empathically and respond to concerns from home and from the pupils themselves to share strengths and work together to find solutions if difficulties arise. Communicate between home and school to ensure a consistent approach. The use of a home-school book can be useful and helps caregivers to support issues in school which may affect the pupil at home, and vice versa. Aim to focus on the positives and not on negative incidents. Share a positive from home at the beginning of the day and a positive from school at the end of the day.
- Model and teach expected social behaviour such as taking turns in conversation, how long to talk for, how close to stand, eye contact and not always saying what you think. Talk about and model interactions with different people (chatting to friends is not the same as talking to the principal). Role play and rehearse everyday social interactions or talk about those in video clips or books.
- Autistic people may struggle to interpret unwritten social cues and may benefit from these being specifically explained or clarified. By valuing differences and diversity in the classroom and modelling understanding of the various difficulties experienced by all children, all pupils will thrive. 'Support for building friendships can start early. All the children in the class can be helped to be more understanding of autism and other needs through stories that have characters with different disabilities and learning needs. Being open to discussing, accepting and celebrating difference should be whole school policy' (McCann, in Hebron & Bond, 2019, p.84).
- Social situations can cause high levels of anxiety for some autistic pupils. Reduce social demands while learning (and learning demands when socialising). Decide if the priority is to work in a pair or group, or complete the learning task. If the social side is the priority, provide structure, support and clear guidelines. It is often useful for pupils to have designated roles with clear expectations around these.
- Support social interactions by providing the pupil with a script to ask to join a game or start a conversation. Encourage other children to invite the pupil to join them in a game.
- Some pupils may find it difficult to read the emotions of others. Begin to talk about and name different emotions using visuals such as photographs, flashcards or emojis, play matching games, pairing the picture to the emotion. Practise pulling faces for the

different emotions or play emotions charades. Explore and talk about how characters in books and on screen may be feeling in different situations. Name the emotions and physical features (body language, tone and facial expressions) which can be seen; for example, 'the teacher has his hands on his hips and is frowning, he is looking at the clock, I wonder how he might be feeling?' Also, help them interpret their own facial expressions; for example, 'you are frowning, I wonder if you are feeling cross?' or 'that's a big smile, are you feeling happy?'

■ Pupils may have difficulty understanding that people have different thoughts and feelings to their own and need help to express their views and to understand the perspective of others. Social Stories™ (Gray, 2015) and Comic Strip Conversations™ (Gray, 1994) are useful in developing social understanding and empathy. They can be used to explain different scenarios or teach different social conventions and explore alternative behaviours should a similar situation arise in the future. Pupils may need support to understand that the friendship is not over following a disagreement or incident and need to be taught strategies for repairing relationships if things have gone wrong (see p.11–12).

■ Some autistic individuals struggle to make connections or generalise information; for example, rules or skills taught in one classroom may not be transferred to other areas of the school and may need to be taught in the hall and computer room as well.

■ Swearing often gets autistic pupils in trouble at school. Discuss how they will probably hear (and may even use) swear words in the playground, away from adults, but it is not appropriate to use that language in the classroom or around adults, and swearing at someone is not acceptable. They may also need teaching which words are much worse than others and that using them can make people very upset or angry.

## *Communication*

■ An autistic pupil can struggle to screen out sensory material and focus on the necessary information, particularly in a busy classroom, leading to information overload. Attract attention and use the pupil's name before giving instructions or beginning communication.

■ Use a calm and predictable, neutral tone of voice.

■ Keep verbal instruction short and clear, avoiding open-ended questions. Ask one question or deliver one instruction at a time and allow processing time. Break longer questions or instructions into smaller chunks and check for understanding. Use, repeat and emphasise specific keywords. If necessary, repeat using the same tone and words (changing the tone or words changes the message, thus increasing the processing time).

- Some autistic people have difficulties interpreting tone of voice. Explore how the same word or sentence can mean different things based on tone of voice. Play games and say a word in a variety of different voices; for example, say 'OK' and sound happy, angry, scared, excited and sad. Alternatively, read books and select sentences to read with a different tone of voice. Pupils could try recording themselves or others doing this and match an emotion picture to the tone.
- Teach appropriate eye contact if appropriate, but do not insist on this, as it can be difficult, overwhelming or even painful for an autistic individual. If focused on maintaining eye contact, a pupil may not be able to concentrate on anything else, such as listening. Establish alternative ways of ensuring the pupil is engaged and listening.
- Use consistent, positive, direct language which is clear and accurate, using visual supports where appropriate. Say (or at least explain) what you mean and if you say you will do something, do it. You may need to reframe language to enable this; for example, if a child hears, 'I'll be back in a minute' they will expect you to return in 60 seconds. Try using modal verbs to indicate that there may be an element of change, such as: 'we should be going out to play, as long as it doesn't rain'.
- Autistic pupils may take language very literally. Sarcasm, idioms, nuances, metaphors, irony and ambiguous phrases can cause much confusion. Notbohm (2005, p.xxiv) explains this clearly: 'It's very confusing for me when you say, "Hold your horses, cowboy!" when what you mean is, "Stop running." Don't tell me something is "a piece of cake" when there's no dessert in sight and what you mean is, "This will be easy for you to do." When you say, "It's raining cats and dogs," I see pets coming out of the sky. Tell me, "It's raining hard."' Use clear, direct language; for example, say 'sit on the carpet' rather than 'would you like to sit on the carpet?' The former is direct and unambiguous, whereas the latter sounds like they have a choice and you may get an honest (unintentionally rude) response ('no').
- Offer the pupil support for communicating their needs, such as a help card, break card, exit strategy, stress scale or other visual prompt. (It may also be useful to give the pupil a means

of communicating that they do not require help and are working independently to avoid interrupting them and causing frustration.)

- Offer clear, positive choices to increase feelings of control; however, limit these to two or three, as too many choices can feel overwhelming or the decision-making can increase anxiety.
- Autistic pupils often have unique and interesting ways of seeing and interpreting situations and can add a different perspective, so communication is essential. Be curious and interested in them and their views.

## Use visual supports

One of the most essential strategies is to support verbal communication with visual supports to assist understanding and reinforce rules, routines, behaviour expectations, instructions and learning tasks. 'I used to think adults spoke a different language. I think in pictures. Words are like a second language to me' (Grandin, 2006). Visual supports can be used in various situations with all ages to support learning, communication and language development, foster independence, increase confidence and lessen anxieties. They can be used in different formats, such as pictures, symbols, flow charts, photographs, labels, timers, concrete items, gestures or written words. A visual explanation is memorable and can be re-referred to as needed, so is incredibly effective. Notbohm (2005, p.xxvi) explains how visual timetables support daily: 'A visual schedule is extremely helpful as I move through my day ... it relieves me of the stress of having to remember what comes next, makes for smooth transition between activities, and helps me manage my time and meet your expectations.'

---

**Personal case example:**

During the Covid-19 pandemic, I have been struck by just how many visual supports are being used to support us to navigate this scary and ever-changing world we find ourselves in. When going shopping, in the workplace, in schools, even on the street, visual supports are there to remind us of what is expected and necessary to keep us safe. We have been given very clear and strict messages of where we can stand and how close we can be to other people and these are reinforced wherever we go.

> Visual supports help with understanding the current guidelines and rules, show what is expected in terms of one-way systems and the wearing of masks. When going to previously familiar, now changed places, I certainly have relied on the visual cues and have physically breathed a sigh of relief when they help me understand exactly what to do and where to go.
>
> I hope that we can learn from some of these adjustments and use visual supports to clearly teach social expectations as we move forward.

- Using a personal visual timetable or *Now and Then* board (see p.15) removes uncertainty and helps a pupil understand what is happening each day. Include pictures of key adults and places.
- The concept of time is often difficult for an autistic child to comprehend. Give verbal and visual warnings about upcoming changes and transitions, such as 'five minutes and then tidy-up time'. Show a five-minute timer so they can see how much time they have left. Include timings using pictures of the actual classroom clockface on the visual timetable to help pupils understand their day.
- Label equipment and resources clearly, using words and photographs, so pupils can easily navigate the classroom and locate resources. Support organisation and sequencing skills by providing lists of resources that they will need and in which order.

## Teaching and learning

For autistic pupils, the learning needs to be made concrete, appropriate, structured and visual. Careful differentiation is needed, not only of tasks but of communication, presentation and visual supports.

- Ensure clear objectives and success criteria are presented visually. Offer visual supports to encourage independence, such as writing frames, story maps and word mats.
- Break tasks down into simple, single steps, presented visually as a checklist (see p.249–50). A timer can be useful so they know how much time they have to complete each step.
- Keep verbal inputs short and, where possible, multi-sensory – include visual supports, physical activity and movement, demonstrations, pictures, modelling and artefacts to hold.

■ Ensure any handouts or worksheets are uncluttered and distraction-free, containing only the required information.

■ 'To do' and 'finished' folders can help pupils develop independence and focus and engage in a range of learning tasks. The 'to do' folder contains tasks (related to the topic or subject) that the pupil can achieve independently. As each step is completed it is placed in the 'finished' folder. Similarly, use stationery trays, where each tray contains an activity and the pupil works through the trays from top to bottom. Alternatively, they can be used as a reward system, which the pupil can access independently, containing puzzles, games and activities linked to their interests.

■ Be aware of parts of the curriculum that autistic pupils may find particularly difficult to understand, such as inference when reading, metaphor or idioms in English, word problems in Maths or the concept of time in History. Provide extra support, visual cues and clear explanations.

■ Manage homework expectations and communicate with caregivers. Homework is often very challenging, as a pupil's perception may be that they have completed their learning at school. Homework clubs, research or creative projects, practical tasks and life skills work (such as paying for shopping, asking for and purchasing a train ticket, estimating costs and working out how much change is required) are often more effective and productive.

■ Incorporate special interests into learning tasks and research projects where possible, encouraging the pupil to share their knowledge.

■ Support executive function (see p.14–15).

## *Environmental considerations*

■ Classrooms are busy and bright and can cause sensory overload. Increase awareness of the sensory environment (noise, crowds, lighting, smells, textures) by using an environmental checklist (see 'tool kit') and reduce sensory stimulation and distraction, where possible (see the 'Sensory Processing Disorder (SPD)' chapter). 'the ordinary sights, sounds, smells, tastes and touches of every day that you may not even notice can be downright painful for me. The very environment in which I have to live often seems hostile. I may appear withdrawn or belligerent to you but I am really just trying to defend myself' (Notbohm, 2005, p.xxi).

■ Many people need movement to help them to focus and regulate. Support sensory sensitivities which may affect processing and can lead to overwhelm, by planning regular sensory and movement breaks into the day and provide a range of calm tools and, where possible, allow movement whilst listening and working (see the 'Sensory Processing Disorder (SPD)' and 'Self-regulation' chapters).

- Provide the pupils with an exit strategy and ensure access to a safe, quiet space (see p.42). Rehearse and model using the safe space when the pupil is calm through role play and walkthroughs. Take a photograph to use as a visual reminder. Ensure they know when they can use it and for how long.
- Allow for a reset time first thing in the morning, after breaks and before going home. Using calming sensory items and time to de-brief and off-load with a trusted adult can help a pupil talk through any concerns or difficulties, lessen anxieties and stop them from focusing on unresolved issues, which can be a barrier to learning and cause increased stress.

## Unstructured times

Unstructured times should be managed carefully as social times often cause increased anxiety for autistic pupils. Furthermore, the increased crowds, sounds and smells can be overwhelming for those with sensory sensitivities.

- Have a predictable routine for break and lunchtimes, with clear rules and expectations presented visually.
- Offer a quieter area to eat in or allow the pupil to eat slightly earlier or later to avoid crowds, noises and smells. Similarly, offer a safe, quiet zone to access if the playground becomes overwhelming. Rehearse, when the pupil is calm, where and who to go to and provide a visual reminder such as a photograph. Provide a range of activities and clubs around the pupil's interests at break and lunchtimes or ask the pupil to help run these.
- Provide a key adult at break and lunchtimes and have a photograph as a reminder. The key adult can remind the pupil of playground expectations, teach, practice and support turn-taking, teach some simple structured games and explain the rules of popular sports or games. They can also teach the pupil scripts and encourage other children to invite the pupil into their games.
- Implementing a buddy or mentor system may increase confidence and decrease anxieties at social times.

- Provide support for wet break times, offering a list of activities to choose from. The noise and lack of clarity around expectations can be overwhelming and frustrating.
- Support may be required for PE lessons, such as preparing the pupil for going to the hall or field. Rehearse beforehand and build up gradually if it is an area that creates anxiety. The pupil may also need to be given an alternative place for changing, away from crowds. Be aware of sensory sensitivities around clothing and change of footwear (see the 'Sensory Processing Disorder (SPD)' chapter). A mini schedule for PE lessons may be supportive, for example, outlining the warm-up activities, the main lesson and cool-down, what equipment will be used and who they will be in a group with. Pupils could be given the job of choosing stretching or warm-up activities from a selection of picture cards to give them some ownership and increase their sense of control.

## Rewards and consequences

- Ensure rules and routines are displayed visually and the reasons for each is clearly explained and understood.
- Be consistent and predictable in the application of rewards and consequences.
- Feedback and rewards should be immediate, where possible. Offering specific interests as rewards or motivators can be effective. However, do not take special interests away as a sanction, as this can cause distress. Interests often help pupils to calm and regulate; removing them will increase dysregulation.
- Sanctions are often not clearly understood or seen as logical by pupils. Be curious and try to identify triggers and the need being met by their behaviours. Establish if environmental adaptions need to be made, which key skills need teaching, if support is needed with communication or with social understanding, and whether the behaviour is being driven by anxiety, confusion or frustration. For example, a pupil displaying excessive movement or looking out of the window or with their head on their desk may be attempting to block out sensory stimuli so that they can engage and listen, yet this may be interpreted by staff as inattention and a lack of engagement. By being curious and listening to the experiences of pupils, understanding and acceptance are increased and pupils can be supported rather than reprimanded.

# Resources, further information and 'tool kits'

## Websites

www.autism.org.uk Support, guidance and advice from the National Autistic Society

https://www.autismawareness.com.au/could-it-be-autism/autism-and-girls/ Information on autism and girls

www.autismeducationtrust.org.uk Information advice, resources and training

http://www.autismtoolbox.co.uk/ Information, resources and training

https://theautisticadvocate.com/2018/05/an-autistic-burnout/ First-hand experience of autistic burnout

https://autisticnotweird.com/ Insights from an autistic teacher, author and speaker

https://www.creativeeducation.co.uk/courses/promote-emotional-regulation-in-autistic-children/ On-demand video course to support adults to promote emotional regulation

https://www.jodiesmitten.co.uk/autistic-masking Links to further information on masking

www.nasen.org.uk Information, advice, resources and training

## Environmental checklists

Sensory Audit for Schools and Classrooms – https://www.aettraininghubs.org.uk/wp-content/uploads/2012/05/37.1-Sensory-audit-tool-for-environments.pdf

Checklist for autism friendly environments from the South Yorkshire Partnership NHS Foundation Trust – https://positiveaboutautism.co.uk/uploads/9/7/4/5/97454370/checklist_for_autism-friendly_environments_-september_2016.pdf

## Books to share with young people

*All Cats Are on the Autism Spectrum* by Kathy Hoopmann

*Can I Tell You about Autism?* by Jude Welton

*Can You See Me?* by Libby Scott

*Different Like Me: My Book of Autism Heroes* by Jennifer Elder

*M Is for Autism* by The Students of Limpsfield Grange School and Vicky Martin

*M in the Middle: Secret Crushes, Mega-Colossal Anxiety and the People's Republic of Autism* by The Students of Limpsfield Grange School and Vicky Martin

*The Reason I Jump: One Boy's Voice from the Silence of Autism* by Naoki Higashida

*The Secret Life of Rose: Inside an Autistic Head by* Rose Smitten and Jodie Smitten

## Books for adults

*Autism in the Early Years: A Practical Guide (Resource Materials for Teachers)* by Val Cumine

*Education and Girls on the Autistic Spectrum* by Judith Hebron and Caroline Bond (editors)

*Supporting Autistic People with Eating Disorders: A Guide to Adapting Treatment and Supporting Recovery* by Kate Tchanturia

*Teaching Play to Children with Autism: Practical Interventions Using Identiplay* by Nicky Phillips and Liz Beavan

*Reframe Your Thinking around Autism: How the Polyvagal Theory and Brain Plasticity Help Us Make Sense of Autism* by Holly Bridges

*Thinking in Pictures* by Temple Grandin

*The Spectrum Girls Survival Guide* by Siena Castellon

*Ten Things Every Child with Autism Wishes You Knew* by Ellen Notbohm

*Avoiding Anxiety in Autistic Children: A Guide for Autistic Wellbeing* by Luke Beardon

## Podcasts

Sarah Jane Critchley – *Autism in Girls* https://www.thesendcast.com/autism-in-girls/

Pooky Knightsmith and Jodie Smitten – *What Is Autistic Masking and Why Does It Matter?* https://pookyh.buzzsprout.com/1183931/4340186

https://www.nccd.edu.au/professional-learning/classroom-adjustments-autism

# References

Arky, B. (undated) *Why Many Autistic Girls Are Overlooked* [online] Child Mind Institute. Available at: https://childmind.org/article/autistic-girls-overlooked-undiagnosed-autism/ [Accessed 9 September 2020]

Baron-Cohen, S. (2003) *They Just Can't Help It* [online] The Guardian, 17 April. Available at: https://www.theguardian.com/education/2003/apr/17/research.highereducation [Accessed 8 January 2021]

Bridges, H. (2018) *Reframing Autism* [online] The Art of Autism, 12 November. Available at: https://the-art-of-autism.com/reframing-autism/ [Accessed 16 March 2021]

DSM-5 of the American Psychiatric Association (2013) *Diagnostic and Statistical Manual of Mental Disorders* Fifth Edition. Arlington

Egerton, J. & Carpenter, B. (2016) *Girls and Autism: Flying Under the Radar* [online] Nasen.org.uk, 30 March. Available at: https://nasen.org.uk/resources/girls-and-autism-flying-under-radar [Accessed 9 December 2020]

Grandin, T. (2006) *Thinking in Pictures – and Other Reports from My Life with Autism* Bloomsbury Publishing, London

Gray, C. (1994) *Comic Strip Conversations™* Future Horizons, Arlington

Gray, C. (2015) *The New Social Story Book™: Over 150 Social Stories That Teach Everyday Social Skills to Children and Adults with Autism and Their Peers* Future Horizons, Arlington

Healthylondon.org (2017) *Children and Young People with Autism Spectrum Disorder – Case for Change* [online] Available at: https://www.healthy london.org/wp-content/uploads/2018/11/Children-and-young-people-with-austism-spectrum-disorder-case-for-change-Oct-2017.pdf [Accessed 8 January 2021]

Hebron, J. & Bond, C. (Eds) (2019) *Education and Girls on the Autistic Spectrum – Developing an Integrated Approach* Jessica Kingsley Publishers, London

Lai, M., Lombardo, M., Ruigrok, A., Chakrabarti, B., Auyeung, B., Szatmari, P., Happé, F., Baron-Cohen, S. and MRC AIMS Consortium (2017) *Quantifying and Exploring Camouflaging in Men and Women with Autism* Sage Journals: Autism, 21(6), 690–702 [online] Available at: https://journals.sagepub.com/doi/pdf/10.1177/1362361316671012 [Accessed 10 December 2020]

Notbohm, E. (2005) *Ten Things Every Child with Autism Wishes You Knew* Future Horizons, Arlington

Smitten, J. (2021) *Supporting Autistic Children and Young Peoples' Mental Health* at the Acceptance Matters Virtual Conference by the North East Autism Society, UK

Szalavitz, M. (2016) *Autism – It's Different in Girls* Scientific American, 1 March [online] Available at: https://www.scientificamerican.com/article/autism-it-s-different-in-girls/ [Accessed 9 December 2020]

Wild, S. (2016) *Limpsfield Grange School: Teaching Autistic Girls* [online] National Autistic Society, 9 December. Available at: https://www.autism.org.uk/advice-and-guidance/professional-practice/autistic-girls-education [Accessed 4 January 2021]

## Checklist to support pupils with autism

| STRATEGY | COMMENTS |
|---|---|
| **Please also refer to the 'Behaviour is communication', 'Self-regulation' and 'Sensory Processing Disorder (SPD)' chapters** | |
| **A strength-based approach** | |
| Value and celebrate neurodiversity – 'difference' not 'deficit' | |
| Focus on and communicate strengths and successes and use positive language | |
| Research and celebrate successful autistic people | |
| Encourage pupils to share interests and knowledge | |
| **Reduce anxieties (see the 'Anxiety' chapter)** | |
| Awareness of and support for triggers and support to reduce stress | |
| Name and label emotions, use a stress scale and calming tools and access to a safe space | |
| Predictable routines, visual timetables, support around transitions and change | |
| Awareness of and support for sensory sensitivities | |
| **Social learning and relationships** | |
| Build understanding, accepting and trusting relationships, using strengths and interests to build rapport | |
| Work in collaboration with caregivers and pupils | |
| Model and teach expected social behaviour and clarify unwritten social cues | |
| Clear guidelines and support for group work – reduce social demands when learning and learning demands when socialising | |
| Teach emotions | |
| Support pupils to express views, to understand the perspective of others and how to restore relationships after an incident | |

*(Continued)*

## Continued

| STRATEGY | COMMENTS |
|---|---|
| Support generalising or connecting information and learning | |
| **Communication** | |
| Use pupil's name to attract attention | |
| Short, clear, single-step verbal instruction and allow processing time | |
| Teach changes in tone of voice and do not insist on eye contact | |
| Positive, direct, accurate language – say what you mean | |
| Support with communicating needs – help cards, break cards, stress scales | |
| Offer two or three positive choices | |
| **Use visual supports** | |
| Present information as visually as possible, e.g. visual timetable and *Now and Then* board, stress scale, timers, lists, pictures, labels | |
| **Teaching and learning** | |
| Clear objectives and success criteria presented visually | |
| Break tasks down into simple single steps, presented in a checklist | |
| Keep verbal inputs short and multi-sensory, where possible | |
| Uncluttered handouts or worksheets | |
| 'To do' and 'finished' folders for independent activities | |
| Support with homework | |
| Use special interests as motivators | |
| Support executive function (see p.14–15) | |
| **Environmental considerations** | |
| Use an environmental checklist and reduce stimulation and distractions | |
| Support sensory sensitivities and offer sensory tools and regular sensory and movement breaks | |
| Exit strategy and safe space | |

| STRATEGY | COMMENTS |
|---|---|
| Calming, reset time in mornings, after break and before going home | |
| **Unstructured times** | |
| Predictable routines and clear rules for break and lunchtimes with access to quieter areas and buddy/mentor and trusted key adult | |
| Support for wet breaks and PE | |
| **Rewards and consequences** | |
| Rules and routines displayed visually and are clearly explained | |
| Consistent approach, offer special interests as rewards or to regulate, at times, but do not take away as a consequence | |
| Establish what the behaviour was communicating and teach skills, language and social understanding | |

# Chapter 7

# Bereavement, grief and loss

Grief is a natural response to a death or significant loss and an important part of the healing process. There are different types of grief, caused by a range of circumstances, which are experienced by individuals in many different ways. Grief is usually the most intense following the death of a loved one. However, pupils may experience grief following other losses or may grieve for someone who is still alive; for example, looked-after children may grieve the loss of their birth family. Feelings of grief and loss may be due to parental separation or for a family member who is ill and their life together has transformed. Pupils may also grieve after a momentous change such as moving house or school, the loss of a friendship or the death of a pet.

## Presentations of grief and loss

Following a death or loss, pupils may display significant changes in behaviour. Grief responses will be different for each individual; however, recognising some of the ways that grief may present is essential in supporting pupils to understand and manage their feelings. 'There is no right way for the pupil to feel; remember that every child will experience grief in a different way to the next' (Moore, 2020).

DOI: 10.4324/9781003146292-8

Possible presentations of grief and loss may include:

- Irritability, frustration or anger
- Increased anxiety (including separation or health anxiety and panic attacks)
- Hyper-vigilance and feeling unsafe or insecure
- Increased impulsivity
- Difficulty concentrating or maintaining focus
- Forgetfulness
- Withdrawal
- Loss of self-confidence
- Feeling overwhelmed or out of control
- Regression to earlier developmental behaviours (such as toddler talk or toileting issues)
- Difficulties sleeping
- Changes in eating patterns
- Feelings of loneliness
- Depression
- Guilt
- Nausea, headaches or stomach aches

Children may mask grief or anxiety or communicate it through negative behaviours and struggle to know how to get their emotional needs met appropriately.

Everyone will respond to grief and loss very differently, so how an adult responds to a pupil will depend on the individual. The most important thing is to be there for them, listen and let them express their feelings.

# Suggestions for supporting pupils in school

Below is a range of activities to support pupils to reflect on and talk about their feelings and experiences of grief and loss. There is a checklist at the end of this chapter.

## Relationship and communication

- Keep (or establish new) routines, structure and predictability to increase feelings of safety and present these visually, where possible.
- Arguably, the most important support an adult can give a pupil is to acknowledge their feelings and show that they are there and

that they care. Grief, loss and death are often seen as taboo subjects, with people worrying about upsetting children by talking about them. However, it is necessary to enable and offer the pupil opportunities to talk about their grief and their needs and for adults to be there to listen with empathy and understanding. 'Discussing a death with a child can seem like a very tall order but remember; nothing you say will make it worse, the worst has already happened' (Winstonswish.org, 2020).

■ Ensure a trusted adult regularly checks in with the pupil throughout the day to find out how they are and enable them to share their feelings, worries and concerns. 'It is always better to say something than nothing when a child is hurting' (Knightsmith, 2020a).

■ Pupils may wish to express themselves but not know how to, needing adults to support and guide them. Wondering aloud techniques (Bombèr, 2011) or emotion coaching (Gottman & DeClaire, 1997) (see p.34–5) can help to label and validate all of their intense feelings. 'Never assume anything. Always ask the pupil questions to find out what they are thinking and feeling' (Moore, 2020).

■ Children may feel guilty about feeling anger or happiness after a loved one has died. They need to know that it is normal and natural to experience this wide range of feelings. The analogy of a roller coaster may help them see the many different emotions they feel throughout each day and begin to name and talk about these.

■ Pupils may feel confused about the range of feelings that they are experiencing following a loss. Treisman (2017, p.29) discusses exploring such mixed feelings creatively by creating a feelings patchwork, jigsaw or rainbow, or mixing paints, making a kaleidoscope or mixing ingredients in cookery.

■ Support pupils to express and put their feelings into words. Ask the pupil what colours they associate with a range of emotions (such as angry, scared, confused or sad) and use those colours to scribble or draw their representations of their feelings on a large piece of paper. Alternatively, similar colours and verbalisations could be used in a Jackson Pollock-style splatter painting. The pupil uses a brush or stick to splatter paint on a large sheet of paper (preferably outside). Allow the pupil to choose which emotions they are feeling (avoid putting words in their mouth) and the colours they will use to represent these.

■ Use visual prompts and a creative approach to encourage pupils to express their feelings, such as through pictures, puppets, role play or cartoons. Knightsmith (2020b) suggests using emojis as a quick, simple, visual and familiar way for children to express their range of feelings.

■ Knightsmith (2020b) suggests a 'grief brainstorm' for pupils to explore their own feelings around grief, including using words and colours to describe their grief, drawing it and exploring the size of it and where in their body they are feeling the grief.

■ Give pupils the opportunity to talk about their worries and concerns. Many worries may centre around practical issues and changes to routines. Use worry boxes (see p.251) or similar to express their feelings. Help them 'name it to tame it' (Siegel & Payne Bryson, 2012) by voicing and naming their worries to manage and reduce them. 'When we can give words to our frightening and painful experiences – when we literally come to terms with them – they often become much less frightening and painful. When we help our children name their pain and their fears, we help them tame them' (Siegel & Payne Bryson, 2012, p.27)

■ Young children tend to be very literal thinkers. therefore, use concrete, accurate, age-appropriate language when talking about the loss or death so there is no ambiguity. 'Try to avoid using euphemisms such as "gone to a better place", "gone to sleep" etc. – this can be extremely confusing, particularly for younger children and may lead to a misinterpretation that their loved one will return. For older children this could lead to frustration and may prevent them from talking openly about the death' (Mosaic Family Support, 2018, p.12).

■ Plan in advance with the pupil what to do if they become upset or overwhelmed (and what this feels like). Provide an exit strategy and access to a safe space, trusted adult and a range of calm tools. When the pupil is calm, trial a range of calming strategies together which can help them in times of overwhelm, such as breathing exercises, stress toys, exercise, mindful colouring and reading (see the 'Self-regulation' chapter). Take photos of these and record them as a visual reminder in times of escalation. Rehearse the strategies regularly when the pupil is calm. Model healthy coping and calming strategies.

■ Allow and encourage pupils to cry! It can help to release tension and is a natural response to sadness and overwhelm. It can be a healthy coping mechanism for emptying their 'stress bucket' (see p.88). Pupils need to feel safe enough to cry alongside an understanding, supportive, trusted adult. They need to be encouraged to show their emotions and often can feel better afterwards. Use music, dance, poetry, drama, art, song or film to explore sadness. Julie Monaghan at Mosaic Family Support suggested, in conversation in 2020, that there is a need to 'reframe crying' and see it in a different way, as a form of release and a possible tool to help to cope and manage grief.

- It might be useful to talk about grief as a natural and necessary part of the healing process. Lois Tonkin's (1996) *Growing Around Grief* model acknowledges that people will not 'get over it' and that this is natural. Their world will, in time, grow around their grief. The grief is portrayed as a circle (which remains the same size) with their world portrayed as a circle around this. The outer circle gets bigger as time passes and life grows around the grief. Barbara Monroe illustrates this practically with grief portrayed as a ball in a jar. The ball is always the same size, but the jar gets bigger as the world around the grief grows. Alternatively, there is the Fried Egg model of grief; grief is the yolk, the size of which stays the same, yet the size of the white changes in time, as life continues around the grief. One or more of these models may be helpful to explore visually with young people, and lots of images and explanations can be found online.

---

**Personal case example:**

Personally, since my lovely mum died, I have found grief counsellor Lois Tonkin's (1996) *Growing Around Grief* model and the other models outlined above, very supportive. I did not (and do not) want to 'get over it'; however, I do want to remember the happy times and the memories with fondness rather than immense sadness. For me, these models allow me to do that and to see that it is possible, moving forwards. The grief will always be there and will, at different times, increase and decrease in its intensity as I continue to live with and around the grief.

---

- The grieving process is cyclical and grief comes in waves, with strong feelings being revisited as pupils grow. Grief may be re-triggered months or years later, particularly as children's understanding of their loss develops. Ensure that all staff who work closely with the pupil are aware of their loss. Be mindful of birthdays, anniversaries and other key milestones which may be potentially difficult days for the pupil to manage. If the pupil displays a sudden change in behaviour, it may be a trigger to a grief response.
- Support and plan for transitions and separation anxiety using transitional objects, such as bringing in a photograph or special

memory stone. Have a key adult meet and greet the pupil and settle them before going to the classroom, if necessary.

## Exploring memories

'It's important that we create a safe space where it's possible to explore memories and talk about the person who's died openly' (Knightsmith, 2020a). Encourage time to talk about, explore and revisit happy memories through creative activities:

- 'Memory salt jars, memory boxes, making a memory book, journaling – recording thoughts, feelings and emotions, writing a goodbye letter, making a photo frame, decorating a candle jar, drawing or painting their feelings, tearing up lots of newspaper to express anger and frustration, running around the playground to let off "steam", decorating a small stone' (Mosaic Family Support, 2020).
- Write a happy memory or something about the person onto a strip of coloured paper and form these into a paper chain. Knightsmith (2020b, p.33) suggests making a mobile or memory jar to provide the pupil with 'something tangible they can use to revisit memories of the person who died'.
- Decorate a plant pot, with the pupil choosing colours or pictures which remind them of the person that they are grieving. Plant seeds or a bulb in memory of a person who died.
- Create a scrapbook of happy memories and create photo books or photo albums.
- Decorate a wooden disc or heart with pictures and the person's name to hang on a tree (especially relevant at Christmas time, if celebrated).
- Allow pupils the chance to say all the things they wish they had said to the person through letters, cards, videos, blogs, photographs, plays, poems or songs.
- Look after yourself and each other! Discussions may trigger certain personal feelings for staff and remind them of their own losses.

**Case study:**

Daley's grandmother died three years ago. He was very close to her. Daley had ELSA (Emotional Literacy Support Assistant) sessions at the time and he has had a block of counselling. He seemed settled in school. His grandfather has recently remarried. During the past year, Daley's behaviours have escalated. He is unpredictable and runs out of class and runs around the school. He throws equipment, shouts and will not engage in any learning. He has adult support throughout the school day but staff are at a loss as to how to manage his behaviours.

*How can staff support Daley?*

Daley is showing high levels of stress, possibly stemming from unprocessed grief and triggered by his grandfather's recent marriage. Daley will be given time with an experienced, trusted adult to explore his feelings through play and creative means and this will be timetabled into his week. Daley has brought a picture of his grandmother into school and is making a frame to go around this. He has expressed that he is looking forward to taking it home to put on his shelf to look at and talk to before going to bed once he has finished it.

Daley has been given opportunities to revisit memories of his grandmother. Working in collaboration with his parents, it became apparent that Daley's father had perhaps not fully processed his grief. His father has been invited to work with Daley. They have created a jar of memories (see the 'took kit'). Next, they have decided to create a memory box. They will look for photographs, objects and other memorabilia to put into the memory box. Daley will decorate this box with his key adult. Daley has stated that it is nice to talk to his dad about Gran, as he was previously scared of upsetting him, so remained quiet. He is currently not ready to talk about his grandfather's remarriage but knows that staff are available when he wishes to; however, he has been given an outlet to express some of his negative feelings and has thrown wet sponges at the wall and stamped on bubble wrap.

He has been given a safe space to go to, outside of the classroom, if he is feeling overwhelmed, and has been given 'talk' or 'space' cards to give to his key adult, inviting her to support him or give him space, depending on how he is feeling. This was rehearsed with his key adult, in a playful way.

As Daley is beginning to be given opportunities to explore and reflect on his feelings and has a place to go when he feels overwhelmed, his behaviours are settling.

# Resources, further information and 'tool kits'

## *Book for adults*

*Helping Children Cope with Loss and Change – a Guide for Professionals and Parents* by Amanda Seyderhelm

## *Books and resources to share with pupils*

*Always and Forever* by Alan Durant and Debi Gliori
*Blob Bereavement Cards* by Pip Wilson and Ian Long; these help children to express feelings in a visual and non-verbal way.
*Badger's Parting Gifts* by Sue Varley
*Helping Children with Loss* by Margot Sunderland
*Love Will Never Die* by Clare Shaw
*Michael Rosen's Sad Book* by Michael Rosen
*The Day the Sea Went Out and Never Came Back* by Margot Sunderland
*The Girl Who Lost the Light in her Eyes* by Juliet Ttofa
*The Invisible String* by Patrice Karst
*Till We Meet Again* by Julie Muller
*When the Sun Fell Out of the Sky* and *Supporting Children through Bereavement and Loss* Set by Hollie Rankin

## *Websites*

https://www.blobtree.com/ To help pupils explore a range of feelings and emotions
https://www.camrevle.com/pluginfile.php/23711/mod_resource/content/1/Teenagers-Guide.pdf Guide to support teenagers with grief and loss
http://www.childhoodbereavementnetwork.org.uk/campaigns/growing-in-grief-awareness.aspx A free, downloadable bereavement audit to help schools proactively plan how to support pupils with bereavement and loss, plus help, support and information for schools
http://www.childhoodbereavementnetwork.org.uk/media/106761/grief-support-at-school.pdf Useful conversation starters for bereaved pupils to tick off to give school staff and offer appropriate, supportive ways to open up a discussion or offer further support
https://www.childbereavementuk.org/Pages/Category/primary-schools Offers support and information for schools
https://www.cruse.org.uk/get-help/for-schools Offers support and information for schools

https://elearning.creativeeducation.co.uk/courses/supporting-stu
dents-with-bereavement/ Online training modules with a wide
range of practical ideas to help adults in school confidently support children to feel heard, seen and safe

https://www.creativeeducation.co.uk/product/loss-bereavement-acti
vities-to-support-children/ Excellent ideas for adults to use when
supporting pupils to explore their feelings and experiences.

https://www.griefencounter.org.uk/get-support/professionals/schools-
and-educational-providers/ Offers support, guidance and information for schools

https://thegoodgrieftrust.org/professional-advise/ A range of advice
and videos for professionals

https://www.hopeagain.org.uk/ Designed by young people for young
people to help them feel less alone and gain support

https://www.mentallyhealthyschools.org.uk/mental-health-needs/
bereavement-and-loss/ Support and advice for schools

https://www.mentallyheathyschools.org.uk/mental-health-needs/
bereavement-and-loss/

https://mosaicfamilysupport.org/ Dorset-based charity supporting
bereaved children and young people, their families and the professionals working with them. They also offer incredibly useful
advice and training for schools to support bereaved pupils

https://mosaicfamilysupport.org/images/Mosaic_School_Pack_With_
Copywrite.pdf School Bereavement Information Pack contains
lots of useful information for schools, including an example school
bereavement policy, sample letters and advice for schools when
supporting pupils

https://www.traumainformedschools.co.uk Useful resources and
information about their training courses, the Trauma-Informed
Practitioner diploma is a wonderful course with lots of practical
strategies that can be used in schools

https://www.verywellfamily.com/signs-of-grief-in-children-and-how-
to-help-them-cope-4174245 Understanding grief in children

https://whatsyourgrief.com/types-of-grief-2/ Describes seven types of
grief

https://www.winstonswish.org/supporting-you/support-for-schools/
Offers support, training and information for schools

https://www.winstonswish.org/wp-content/uploads/2020/04/Mem
ory-Jars-Winstons-Wish.pdf Instructions for creating a **jar of
memories**

https://youthlight.com/sample/activities_grieving_children.pdf Lots of
activities for grieving children

## Apps

**Apart of Me** is an app designed with the help of the bereaved and child psychologists for young people (nine years and older) who have lost a parent or sibling

# References

Particular thanks to Julie Monaghan at https://mosaicfamilysupport.org/ for her time and invaluable advice and support!

Bombèr, L. (2011) *What about Me? Inclusive Strategies to Support Pupils with Attachment Difficulties Make It through the School Day* Worth Publishing, London

Gottman, J. & DeClaire, J. (1997) *Raising an Emotionally Intelligent Child* Simon and Schuster, New York

Knightsmith, P. (2020a) *Support Bereaved Children* [online] Creative Education. Available at: https://elearning.creativeeducation.co.uk/courses/support ing-students-with-bereavement/ [Accessed 14 May 2020]

Knightsmith, P. (2020b) *Growing Through Grief Activities and Ideas* [online] Creative Education. Available at: https://www.creativeeducation.co.uk/courses/bereavement-indepth-with-pooky-knightsmith/lessons/resource-booklet-growing-through-grief-activities/ [Accessed 28 September 2020]

Moore, M. (2020) *Working with Pupils Who Have Been Recently Bereaved* [online] Attendance Matters Magazine, 9 March. Available at: https://attendance mattersmagonline.co.uk/working-with-pupils-who-have-been-recently-bereaved/ [Accessed 1 April 2021]

Mosaic Family Support (2018) *School Bereavement Information Pack* [online] Available at: https://mosaicfamilysupport.org/images/Mosaic_School_Pack_With_Copywrite.pdf [Accessed 30 June 2020]

Mosaic Family Support (2020) *Supporting Bereaved Children On-line Professional Advice and Support for Those Supporting Bereaved Children and Their Families during the Coronavirus Pandemic Training PowerPoint* [online] Available at: https://mosaicfamilysupport.org/ [Accessed 30 June 2020]

Siegel, D. and Payne Bryson, T. (2012) *The Whole-Brain Child – 12 Proven Strategies to Nurture Your Child's Developing Mind* Robinson, London

Tonkin, L. (1996) *Growing around Grief – Another Way of Looking at Grief and Recovery* [online] Bereavement Care, 7 January, 15(1), 10, DOI:10.1080/02682629608657376. Available at: https://www.tandfonline.com/doi/abs/10.1080/02682629608657376

Treisman, K. (2017) *Working with Relational and Developmental Trauma in Children and Adolescents* Routledge, Oxon

Winstonswish.org (2020) [online] Available at: https://www.winstonswish.org/wp-content/courses/how_to_help_primary/index.html#/id/5ddf8f7461084a06bd07b572 [Accessed 4 December 2020]

## Checklist to support pupils with bereavement, grief and loss

| STRATEGY | COMMENTS |
|---|---|
| **Relationship and communication** | |
| Predictable routines | |
| Acknowledge their feelings and enable them to talk | |
| Regular check-ins with _____ | |
| Name and label feeling (emotion coaching or wondering aloud) | |
| Feelings activities – scribbling/painting to verbalise feelings using colour | |
| Visual emotion prompts – pictures, puppets, cartoons, emojis | |
| Worry boxes/worry monsters to name and tame fears | |
| Use concrete, accurate language | |
| Plan and rehearse use of safe space and calming strategies | |
| Allow and encourage crying as a coping mechanism | |
| Discuss and portray models of grief | |
| Ensure all staff who need to know, do know and are aware of milestones, anniversaries and birthdays | |
| **Exploring memories** | |
| Creative activities to explore and revisit memories such as memory boxes, journals, decorations | |
| Use letters, videos, cards, poems, songs, etc. to say all the things they wish they had said | |
| Look after yourself! | |

# Chapter 8

# Fetal Alcohol Spectrum Disorders (FASD)

Fetal Alcohol Spectrum Disorders (FASD) cover a broad spectrum of preventable neurodevelopmental disorders caused by fetal exposure to alcohol, causing permanent changes to brain structure, affecting executive function and development. 'FASD alters the way that the brain is structured and how neural pathways are linked' (Roberts, 2020).

Research suggests that up to 17 per cent of children in the UK may have FASD (McQuire et al., 2019).

FASD is a spectrum disorder so symptoms vary between each individual and can range from 'mild to profound' (Blackburn et al., 2012).

Although individuals can show physical symptoms of FASD which 'include facial differences, growth deficiencies, major organ damage, and skeletal damage, as well as hearing and vision impairments' (Blackburn et al., 2012 p.1), most people with FASD present with no obvious visible differences, leading to it often being described as a 'hidden disability'. Approximately 10 per cent of people diagnosed with FASD have the associated facial features. However, most do have a range of cognitive difficulties and may have had delays in reaching key developmental milestones. Damage to the brain whilst in the womb can result in 'a range of developmental, learning, behavioural, social, emotional and sensory difficulties which create barriers to learning' (Blackburn et al., 2012, p.28).

## Main presentations of FASD

The range and severity of symptoms will present differently for each individual. However, people with FASD usually display some of the following symptoms, often linked to delayed executive function (see p.14–15):

- Extreme, unpredictable or unexplained behaviours
- Sudden emotional reactions and difficulties with emotional regulation
- Hypervigilance
- Anxiety
- Hyperactivity
- Inattention and loss of focus
- Impulsiveness
- Fixations or obsessions on people or objects
- Memory difficulties or gaps
- Difficulties making and maintaining friendships and reading social cues
- Sensory processing difficulties (see 'Sensory Processing Disorder (SPD)' chapter)
- Low self-esteem
- Language and processing difficulties
- Difficulties with planning, sequencing, problem-solving and organisation
- Lack of cause and effect thinking
- Difficulties understanding the concept of time and time management
- Lack of understanding around risks or danger
- Confabulation – likely to fill in gaps in knowledge or understanding with fabrications that they may believe to be true

Their developmental age often presents as half their chronological age, particularly socially or emotionally. Malbin (2013) refers to this as *dysmaturity*. Pupils are described as having a 'spiky profile', displaying at or above age-related skills or knowledge in certain areas, and well below average in other areas. Pupils with FASD also find it difficult to generalise learning, meaning that what they know and understand in one setting or classroom may not be transferred to another.

**Case study:**

Tron was diagnosed with FASD two years ago at the age of eight. He often gets into trouble at school because of his risk-taking and impulsive behaviours. Tron is desperate to play and fit in with his peers but often doesn't seem to know how. He appears to sabotage relationships by hitting out and hurting others. When he approaches others on the playground it is usually with a hit or a kick. He doesn't understand why his peers won't play with him and will shout, throw things and then cry, saying that nobody likes him.

Tron loves most sports and is fantastic at football. However, at times, he seems to deliberately kick the ball out of play, causing outrage from his teammates. Tron is also incredibly good at drumming, playing in a band with older pupils.

His reading is above average and in class discussions he is very articulate and often astounds the teacher with his creative ideas. He struggles with written tasks and does not usually get started on his written work. When he does start, he writes two or three words before the book is thrown on the floor. If an adult writes his ideas down, he will remain focused for much longer periods of time. If an adult is too busy to scribe for him or asks him to work independently, he will leave the classroom and is often found up a tree or climbing the fence with the aim to leave the site.

*What could staff do to support Tron?*

Key staff have worked hard to understand Tron's needs. They have started to build much more positive relationships with him and see the person underneath some of his behaviours.

Restorative conversations have been introduced, after an incident. Staff explore Tron's feelings, and also support him to see the perspective of others and the impact that his actions can have on other people.

Staff are also focusing on his strengths and achievements and pointing these out at every opportunity. He has been made sports captain for his school team and his band have played in an assembly. He has, alongside the drumming teacher, helped with drumming lessons for beginners.

Tron is currently trialling a dictation program to help him get his ideas down and reduce the need for writing (at times). This has increased his confidence in English and he has produced some imaginative creative writing.

Many pupils with FASD will have a range of complex needs and often are diagnosed alongside other comorbid conditions such as autism, (Attention Deficit Hyperactivity Disorder (ADHD), Sensory Processing

Disorder (SPD), Oppositional Defiant Disorder (ODD), attachment disorders or eating disorders.

# Supporting pupils with FASD in school

Schools often need to change how they have traditionally worked and be flexible around (or make changes to) existing school behaviour policies to best support pupils with FASD. Staff need to 'view the challenges they face through the lens of brain differences and not simply as behavioural issues' (NHS Ayrshire & Arran, 2019). It needs a whole-school approach, with all staff involved, rather than adjustments only made within the classroom. 'It's about the children or the students feeling a sense of belonging from the time they arrive at the front gate' (Basaraba, in Senelmis et al., 2019).

Pupils with FASD usually have damage to the brain's frontal lobe, affecting executive functioning (see p.14–15). Executive function impacts learning, behaviour, daily life and independence in various situations (Blackburn, 2020). Because the brain affected by FASD processes differently, it can be a significant barrier to learning. 'It does not have to be a barrier because it is not that those affected cannot learn but rather that they learn in a different way to their peers' (Roberts, 2020). As adults, it is essential to understand these differences in order to support pupils; it is about staff 'trying differently rather than harder' (Malbin, 2002). 'Trying harder to change neurobehavioral symptoms exacerbates frustration. Recognizing brain function and providing accommodations prevents problems' (Malbin, 2013).

Below is a range of strategies that have been tried and tested and found to support pupils with FASD in school. There is a checklist at the end of this chapter.

## *A strength-based approach*

'A positive educational experience is key' (Blackburn, 2017). 'The classroom teacher is probably the most important determinant of success for an individual pupil with FASD. Reframing the "behaviours" is the most important first step' (Cunningham, 2012). Staff need to understand that the brains of pupils with FASD work differently and support them in gaining the skills to overcome their challenges. 'It is not that pupils with FASD "won't" behave, they "can't" behave' (Cunningham, 2012, p.3).

FASD has symptoms that cause challenges for pupils, particularly in terms of behaviour and learning. It is important to understand and support these, yet it is essential to communicate and focus on the pupil's many strengths and successes.

- When teaching children (and adults) to understand the condition, communicate brain differences rather than deficits. Adult responses strongly influence pupils' behaviour and attitudes towards difference. Therefore, it is essential that adults in school model tolerance, acceptance and patience.
- Pupils with FASD tend to have strengths in hands-on, practical tasks (enjoying making things, drawing and design, building and construction tasks and puzzles). Many are sociable, engaging, articulate and have good verbal abilities and have shown compassion when working with children and animals. Many pupils with FASD have a strong sense of fairness and morals. Many pupils display strengths in literacy and practical subjects such as art, performing arts, sport, mechanics, technology and computer science. Long-term visual memory can also be a strength (Blackburn, 2020; Cunningham, 2012). They often have a good sense of humour and creativity along with a desire to please (NHS Ayrshire & Arran, 2019).
- Focusing on strengths is essential to build self-esteem. 'These strengths will become the foundations on which to develop personalised curricula, to encourage and develop further strengths, and so build emotional resilience' (Blackburn et al., 2012, p.29). Celebrate these successes and share them regularly with caregivers. Low self-confidence is often associated with FASD. Give roles and responsibilities based on the pupil's strengths and interests, to increase their sense of self-worth and feelings of belonging. Boost self-esteem by using a positive home-school book, sending positive postcards home, or creating a scrapbook of successes or a success jar. In communication, aim for ten positive comments for every (perceived) negative.

## Relationships

- Relational approaches are essential and need to be built on trust and a clear understanding of the pupil's strengths and challenges. Collaborate and work with the pupil to understand their needs and what works for them. 'Only by understanding their pupils, what they can do and what they find difficult, can adults in schools make the reasonable adjustments necessary for a student to achieve. These adjustments often are not huge, but the rewards can be great' (Roberts, 2020). Involve them in discussing solutions to difficulties.

- Empathy is essential, yet impossible without genuine under-standing. Work in close collaboration with caregivers, any out-side agencies involved and with other staff who work closely with the pupil. Establish positive relationships with the pupil and their family, built on understanding and trust. Caregivers know the pupil best and can share their experiences. Discuss strengths and successes as well as challenges the pupil may have. Many families have had negative experiences with the school system and may have felt blamed or criticised in the past. It is crucial to get out of any negative spiral that may have arisen. A consistent approach is the most effective, so sharing good practice, using consistent vocabulary and visual supports is essential (but often overlooked).
- Avoid confrontations and pick your battles. Establish priorities in collaboration with key staff and caregivers to focus on what is cur-rently important for the pupil (see the Priority Rating Scale, p.247).
- Support pupils to build and maintain friendships. Pupils with FASD may need social cues taught explicitly to them in order to understand them fully. Teach, model and rehearse social skills such as personal space, taking turns in conversations and using words rather than touch (a script might be useful here). Model appropriate behaviour, teach appropriate ways to manage frus-tration and disappointment and how to gain someone's attention in an acceptable way (Zieff & Schwartz-Bloom, 2008).
- Model, guide and support pupils and become their 'external brain' (NHS Ayrshire & Arran, 2019). Developmental differences in exec-utive functioning mean that pupils may need support to control their impulsiveness. Teach 'stopping and thinking' by providing and modelling the use of a *stop, breathe and think* card.
- Pupils will need to regulate emotionally alongside an understand-ing, trusted adult, focusing on co-regulation rather than self-regulation, particularly initially. Teach self-regulation strategies (see the 'Self-regulation' chapter) by co-regulation and model-ling. Pupils with FASD need to develop 'interdependence' rather than 'independence', which is critical for their future success (Cunningham, 2012). We need to teach pupils how and whom to ask for help or support and praise their successes when they achieve this (Noble, 2010).

## Communication

- Allow processing time (silently count to ten) before expecting a response. Malbin (2013) describes pupils with FASD as 'ten second children in a one second world'. Slow down, reduce the number of words used and increase the use of visuals supports.

■ Establish predictable and consistent routines and warn pupils of any changes. Use clear and simple visual cues, such as timers and visual timetables, to support memory difficulties and alleviate anxiety. Use photos rather than picture symbols and include timings by displaying a picture of the classroom clock. Visual timetables are more effective on the pupil's desk than relying on a whole class one.

■ Display visuals of behaviour expectations (photographs of the pupil engaging in the expected behaviours, such as good sitting or good listening, are often more effective than pictures or symbols, which are more abstract and less easy to understand or process). Use the same visual cues across all settings (every classroom and at home).

■ Ensure consistent use of language and vocabulary from every adult, in every classroom and at home. For example, all agree to say 'tidy up' rather than 'pack away', 'put your things away' or 'clear up' so the pupil only needs to process one set of verbal instructions.

■ Keep rules simple, concrete and easy to follow, and rehearse these regularly. Again, all adults need to be consistent and use the same words for the same rules, reducing the amount that needs to be remembered (Blackburn et al., 2012). Ensure a consistent approach across the school (and at home, where applicable) by having the same rules in each class, presented in the same way, using the same words and pictures.

■ Use the pupil's name to attract their attention before giving an instruction or initiating conversation.

■ Remain calm and smile.

■ Use direct language, say exactly what you mean, avoiding metaphors, idioms and ambiguous language.

■ Use positive language, avoiding 'don't' and 'no' where possible (unless it is an issue of immediate safety) and reframe communication into positives. Tell the pupil the expected or desired behaviour (rather than focusing on the undesired behaviour); therefore, 'don't run' becomes 'walk'. This will help the pupil remember and focus on the behaviours that you do want to see and create a more positive atmosphere.

■ Keep verbal instructions and lesson inputs short, using simple single steps (Blackburn et al., 2012) and reinforce these using visual prompts where possible.

■ Ask pupils to repeat key information or instructions, using their own words, to check for understanding (Blackburn et al., 2012, p.48).

- Differentiation is needed, not only in terms of the curriculum but also when communicating with a pupil with FASD. Take the pupil's developmental age into consideration and adjust expectations accordingly; it is necessary to *think younger*. 'The better the fit between expectation and ability, the less stress. Dysmaturity is a classic sign of FASD. This is VERY confusing for parents and teachers. All modifications should be planned around where the pupil seems to be developmentally' (Cunningham, 2012).
- Observe pupils in order to recognise triggers and patterns of behaviour and put in support around these. 'Focused observation is important to gain an understanding of how individuals with FASD experience stress, relieve tension, cope with obstacles and react to change. This can inform us about how to provide a supportive environment that leads to achievement' (NHS Ayrshire & Arran, 2019).
- Rehearse or role play scenarios that the pupil often struggles with or that are different from the usual routine. For example, rehearse going to the hall and sitting down for assembly, role play going to the changing rooms and then out on the field for PE, and ensure the pupil knows where the equipment is, and where or who to go to if they are feeling overwhelmed. 'Role play may be a useful tool. Try practising appropriate behaviours, maybe before a specific situation or transition that may be challenging, or after a situation where behaviour was not appropriate' (Sharp & Sharp, 2020).
- Pupils with FASD often have difficulties with change and will need support around transitions. Cunningham (2012) suggests providing 'transition buddies to get them through changes in routine'. Reminder cards and transitional objects can be helpful (see p.91). Pupils with FASD will almost certainly need an enhanced transition plan when changing key stage or when moving schools.
- Avoid asking why. Pupils usually will not know why they have acted in a certain way or be able to communicate these reasons. Using the word 'why' can also sound accusatory.

## *Teaching and learning*

Difficulties with executive function mean that pupils may underperform and not reach their full potential academically. They will need support and strategies around planning and prioritising, flexible thinking, working memory, understanding cause and effect, and organisational skills (see p.14–16).

- Collaborate with other adults working with the pupil to ensure consistent and predictable routines, vocabulary, expectations and approaches.
- Support pupils to start tasks and provide structure to help orga-nise thoughts and ideas logically. Keep instructions concrete and specific and provide visual cues where possible. Pupils with FASD learn best by doing and need to be repeatedly shown how. Show pupils exactly what is expected, rather than just telling them. Show work samples and model each step. Lack of engagement may mean that instructions were too ambiguous (NHS Ayrshire & Arran, 2019).
- Aim for short, sharp bursts of work followed by a quick movement or sensory break.
- Many pupils are unable to keep still and to listen at the same time. If asked to remain still, this may take all of their energy or attention. Allow fiddling or doodling whilst listening (see the 'Self-regulation' chapter).
- Offer limited positive choices to increase feelings of control and to reduce the chance of a negative choice being made. Choices may be about how or where to complete a task, such as which writing implement to use, choice of pencil grip, choice of where to com-plete the task or choice of paper colour.
- A good verbal ability can often mask a lack of, or gaps in, under-standing. Use concrete concepts and real examples rather than abstract ones, wherever possible, particularly in Maths tasks. 'Neuroscience shows that, with FASDs, the brain's parietal lobe can be significantly reduced. This area controls numeracy and mathematical computation' (Blackburn et al., 2012, p.93). Ideas include using real money and role play scenarios when teaching money, and real clocks and calendars when teaching time. Use 'number lines, an abacus for understanding place value and real objects for counting in sequence' (Blackburn et al., 2012, pp.47–48). Provide hands-on, practical, multi-sensory tasks, where pos-sible, so pupils are learning by doing.
- Where worksheets are used, make them clear and straightfor-ward, removing excess information and unnecessary pictures or distractors. Alternatively, cut them up and give one piece of infor-mation or question at a time. Provide a copy of the key points for them to highlight and visual prompts such as pictures, photos, diagrams and flow charts, to aid memory.
- Use the pupil's interests to motivate and to foster their curiosity and create 'personal learning pathways' (Blackburn et al., 2012)

to increase pupil engagement. 'Using evidence-based knowledge of a child's successful learning pathways, strategies can be identified, high expectations set, and incremental progress recorded on their journey towards optimal engagement in learning' (Blackburn et al., 2012, p.76).

▪ Pupils with FASD may have difficulties with fine motor control and hand–eye coordination. Trial a range of writing implements or pencil grips. Reduce the amount of writing expected by providing tasks where pupils write captions for pictures or posters, fill in speech and thought bubbles, use cloze procedures or provide sentence starters. Offer alternative methods of recording, particularly where writing is a trigger, such as videos and voice recordings, taking photographs, typing on the computer or using scribes.

▪ Adults need to understand that confabulation seems as if the pupil is lying but it is likely that they are filling in gaps in their knowledge or memory. They may be masking a lack of understanding and telling you what they think you would like to hear or desperately trying to fit in (Brooks, in Senelmis et al., 2019). 'To the outsider, it sounds like lying, fabrication, or fantasy. To the person who is confabulating, it seems real' (FAFASD, 2018). 'Strategies to help with confabulation: stop blaming, accusing, and shift your understanding of the false information from lying to a brain-based symptom. A positive, trusting relationship can help when the person who is confabulating needs support. Educate the person with an FASD about confabulation as well as his/her support system' (FAFASD, 2018).

▪ Provide support and adjust expectations around homework. Where possible, set home learning activities around life skills. Pupils with an FASD often have particular difficulties understanding money and time. Practical activities could include shopping tasks in collaboration with caregivers, counting out money in a money box, paying for a bus ride, using clocks to tell the time, and planning using diaries, clocks or calendars. Cooking activities are helpful for following sequences, using measuring practically as well as being an essential life skill. Break more formal homework into step-by-step chunks, provide a checklist and include movement breaks.

▪ Step-by-step learning, repetition, and using memory aids have been successful in facilitating learning with students with FASD (Zieff & Schwartz-Bloom, 2008). Provide, model and practise the use of visual cues such as vocabulary mats with pictures, key information cards, number lines, timelines, practical equipment,

topic-related artefacts to hold, talking tins, teach mnemonics, colour-coding and arrows in note-taking.
■ Support executive functions (see pp.14–15 and 22–3).

## *Environmental considerations*

■ Pupils with FASD tend to have difficulties managing sensory information (Pennell, 2020) and a calm, nurturing, structured learning environment is vital (NHS Ayrshire & Arran, 2019). Staff need to create an environment where all pupils feel 'emotionally safe' by being creative, flexible and nurturing (Zieff & Schwartz-Bloom, 2008). 'Be aware that unwanted behaviour is a cue that some element of the environment needs to be adapted. Since children with FASD are unable to change their neurological challenges, it is up to the educator to make the necessary changes' (NHS Ayrshire & Arran, 2019).
■ Where possible, reduce stimulation and distractions. 'Be ready to change the environment, you can't change the child's brain' (Sharp & Sharp, 2020). Work stations in a quieter area of the classroom can be a useful choice for some activities. It should always be regarded as a supportive rather than a punitive measure. Avoid sparkly, moving or dangling displays, which can be distracting or overwhelming.
■ Be aware of the sensory environment (noise, crowds, lighting, smells, textures). Calm the nervous system and support sensory sensitivities to avoid a pupil feeling overwhelmed by planning regular sensory and movement breaks and providing a range of calm tools (see the 'Self-regulation' and 'Sensory Processing Disorder (SPD)' chapters). It would be useful to complete a sensory checklist or request an Occupational Therapist assessment to enable the implementation of strategies to calm the sensory system or manage or avoid certain triggers.
■ Sensory resources such as wobble cushions, ball chairs, weighted lap pads or resistance bands on the chair legs can be highly effective in allowing movement whilst sitting (see the 'Self-regulation' chapter). 'Children with FASD may constantly move in their chairs, fall off their chairs, avoid sitting or only remain seated for short periods of time during class activities. Children will often try to lean against a wall, furniture or other people for support in a constant effort to keep upright' (NHS Ayrshire & Arran, 2019). Allow pupils to stand to work, pace whilst listening, sit on a beanbag or lie on the floor with a clipboard to take notes or read. Some pupils benefit from standing desks or easels.

■ Provide the pupils with an exit strategy and ensure access to a safe, quiet space (see p.42).

## *Unstructured times*

It is important that unstructured times are managed carefully. Be aware that social times often cause increased anxiety and the increased crowds, sounds and smells can be overwhelming for those with sensory sensitivities.

■ Pupils with FASD are usually impulsive, with little sense of danger or risk. They will need supervision and support at unstructured times.
■ Have a predictable routine for break and lunchtimes, with clear, consistent rules and expectations, presented visually. Ensure all staff (including lunchtime supervisors) are using the same language and have the same expectations.
■ Offer a quieter area to eat in or allow the pupil to eat slightly earlier or later to avoid crowds, noises and smells. Similarly, offer a safe, quiet zone to access if the playground becomes overwhelming. Rehearse, when the pupil is calm, where and who to go to and provide a visual reminder. Provide a range of activities and clubs around the pupil's interests at break and lunchtimes, taking time to teach and explain the rules of some simple games.
■ Provide access to a key adult at break and lunchtimes. Take photographs as a non-verbal reminder. The key adult can remind the pupil of playground expectations, teach, practise and support turn-taking, teach scripts and also encourage other children to invite the pupil into their games.
■ Implementing a buddy or mentor system may increase confidence and decrease anxieties at social times.
■ Support and understanding may be required for PE lessons. A pupil may struggle with fine and gross motor skills and need adjustments made to enable them to feel successful and engage fully. Additional support may be needed in preparing the pupil for going to the hall or field. Be mindful of sensory sensitivities around changing, clothing and changes of footwear (see the 'Sensory Processing Disorder (SPD)' chapter).

## *Rewards and consequences*

Pupils with FASD often display impulsive behaviour and do not always think about possible consequences or the implications of their actions.

Certain rewards or consequences may be successful to begin with, but then lose their effectiveness (NHS Ayrshire & Arran, 2019). Many pupils do not learn from sanctions and react negatively when they are imposed upon them. Brain-based differences, memory difficulties and difficulties linking cause and effect may mean a pupil cannot understand reasons for the sanctions, which may lead to further inappropriate behaviour (Sharp & Sharp, 2020).

- Cause and effect or planned consequences are often an abstract concept for pupils with FASD and, therefore, difficult to understand and predict. Pupils may repeat negative behaviours and not learn from previous consequences (Sharp & Sharp, 2020). Teach and model expected behaviour and how to make positive choices. Show that their actions will have a consequence or an effect on themselves or others by using flow charts, pictures, role play and Comic Strip Conversations™ (Gray, 1994) or Social Stories™ (Gray, 2015).
- Consequences need to be practical, fair, logical, concrete, immediate and simple, for example, tidying up after throwing equipment. Avoid removing a treasured item like an electronic device that might also help self-regulation (Sharp & Sharp, 2020). Also avoid the removal of specific interests or activities linked to a pupil's strengths and successes, such as removing football for a pupil whose area of strength that is.
- Provide support rather than sanctions and teach pupils the skills they need. Avoid sanctions for behaviours that the pupil has no control over and teach necessary skills instead. 'NEVER punish brain-based behaviour. Punishment doesn't work and almost always will cause the Secondary Effects!' Secondary effects being 'defensive behaviours which develop over time in response to a non-supportive environment' (Cunningham, 2012).

## Resources, further information and 'tool kits'

### Books

*Damaged Angels* by Bonnie Buxton
*Educating Children and Young People with Fetal Alcohol Spectrum Disorders – Constructing Personalised Pathways to Learning* by Carolyn Blackburn, Barry Carpenter and Jo Egerton – hugely informative with lots of useful strategies for school staff
*Fetal Alcohol Spectrum Disorders – Interdisciplinary Perspectives* by Barry Carpenter, Carolyn Blackburn and Jo Egerton

*Developing Inclusive Practice for Young Children with Fetal Alcohol Spectrum Disorders: A Framework of Knowledge and Understanding for the Early Childhood Workforce* by Carolyn Blackburn

*Trying Differently Rather Than Harder: Fetal Alcohol Spectrum Disorders* by Diane Malbin

*Understanding Fetal Alcohol Spectrum Disorder: A Guide to FASD for Parents, Carers and Professionals* by Maria Catterick and Liam Curran

## Websites

http://www.betterendings.org/strategies_not_solutions.pdf Strategies to support

https://www.creativeeducation.co.uk/courses/spot-and-support-those-with-foetal-alcohol-spectrum-disorders-fasd/ On-demand course to support those with FASD

https://fascets.org/ A range of information and resources

http://www.fasdnetwork.org/ Information and resources for teachers, parents and young people

https://lcfasd.com/resources-about-fasd/ Support and success stories

https://nationalfasd.org.uk/ UK national organisation for FASD, raising awareness and offering support and advice

https://www.nhsaaa.net/media/8391/fasd_whateducatorsneedtoknow.pdf A wealth of information and suggestions

https://www.saskfasdnetwork.ca/resources A range of advice and strategies to support

https://www.sign.ac.uk/assets/pat156_fasd.pdf A booklet for families

https://sites.duke.edu/fasd/ A guide for teachers

## Podcasts

https://www.acamh.org/blog/fasd-podcast/ Informative discussion about FASD

https://www.nccd.edu.au/professional-learning/classroom-adjustments-fetal-alcohol-spectrum-disorder-fasd Personal experiences and suggestions for reasonable adjustments within the school

# References

Blackburn, C. (2017) *Teaching a Pupil with FASD* [online] The National Organisation for FASD. Available at: https://nationalfasd.org.uk/documents/FASD%20in%20Focus%20EducationProfile.pdf [Accessed 16 June 2020]

Blackburn, C. (2020) *FASD in Focus – Education Profile* [online] The National Organisation for FASD. Available at: https://nationalfasd.org.uk/documents/FASD%20in%20Focus%20EducationProfile.pdf [Accessed 12 January 2021]

Blackburn, C., Carpenter, B. & Egerton, J. (2012) *Educating Children and Young People with Fetal Alcohol Spectrum Disorders – Constructing Personalised Pathways to Learning* Routledge, Oxon

Cunningham, M. (2012) *Building Educational Success for Pupils with FASD Foetal Alcohol Spectrum Disorders* [online] Available at: http://www.fasdnetwork.org/uploads/9/5/1/1/9511748/educational_success_fas.pdf [Accessed 13 January 2021]

FAFASD (2018) *FASD Fact #14: Confabulation Is Not Lying* [online] Available at: https://fafasd.org/fasd-fact-14-confabulation-not-lying/#:~:text=Confabulation%20is%20when%20the%20brain,of%20understanding%20or%20of%20memory.&text=Confabulation%20is%20common%20for%20many,to%20a%20brain%2Dbased%20symptom [Accessed 17 January 2021]

Gathercole, S. & Packiam Alloway, T. (2007) *Understanding Working Memory: A Classroom Guide* [online] Harcourt Assessment. Available at: https://www.mrc-cbu.cam.ac.uk/wp-content/uploads/2013/01/WM-classroom-guide.pdf [Accessed 11 October 2017]

Gray, C. (1994) *Comic Strip Conversations* Future Horizons, Arlington

Gray, C. (2015) *The New Social Story Book: Over 150 Social Stories That Teach Everyday Social Skills to Children and Adults with Autism and Their Peers* Future Horizons, Arlington

Malbin (2002) *Trying Differently Rather Than Harder: Fetal Alcohol Spectrum Disorders* FASCETs Inc USA

Malbin, D. (2013) *Linking Brain Function with Behaviors: Understanding and Application of a Brain-Based Approach* [online] 21 November. Available at: https://www.fasdwaterlooregion.ca/assets/documents/Diane-Malbin.pdf [Accessed 14 January 2021]

McQuire, C., Mukherjee, R., Hurt, L., Higgins, A., Greene, G., Farewell, D., Kemp, A. & Paranjothy, S. (2019) *Screening Prevalence of Fetal Alcohol Spectrum Disorders in a Region of the United Kingdom: A Population-Based Birth-Cohort Study* Preventive Medicine, 118, 344–351. Available at: https://www.sciencedirect.com/science/article/pii/S0091743518303323 [Accessed 2 April 2021]

NHS Ayrshire & Arran (2019) *Understanding Fetal Alcohol Spectrum Disorder (FASD) What Educators Need to Know – for Education Staff Working with Children and Young People with FASD* [online] Available at: https://www.nhsaaa.net/media/8391/fasd_whateducatorsneedtoknow.pdf [Accessed 12 January 2021]

Noble, J. (2010) *Independence vs. Interdependence* [online] Available at: http://fasdforever.com/why-independence-and-fasd-is-not-always-a-good-thing/# [Accessed 14 January 2021]

Pennell, J. (2020) *FASD in Focus – Sensory Integration* [online] The National Organisation for FASD. Available at: https://nationalfasd.org.uk/documents/FASD%20in%20Focus%20EducationProfile.pdf [Accessed 12 January 2021]

Roberts, B. (2020) *FASD in Focus – Tips for Educators* [online] The National Organisation for FASD. Available at: https://nationalfasd.org.uk/documents/FASD%20in%20Focus%20EducationProfile.pdf [Accessed 12 January 2021]

Senelmis, S., Basaraba, D., Brooks, C. & Russell, A. (2019) *Classroom Adjustments: Fetal Alcohol Spectrum Disorder (FASD)* [podcast] 11 February. Available at: https://www.nccd.edu.au/professional-learning/classroom-adjustments-fetal-alcohol-spectrum-disorder-fasd [Accessed 5 January 2020]

Sharp, A. & Sharp, S. (2020) *FASD and Trauma: Parenting Tips for Foster Carers* [online] Available at: *https://www.thefosteringnetwork.org.uk/sites/default/files/content/fasdandtraumaforfostercarersfinal.pdf* [Accessed 19 July2021]

Zieff, C. & Schwartz-Bloom, R. (2008) *Understanding Fetal Alcohol Spectrum Disorders (FASD) A Comprehensive Guide for Pre-K-8 Educators* [online] Duke Institute for Brain Sciences. Available at: https://sites.duke.edu/fasd/introduction/ [Accessed 14 January 2021]

## Checklist to support pupils with FASD

| STRATEGY | COMMENTS |
|---|---|
| **Please also refer to the 'Behaviour is communication', 'Self-regulation' and 'Sensory Processing Disorder (SPD)' chapters** | |
| **A strength-based approach** | |
| Communicate brain 'difference' not 'deficit' | |
| Focus on and celebrate strengths | |
| Give roles and responsibilities based on strengths and interests and boost self-esteem | |
| **Relationships** | |
| Build trust, collaborate with pupils, caregivers and outside agencies and all staff who work with the pupil – consistent approach | |
| Avoid confrontations, pick battles and focus on priority behaviours | |
| Support to build and maintain friendships | |
| Model, guide and support pupils, become their 'external brain', provide co-regulation and aim for interdependence | |
| **Communication** | |
| Allow processing time | |
| Predictable routines and visual cues consistent in all settings | |
| Use consistent vocabulary and simple rules across all classrooms and settings | |
| Use the pupil's name to attract attention | |
| Remain calm and smile | |
| Use direct, clear language | |
| Use positive language (avoiding 'don't and 'no' where possible) | |
| Short verbal instructions and lesson inputs, use visual cues where possible | |
| Ask pupil to repeat key information | |
| Spot triggers and put in support at these times and support for change and transition times | |
| Avoid asking 'why' | |

*(Continued)*

## Continued

| STRATEGY | COMMENTS |
|---|---|
| **Teaching and learning** ||
| Consistent and predictable routines, expectations and approaches across all lessons, with all adults | |
| Support to start tasks and structure and organise thoughts, show and tell pupils how to do something and repeat regularly | |
| Short, sharp bursts of work followed by a movement or sensory break | |
| Provide fiddle tools or doodle books | |
| Offer two or three positive choices, such as how or where to complete a task | |
| Use concrete and real examples, where possible | |
| Clear and simple worksheets or present one question at a time and provide a copy of key information | |
| Use their interests to motivate and foster curiosity. Create personal learning pathways | |
| Trial pencil grips, reduce the amount of writing or provide alternative methods of recording, at times | |
| Understand confabulation as filling in gaps or masking a lack of understanding | |
| Provide support and reduce expectations around homework | |
| Support executive function (see pp.14–15 and 22–3) | |
| **Environmental considerations** ||
| Reduce distractions and stimulation | |
| Be aware of environment, reduce sensory overwhelm and provide calm tools | |
| Trial wobble cushion, weighted lap pad, resistance band on chair legs or alternative seating or standing to work | |
| Provide exit strategy and safe, quiet space | |
| **Unstructured times** ||
| Supervision and support at unstructured times | |

| STRATEGY | COMMENTS |
|---|---|
| Predictable routine at break and lunchtimes and access to quiet area and key adult/ buddy system | |
| Support for PE | |
| **Rewards and consequences** | |
| Show consequences visually. They need to be immediate, logical and simple. Provide support rather than sanction | |

# Chapter 9

# Oppositional Defiant Disorder (ODD)

Oppositional Defiant Disorder (ODD) is an ongoing or recurrent pattern of opposition and defiance, usually towards people in authority. It is described as 'a pattern of angry/irritable mood, argumentative/defiant behavior, or vindictiveness lasting at least six months' (DSM-5 of the American Psychiatric Association, 2013). ODD is a behavioural diagnosis (meaning there is no definitive brain scan or blood test). It features in both the ICD 10 (the guide used by the World Health Organization) and the DSM-5 (the guide used by health care professionals in the United States and much of the world).

Each individual's experience will be different, reflecting the uniqueness of each child. For specific information on diagnosis please refer to the DSM-5 of the American Psychiatric Association (2013). 'A closer reading of the full diagnostic criteria suggests that a child who is diagnosed with ODD may be struggling on a number of different fronts, including emotional self-regulation, self-control and interpersonal skills' (Bowler, 2020, p.16).

Pupils with ODD tend to present with the following difficulties:

### 'Difficulty regulating intense emotions' (Bowler, 2020, p.16):

- Seem to lose their temper and become annoyed easily
- May be quick to anger and need support to calm
- May be impulsive and struggle with self-control
- Struggle to express and regulate emotions

DOI: 10.4324/9781003146292-10

**'Difficulty moderating goal-directed behavior'** (Bowler, 2020, p.16):

- May question, argue and struggle to comply with rules and authority
- May struggle to take ownership of mistakes or actions, feel justified in their behaviour and blame others when things go wrong
- May struggle to meet adult expectations (Bowler, 2020, p.20)

**'Difficulty cooperating with others'** (Bowler, 2020, p.16):

- May need support to maintain appropriate friendships, collaborate with and understand the perspective of others
- May interpret social interactions negatively and lack the skills needed to resolve conflicts, tending to solve issues with physical aggression or hostility

ODD often has comorbidities with other conditions, particularly Attention Deficit Hyperactivity Disorder (ADHD) but also anxiety, autism, Sensory Processing Disorder (SPD) and Tourette Syndrome.

## ODD in the classroom

A pupil diagnosed with ODD appears to resist control and challenge authority, with pupils often presenting with increased defiance the more control is imposed. Behaviour may appear as a desire to elicit a reaction or emotional response from the adult and is often described as 'challenging' by school staff. Pupils often lack the motivation to engage in a task, may interrupt and disrupt the learning of others and seem to struggle with impulse control.

The most effective way of supporting a pupil with ODD is to reflect on what the pupil is finding difficult and why. Then consider what support can be offered, what adjustments can be made and what skills can be taught. 'Challenge the behaviour and not the person' (Finnis, 2021).

It is necessary to look beyond the behaviour, connect with the child and build a better understanding of their needs in order to offer support. 'That's the problem that the label causes. The label tells us what adults around your child are feeling. They are feeling opposed, and they are feeling defied' (Bowler, in Reber, 2020). When pupils are presenting with anger and aggression, it is necessary to be curious and to understand why they are behaving in that way. Defiance can often be masking other difficulties such as a lack of skill or understanding, difficulty processing information or needing support to regulate emotions.

# Strategies to support pupils with oppositional defiant behaviour in school

Below is a range of strategies that have been tried and tested and found to support pupils who present with oppositional defiant behaviour within the classroom. There is a checklist at the end of this chapter.

## *A strength-based approach*

- Reframe communication around ODD and focus on each individual's strengths and achievements. 'They won't behave or they need help to behave?' (Finnis, 2021). 'Always build on the positives, give the child praise and positive reinforcement when he shows flexibility or cooperation. Recognize the little victories' (ADDitude Editors, 2020). Pupils diagnosed with ODD are often described as entrepreneurial, creative, determined, resourceful and good at practical, hands-on tasks (Abraham & Studaker-Cordner, undated), as well as focused, 'passionate, independent, brave. The world needs rebels, free-thinkers, warriors and leaders' (Bowler, 2020, p.16).
- Encourage participation in a range of clubs and extra-curricular activities to harness strengths and interests outside of the classroom.
- Low self-confidence can be associated with ODD. Give roles and responsibilities based on the pupil's strengths and interests to increase their sense of self-worth and belonging. Ensure they feel like a valued member of the classroom. Celebrate their achievements and successes at every opportunity. 'Children who have disruptive and challenging behaviour are still whole, complex and full of amazing potential. They have specific needs and struggles, but when those children get the right kind of help, they can start to express their gifts and interests in a much healthier way' (Bowler, 2020, p.19). Boost self-esteem by sending a positive message home each day and encourage caregivers to pass a daily positive message onto school. This can make a massive difference and help avoid or escape from a negative spiral of behaviour.

**Case study:**

Sandy was a pupil in Year 9 with ODD and ADHD. She had been excluded from several schools and just started at a mainstream secondary school after a year in a pupil referral unit. Sandy struggled with the transition and was in and out of lessons. When she was in lessons she was very disruptive, defiant and aggressive. She was at risk of permanent exclusion due to an ever-increasing number of fixed-term exclusions.

*How could school be made a more positive experience for Sandy?*

Staff worked collaboratively with Sandy's caregiver and discovered that, outside of school, Sandy had secured a Saturday job with a local painting and decorating firm. She got up early, worked hard all day and was highly praised by her boss for her effort and high standard of work. Staff in school built on this strength and her timetable was personalised to give her time helping the site manager each week. Sandy helped sweep up, fix things and paint areas of the school. She built up a positive relationship with the site manager and developed a sense of belonging in the school. She took visible pride in showing her key adults and caregiver the areas of the school that she had helped to improve.

Sandy had previously rejected the safe space offered. Staff agreed that, if overwhelmed, she could go outside to a designated safe zone. She was given a broom, litter picker and gloves. When feeling frustrated or overwhelmed, she could go and use these to help her to regulate and the site manager would check in with her, when available. The aggressive incidents decreased and Sandy remained in school to complete her GCSEs and has now started an apprenticeship with her employer.

■ Aim to give ten positive comments for every (perceived) negative during interactions.

## Relationships and communication

■ Adult awareness and understanding of the pupil's difficulties are critical. Build trusting, positive relationships based on the PACE approach (see p.65–6). A small team of key adults to check in with the pupil throughout the day to praise them and be their champion is effective.

■ Form a positive partnership with caregivers and work collaboratively, share strategies and concerns, and listen to them and the pupil about what works well. Actively listen and problem-solve together. Be sure to focus on the pupil's strengths and achievements before discussing any concerns. 'Children with ODD are often judged harshly and badly misunderstood. The same can often be said for parents facing negative judgement from their communities and even from themselves' (Bowler, 2020, p.20).

■ Ensure all staff involved work collaboratively and have clear and consistent expectations, rules and boundaries. All adults must be fair and consistent.

■ Pupils can get into a negative spiral at school. Welcome the pupil into the classroom, engage in positive, meaningful interactions, show an interest in them, and start and end each day positively.

■ Pick your battles and focus on a few targeted behaviours at a time. 'Since the child with ODD has trouble avoiding power struggles, prioritize the things you want [the] child to do' (ADDitude Editors, 2020). 'Choose what you will tactically ignore, what is negotiable, and what needs to be reinforced' (Greene, 2014).

■ Avoid getting drawn into control battles or lengthy negotiations (scripts can be helpful here). Respond calmly and respectfully, using a neutral tone of voice to avoid escalation and inadvertently rewarding negative behaviour with lots of attention.

■ Reframe language to be positive, where possible. For example, instead of 'Stop calling out', say, 'I know you have an amazing answer and I can't wait to hear it once you've put your hand up'. Focusing on solutions and moving the pupil on rather than the problem draws attention to the expected behaviours rather than the negative ones. Use clear, direct and short verbal communications, stating what you want, rather than what you don't want; for example, say 'put your feet on the floor' rather than 'take your feet off the chair', or 'put the ball on the floor' rather than 'don't throw the ball'.

■ Allow processing time. When being met with defiance, be aware that the pupil's default response may be 'no', often driven by fear of failure or the unknown. Avoid persuading or negotiating and allow time for the pupil to process the task or instruction. Modelling and encouragement work better than reprimands.

**Case study:**

Cody was a Year 6 pupil with diagnoses of ADHD and ODD. He struggled with transitions and his first few weeks in Year 6 were proving very difficult. From being very settled at the end of the previous year, Cody was at risk of permanent exclusion and was in a negative spiral.

Cody was struggling to engage in his learning and started sabotaging success on his reward chart as soon as he made a mistake. He threw pens and pencils at the teacher and was rude to staff. He was described as needing constant attention. Every day, he was spoken to by a member of the leadership team because of disruptive and challenging behaviour and spent time sitting on his own, outside the principal's office. His mother described him as depressed.

*How could school be made a more positive experience for Cody?*

Staff worked hard to reframe language and communication around Cody, to focus on the positives rather than his increasing negative behaviours. Lower level behaviours were tactically ignored. Staff started to 'catch him being good' and comment on his successes, ensuring he got lots of attention when he was making the right choices. They also reframed conversation with his mother, reporting positives home rather than the negatives.

Work was broken down into smaller, achievable chunks and presented in a checklist. Mini breaks were planned for him after about ten minutes of work, and movement breaks were implemented before he was expected to sit and listen for a period of time. He was also given a wobble cushion and a doodle pad to support when he needed to sit and listen.

Cody was given a quiet area, just outside of the classroom, with some sensory, calming tools, which he had chosen from a selection. He was able to use this when he was feeling overwhelmed or distracted in the classroom.

He was given positive choices around where to work and choice of equipment, increasing his sense of control. His reward chart was changed to an accumulative reward, rather than one where he had to get a certain number of tokens in one session.

■ Catch the pupil making the right choices and praise small steps towards success. Use specific, direct and sincere praise. However, a pupil with oppositional defiant behaviour may sabotage success by destroying work or hitting out after public praise. If this is the case, try indirect praise such as a sticky note on the desk, giving a token reward or state what you are pleased with and then walk away.

- Remove the audience and discuss an incident in private, once both parties are calm. Use restorative conversations and support the pupil to give their own perspective and then to begin to understand the perspective of others (see p.11–12).
- Learn to spot (and help the pupil spot) their triggers and behaviour patterns and plan to avoid or provide increased support to help the pupil to cope at these times. By lowering anxiety levels, the behaviour improves, as the part of the brain responsible for logical thought and reasoning comes back online (see the 'Anxiety' chapter).
- Teach social skills. 'Help for behavioural problems can involve supporting the young person to increase their positive social behaviours, and controlling their antisocial destructive behaviours' (Royal College of Psychiatrists, 2020).
- Avoid asking 'why?' This can sound accusatory and the pupil usually can't articulate why they have behaved in a certain way. 'Changing "why" to "what" will always help' (Finnis, 2021). Rather than asking 'why did you do that?' ask 'what happened?' or 'what was the impact on yourself and others?' 'What' questions will help you gain greater understanding of the incident and the pupils will be more willing to engage as they sound non-judgemental.

## *Teaching and learning*

- Ensure clear and specific rules and behaviour expectations are displayed, referred to and reviewed regularly. Use non-verbal techniques such as gestures and behaviour visuals to remind pupils of expectations.
- Observe the pupil to gain an understanding of the communicative function behind their behaviour. Be curious and explore what the behaviour is achieving and communicating, for example, control, anxiety, task avoidance, attention or masking the lack of skill, ability or understanding. Then teach the necessary skills, put in support or make necessary adjustments, such as scaffolding the task, offering positive choices, giving positive attention, teaching social skills or changing the environment.
- Support pupils to manage change and transitions (see p.15) and give plenty of notice of upcoming changes using countdowns or timers. Give a sense of empowerment at transition times by giving them a job of tidying up certain equipment or ringing the bell or letting the teacher know when the two-minute timer has finished (watching a sand timer can be calming and regulating for a pupil). Where possible, concede control to an object such as the

timer or bell; for example, 'be ready to line up by the time the
timer runs out'.
■ Many pupils are unable to keep still and listen simultaneously,
and if asked to remain still, this may take all of their energy or
attention. Allow fiddling or doodling, or provide a copy of the notes
to highlight whilst listening.
■ Teach emotions and model regulation strategies (see the
'Self-regulation' chapter).

## Environmental considerations

■ Pupils diagnosed with ODD may have sensory sensitivities (see
the 'Sensory Processing Disorder (SPD) chapter). Reflect on
environmental triggers such as noise, flickering lights, smells
and distractions. Remove or reduce environmental distractions
(for example, close the blinds, turn off flickering lights, turn off
electrical equipment if not in use to reduce buzzing, simplify displays), where possible, or offer sensory supports to help the pupil
feel more comfortable.
■ Offer the choice to use a separate work station, to support concentration, as and when the pupil feels this is necessary.
■ Offer an exit strategy and access to a key adult and safe space
where the pupil can go when feeling overwhelmed. Rehearse the
use of this whilst the pupil is calm. Provide calm tools such as a
stress toy, therapeutic putty, old magazines to tear up, a cushion
to squeeze, colouring, building and a favourite book to read (see
the 'Self-regulation' chapter).
■ Build regular, legitimate movement and learning breaks into each
lesson. Give the pupil heavy work jobs or errands to run out of the
classroom, rather than demanding the pupil leaves the class (see
the 'Sensory Processing Disorder (SPD)' chapter).

## Unstructured times

■ At unstructured times, pupils may need additional adult support
to engage and manage these successfully, such as being taught
specific social skills as well as access to more structured zoned
areas or activities, clubs, safe spaces and key adults.

## Rewards and consequences

■ Rewards are usually more effective than sanctions for pupils with
oppositional defiant behaviour. Try accumulative rewards, where

pupils earn tokens over a period of time and trade them in for a selection of pre-determined rewards. This is often more success-ful than systems where pupils lose their reward if they haven't achieved their work in a certain amount of time, where they can lose interest once they have made a mistake.

■ Consequences should be pre-determined, logical, practical, clear and fair, and they should be set when pupils are calm, before problems occur. Involving pupils in determining appropriate con-sequences can be effective, giving them a sense of ownership and control. Pupils need clear boundaries, within the context of a nur-turing, trusting relationship.

■ 'Are our conversations and dialogues about fear and fault or opportunities, strengths and solutions?' (Finnis, 2021). The focus needs to be on repairing and restoring relationships, teaching appropriate skills and making necessary environmental adjust-ments to help pupils succeed. A pupil who is communicating dis-tress and dysregulation through their behaviour needs support to solve the problem.

■ The focus needs to be on relational approaches and teaching and modelling regulation strategies. 'If your child is over-reacting to stress, and has difficulty controlling his or her emotions, then a warm, attachment-based approach will be more effective in teaching those missing emotional self-regulation skills' (Bowler, 2020, p.25).

■ Support with understanding cause and effect (see p.23).

## Resources, further information and 'tool kits'

### Books

*The Explosive Child* by Ross W. Greene – useful collaborative problem-solving approaches for home and school

*The Parent's Guide to Oppositional Defiant Disorder: Your Questions Answered* by Amelia Bowler – fabulous book for parents, but also for school staff, in understanding children with ODD

*Understanding Conduct Disorder and Oppositional-Defiant Disorder: A Guide to Symptoms, Management and Treatment – Understanding Atypical Development* by Laura Vanzin and Valentina Mauri

### Websites

https://www.additudemag.com/?s=ODD Information, advice, articles and more https://www.weareteachers.com/students-with-odd/ Information and practical advice

## Podcasts

https://www.additudemag.com/podcast-adhd-odd-connection-anderson/
https://tiltparenting.com/2020/09/22/episode-227-amelia-bowler-talks-about-her-new-book-the-parents-guide-to-oppositional-defiant-disorder/

# References

Abraham, K. & Studaker-Cordner, M. (undated) *The Strengths of the Oppositional Defiant Child* [online] Empowering Parents. Available at: https://www.empoweringparents.com/article/strengths-oppositional-defiant-child/ [Accessed 3 February 2021]

ADDitude Editors (2020) *ODD vs. ADHD: The Facts About Oppositional Defiant Disorder and Attention Deficit* [online] ADDitude Magazine. Available at: https://www.additudemag.com/oppositional-defiant-disorder-odd-and-adhd/ [Accessed 3 February 2021]

Bowler, A. (2020) *The Parent's Guide to Oppositional Defiant Disorder: Your Questions Answered* Jessica Kingsley Publishers, London

DSM-5 of the American Psychiatric Association (2013) *Diagnostic and Statistical Manual of Mental Disorders* Fifth Edition. Arlington

Finnis, M. (2021) *Independent Thinking on Restorative Practice: Building Relationships, Improving Behaviour and Creating Stronger Communities* Independent Thinking Press, Carmarthen

Greene, R. (2014) *The Explosive Child: A New Approach for Understanding and Parenting Easily Frustrated Chronically Inflexible Children* Harper Collins, London

Reber, D. (2020) [podcast] Available at: https://tiltparenting.com/2020/09/22/episode-227-amelia-bowler-talks-about-her-new-book-the-parents-guide-to-oppositional-defiant-disorder/ [Accessed 4 February 2021]

Royal College of Psychiatrists (2020) *Behavioural Problems and Conduct Disorder: For Parents, Carers and Anyone Working with Young People* [online] Available at: https://www.rcpsych.ac.uk/mental-health/parents-and-young-people/information-for-parents-and-carers/behavioural-problems-and-conduct-disorder-for-parents-carers-and-anyone-who-works-with-young-people [Accessed 3 February 2021]

## Checklist to support pupils with ODD

| STRATEGY | COMMENTS |
|---|---|
| **Please also refer to the 'Behaviour is communication' and 'Self-regulation' chapters** | |
| **A strength-based approach** | |
| Reframe communication to focus on strengths and successes | |
| Encourage participation in a range of clubs and extra-curricular activities | |
| Boost self-esteem – roles/responsibilities, daily positive messages home | |
| Aim to give ten positive comments for every negative | |
| **Relationships and communication** | |
| Ensure adult awareness of symptoms and understanding of difficulties, build positive relationships | |
| Work collaboratively with caregivers, pupil and other staff | |
| Start and end each day positively | |
| Pick your battles and focus on two or three targeted behaviours | |
| Avoid control battles and lengthy negotiations | |
| Reframe language to be positive and focus on moving the pupil on, stating the behaviour that you would like to see | |
| Allow processing time when met with defiance | |
| Catch them being good and give praise for small steps to success. Be wary of lavish praise; it may need to be indirect | |
| Offer positive choices | |
| Remove audience and discuss incidents in private | |
| Spot triggers and alleviate anxieties around transitions, unstructured times and work tasks | |
| Teach social skills | |
| Ask 'what?' rather than 'why?' | |

*(Continued)*

## Continued

| STRATEGY | COMMENTS |
|---|---|
| **Teaching and learning** | |
| Clear, specific rules and behaviour expectations, presented visually | |
| Observe pupil to understand the communicative function of the behaviour and then teach skills or make adjustments | |
| Provide support around transition and change | |
| Allow fiddling or doodling whilst listening | |
| Teach and model regulation strategies | |
| **Environmental** | |
| Be aware of sensory sensitivities, distractions and environmental triggers | |
| Choice to use a separate work station | |
| Offer an exit strategy, key adult, safe space and calming strategies | |
| Regular movement and learning breaks | |
| **Unstructured times** | |
| Support for unstructured times – teach social skills, offer smaller zones/quiet areas/ clubs and access to key adult and safe space | |
| **Rewards and consequences** | |
| Immediate, accumulative reward system | |
| Pre-determined, logical, clear and fair consequences | |
| Restorative conversations to repair and restore relationships and the teaching of skills and regulation strategies | |
| Cause and effect games | |

# Chapter 10

# Pathological Demand Avoidance (PDA)

Pathological Demand Avoidance (PDA) is increasingly being recognised as part of the autism spectrum. Understanding of PDA, however, continues to evolve. It is still not widely diagnosed definitively and is often dependent on country, county or local authority of residence, and professional understanding and knowledge. It may more commonly be referred to as autism with a 'demand avoidant profile', although it is probably better understood as 'demand anxiety' rather than 'demand avoidance'.

PDA is characterised as an extreme anxiety-driven need to be in control and avoid everyday (perceived or actual) expectations and demands. Anxiety may be displayed by hypervigilance, with the pupil feeling threatened and unsafe and on high alert for expectations and demands.

All individuals are unique and each individual will present differently. However, a pupil with a demand-avoidant profile may:

- Display extreme resistance and avoidance of everyday demands or expectations (including direct, indirect, perceived, implied or even internal demands)
- Have high levels of anxiety
- Be sociable and tend to have good conversational and verbal skills
- Maintain appropriate eye contact

DOI: 10.4324/9781003146292-11

- Use some masking or social mimicry when communicating
- Show empathy, which can seem on a more logical than emotional level
- Need support to make and maintain relationships
- Struggle to interpret unwritten social cues
- Experience intense emotions which are difficult to regulate
- Be impulsive
- Have little recognition of hierarchy or their place within this
- Engage fully in role playing and fantasy
- Have possible early language delay (often caught up very quickly as they get older)
- Display obsessive behaviours which often centre around people rather than objects
- Have low self-esteem
- Lack confidence to engage in activities or try new things
- Have very high expectations of themselves
- Fear failure or making mistakes
- Enjoy spontaneity and the novel
- Be very creative and imaginative
- Show high levels of intelligence
- Have a great sense of humour
- Have sensory sensitivities (see the 'Sensory Processing Disorder (SPD)' chapter)

## Understanding pupils with PDA

School, generally, is particularly demand-heavy and for pupils with PDA it is mostly a distressing, frightening experience. The condition often becomes apparent when children start school as specific expectations tend to increase. The transition from primary to secondary school can also be a trigger point. The child will become more anxious and, therefore, seem more resistant or avoidant. The more demands or expectations, the greater the anxiety. Pupils may be highly creative in their use of strategies to resist demands and avoidance may include ignoring, distracting, excuses, delaying tactics, negotiating, humour, making noises, refusing, withdrawing into fantasy, aggression, violence and obscene language. If demands continue to be placed on the child when they are distressed, they may reach a crisis point or meltdown, whereby they lose control and can no longer cope. This is best described as a panic attack caused by extreme anxiety, overload and feelings of overwhelm.

Pupils with PDA struggle with emotional regulation and behaviour tends to be unpredictable and explosive or implosive. It may present as aggression, violence, throwing items and breaking equipment, or be a more internal presentation of withdrawal, shutdown or self-harm. At this point, logical thought, for the pupil, has vanished and the priority must therefore be on keeping them and others safe. The pupil needs to be supported to reduce these and avoid them wherever possible.

To effectively support a pupil with PDA, it is essential to see beyond behaviour and understand it as a presentation of anxiety or distress. Thompson (2020b) states 'there's no such thing as an overreaction' as it is the body's involuntary reaction to perceived danger; anxiety has triggered the body's threat response and it reacts as if the individual is in danger of their life.

Children with a PDA profile often fail to reach their full potential in school, commonly being out of class and experiencing multiple exclusions. The PDA Society states that 70 per cent of children with a PDA profile of autism regularly struggle to attend school. School avoidance is common and many parents of pupils with PDA end up home-schooling or using unschooling methods. Without understanding and support, this figure will not change. Pupils with PDA need an alternative approach. Traditional teaching methods fail to work and often increase anxiety, thus exacerbating the negative behaviours.

Behaviours are driven by an extreme level of overwhelm and anxiety. What the pupil is experiencing is 'I *can't* do this right now' rather than 'I *won't* do this right now' (even if they could do it yesterday and may be able to do it again tomorrow, at that particular moment in time, they can't).

## Supporting pupils to cope and thrive in school

The word 'strategies' has intentionally been avoided in relation to supporting pupils with PDA, since listening to a podcast with Harry Thomson (2020a), who states that understanding, trusting and positive relationships are far more important. Once staff understand the individual, then the 'strategies' can naturally develop. Pupils may oppose a strategy being imposed on them, and, as with all children, relationship and understanding is the key. Supporting pupils with PDA is much more about an 'approach' or a 'style' of working, based on 'personalisation' and 'flexibility' (Fidler & Christie, 2019, p.31).

Pupils with PDA need particular support, which goes against most natural and instinctive teaching methods. It also differs significantly from those which are generally used to support autistic pupils. A whole school awareness is essential (including office staff, site managers, mid-day supervisors and senior management, as well as teaching and support staff). The PDA Society introduced the concept of the giant panda to help raise awareness and increase acceptance and understanding of people with PDA: 'We chose the panda to be our ambassador because, just like giant pandas, individuals with a PDA profile of autism need very specific support to thrive'.

Below is a range of suggestions that have been tried and tested and found to support pupils with PDA in school. There is a checklist at the end of this chapter.

## A strength-based approach

It is essential to understand the pupil beyond their behaviours and get to know them as a person – their personality, strengths, likes and dreams. 'Whatever the difficulties, this is probably the most interesting and potentially rewarding child you will ever meet, who will challenge your ingenuity and flexibility every working day. This can be a growth experience for you and for your professional skills' (Newson, 2016, p.7).

- Reframe language to use a strength-based approach. Focus on what the pupil is good at and what they can do in the moment. Individuals with PDA are often very creative and imaginative, can think outside the box and be extremely original. Pupils are often highly intelligent and charismatic, with very good expressive verbal skills. They may have a strong memory and a great sense of humour. Andrews (2017) suggests that people in the workplace with PDA have strong team-leading abilities, describing 'a natural confidence and reliability when seeing projects through to completion while identifying and neutralising all possible risks – are guaranteed to bring great success'.
- Parents on the PDA society website have described their children with PDA as:

    - Charming
    - Determined
    - Inquisitive
    - Creative
    - Imaginative
    - Brave
    - Funny

- Unique
- Talented
- Compassionate
- Independent
- Passionate
- Smart
- Loving
- Witty

(www.PDAsociety.org.uk)

## *Relationships*

'Relationship is what makes and facilitates the most change' (Wood, 2020) and the power of a quality, understanding, trusting relationship cannot be emphasised enough.

- Establish positive relationships with the pupil and their caregivers, built on understanding and trust. 'The core principle is about collaboration: working with the child, finding a way to negotiate solutions, adjusting expectations, compromising on outcomes and collaborating closely with parents and others' (Fidler & Christie, 2019, p.31). Empathy is essential yet impossible without genuine understanding, so collaboration is key. Caregivers can provide insight into the pupil's needs, strengths and triggers. Include the pupil's (and caregiver's) strengths and successes in these meetings and encourage them to express what works well for them. Many families have had negative experiences with the school system and may have previously felt blamed or criticised. It is crucial to escape any negative spiral that may have arisen.
- Listen to parental concerns as well as to the pupil. Young people may mask (see p.121–3) and behaviour seen in school is often very different from the presentation at home. Reports of outbursts and meltdowns at home are often a response to stress at school; anything done to lessen anxieties throughout the school day will help. 'Just because a child isn't exploding at school doesn't mean that school isn't contributing to explosions that occur elsewhere. Lots of things can happen at school to fuel explosions outside of school: being teased by others, feeling socially isolated or rejected, feeling frustrated and embarrassed over struggles on certain academic tasks, being misunderstood by the teacher' (Greene, 2014).

■ Adults need to be very aware of their own emotional levels and remain consistent and calm when working with a pupil with PDA. Avoid confrontations wherever possible. 'If the adult isn't part of the solution, they will become part of the problem!' (Fidler & Christie, 2019). After an incident, adults need to self-reflect and consider how their actions may have contributed, not with a sense of blame or self-deprecation, but with a view of possibly doing and saying things differently to improve things in the future.

■ After an incident, relationship restoration and repair need to be a priority (see p.11–12). 'Be willing to apologise even when it isn't your fault. If a student is upset with me, they are unlikely to work for me. Fixing that relationship is important. I usually start our conversation with, "I'm sorry I upset you, that wasn't my intention." It's a great start to putting things right and makes students much more receptive to continuing the conversation' (Hatton, 2017). Start each lesson with a clean slate and avoid revisiting previous challenges; let it go and move on. Apologise if something said or done appeared to make the situation worse. Have a conversation after an incident (when both parties are calm) and ask what worked well and what the pupil thinks might work better next time.

## Reduce anxieties

Escalating behaviour for a pupil with PDA is likely to be communicating increased stress and a need for a sense of control and safety. 'In order to successfully eliminate, or at least reduce outbursts or meltdowns one must make sufficient efforts to minimise anxiety levels before anything else. When anxiety is heightened then the likelihood of being triggered, and potentially having a meltdown, is increased' (Thompson, 2019, p.81). The simplest way to decrease anxiety is by reducing demands and increasing their sense of control.

■ Identify potential triggers and plan to put strategies in place to pre-empt difficulties and avoid or support pupils around these. Through effective relationships, adults will be in a better position to support the de-escalation process. Use empathy and understanding whilst employing various diversion techniques such as appropriate humour, distraction, breaks, changes of scene or activity and reduce expectations related to the pupil's tolerance levels in the moment.

■ Lower anxieties and be aware of the pupil's stress bucket (see p.88). 'PDA isn't solely about demand avoidance, as it really depends on the PDAer's anxiety levels at any given moment' (Thompson, 2019, p.80). Each (real or perceived) demand or expectation fills the bucket: reduce demands to reduce anxiety. Demands and sensory issues may start filling the stress bucket first thing in the morning (demands of getting out of bed, getting dressed, eating breakfast, leaving the house and the sensory difficulties with school uniform, transport – the seat, the smell, the seatbelt, the radio) all mean heightened anxiety and sensory overload for a pupil before even arriving at school. At crisis points, adults need to think 'how can I reduce this child's distress and increase their sense of safety?' rather than 'how can I change this behaviour?' Remove anything that may be causing sensory overwhelm (such as light and noise) or that could cause harm, and focus on safety and recovery.

- Have a trusted adult 'meet and greet' the pupil in the mornings, check in with them and settle them, ready for learning. They may need a calm, quiet time to reset before entering the classroom (or even the school – a walk around the grounds with a key adult is often helpful to de-stress, decompress and reset before entering the building). Similar support at the end of the day (and at key trigger points) can help build relationships and ease anxiety.
- Pupils need to feel safe and comfortable from when they first enter the school environment. Ensure the office and site staff and everyone on the gate know how to communicate successfully with the pupil.
- Work together to trial and create a bank of calming strategies which work for the pupil, and take photographs to create calm cards, which can be used when anxiety is heightening. Practise the skills when they are calm, before they need to use them (see the 'Self-regulation' chapter). Pupils will need co-regulation, with the adult modelling and supporting through the process, to help them to understand themselves and their emotions.
- Pupils will need access to their own safe space and calm tools (see p.42). Again, rehearse the use of this when the pupil is calm and take a photograph as a visual reminder.

## *Communication*

Communication with a pupil with PDA is paramount to success and differs from how a teacher may usually communicate with a pupil. Duncan (in Christie et al., 2012, p.130) explains, 'If someone asks me to do something I'm likely to say no ... that's me all over isn't it?! But I'm also like a cat. It all depends on how you ask me. If you ask me in the right way, it's like stroking a cat's fur the way it grows. I may even purr! But if you ask me in the wrong way, it's like stroking a cat's fur backwards. I'm likely to hiss!'

- Use non-threatening and positive language, reducing demands and avoiding confrontation. Changing the interactions with pupils with a demand avoidant profile makes a huge difference and reduces anxiety levels (reducing negative or challenging behaviour).
- Be aware of 'hierarchy blindness'; pupils with PDA may not recognise social hierarchy or authority. A child with PDA often gets on better with those older or younger than themselves or may talk and act like the teacher, not regarding themselves as a child within the classroom. Treating them like an equal or a colleague or asking them to teach another pupil, a puppet or an adult can work well. Collaborating with them and learning together or negotiating to solve challenges is often effective. Giving a selection of tasks for the pupil to 'feed back' on makes the child feel equal, allowing them to choose and try activities out, rather than the learning being forced upon them.

---

**Case example:**

Kandi was a Year 5 pupil. During a Science week, she was given the teacher's planning and some sticky notes and highlighters. She was asked to let the teacher know which tasks would work well and if any could be improved. She was then able to engage in some of these tasks as she felt included in the process.

---

- Praise can be perceived as a demand or a way of imposing control. A pupil may destroy work if it is commented on or praised as this implies compliance with the given expectation. It is often necessary to think of alternative means by which to offer praise. The most effective ways are usually immediate, small and indirect, such as through a puppet or a message hidden in a book or pencil case, or talking to another adult, in earshot of the pupil; for example, 'Ella did really well today, she worked out those Maths answers way before I did'.
- Teach pupils how to ask for help; for example, a help card or a coloured cube on the table causes less anxiety than putting a

hand up. Additionally, an 'I need to be left alone right now' card can also be supportive and avoid the fear of social overload.

■ Complex language and appropriate humour can help pupils with PDA as they can provoke intrigue and interest or be a means of negotiation and distraction. Fidler and Christie (2019, p.51) give the example: 'I can see the others are starting to clear up. It must be nearly time for assembly. I can help you tidy if you like. Do you want to put your drawing pencils away in your tray or are you going to leave them on your desk? ... By the way did you notice that bird's nest that Miss found? It's on the table outside the hall. We can look at it on the way to assembly. I was thinking of putting a chocolate egg in it to give her a surprise! What do you reckon?'

■ Be proactive and pre-plan some responses to a pupil's avoidance approaches, using humour, where appropriate. For example, if a pupil says, 'I can't write, my arms don't work', the adult could respond with 'ah, OK, I wonder how much of this we can write with our feet or type with our nose then', or if they say, 'I can't write, I'm a cat', a response could be 'Ooh, I wonder if there are any cats who can write or if you will be the first. I am going to Google "writing cats" later and see what I find out. I wonder if they would use their mouth, paw or tail?'

■ Teach positive self-talk and help pupils (and adults) remember that 'I can't' (or 'I won't') means 'I can't right now, but I may be able to later or tomorrow'.

■ De-personalise requests and use non-verbal or visual ways to give instructions such as messages, emails, notes, letters, time-tables, timers, posters, role play, or puppets.

■ Reframing the language used is probably the most effective approach for pupils with a demand-avoidant profile. Renaming tasks and activities can help (use 'invitations', 'challenges' or 'missions' rather than 'learning' or 'work'). Avoid direct com-mands and reduce and modify demands – think compromise, conversation and curiosity over confrontation. Use language that sounds like an invitation, suggestion or shared challenge. Act bewildered, treat the pupil as an equal and wonder aloud. Some useful phrases are:

  ■ *I wonder what the best way to do this is?*
  ■ *Do you think ...?*
  ■ *I think I need the help of an expert for this*
  ■ *I'm really good at this; no one can ever beat me*
  ■ *I don't even know where to start*
  ■ *How do you feel about ...?*

- *If you have the time, would you …?*
- *If you're happy to …*
- *What shall we do first?*
- *What would you do if you were me?*
- *What would work for you?*
- *I wonder if there is a different way of approaching this?*
- *I noticed that …*
- *I wish I knew how to …*
- *How on earth are we going to do that?*
- *I have three different answers to this question; I wonder which one is right?*
- *I wonder how Buzz Lightyear would go about this?*

- Allow processing time before expecting a response.

## *Teaching and learning*

Teaching and learning need to be personalised and led by the pupil's interests. 'It's never a direct route from A to B, so be prepared with strategies and resources to gently lead the child to where you want them' (Syson & Gore Langton, undated). It requires a creative, flexible and self-reflective approach. Staff need to maximise learning opportunities and cooperation through curiosity, negotiation, collaboration and compromise, with positive communication and relationship at the heart. 'The whole emphasis needs to be on doing things with the child rather than to them' (Fidler & Christie, 2019).

- Extend the pupil's window of tolerance by teaching them the skills needed for difficult situations. Relationship, empathy and understanding are essential so that staff can adjust their expectations and demands based on the pupil's capacity to cope in that moment. Adults need to understand that it is not that they are deliberately refusing to engage; it is that in that moment they don't have the capacity to cope; they 'can't' as opposed to they 'won't'.
- It is necessary to foster a love of learning and spark interest within the pupil. Begin with an engaging starter activity to 'hook' their interest, and then leave some information, books, worksheets, websites, pictures or artefacts just 'randomly' lying around for pupils to research and explore further.
- Allowing a degree of autonomy over the curriculum can be effective. Encourage the pupil to suggest activities (or give a limited list of options to avoid feeling overwhelmed); for example, if the

objective is to count to 20, the pupil may go outside and count the leaves, complete an exercise in a workbook, count the dinosaur figures, count how many jumps they can do before the timer reaches 20 or count how far they can get in 20 steps. 'I usually like to give two options, when it comes to tasks and to make those options open to the whole class. I'll then negotiate further with individuals if needed. The key is to keep in mind your objective rather than your lesson. If your aim is to improve writing, and your student is happy to write, does it really matter what they write about?' (Hatton, 2017).

■ Offer suggestions that can be adapted to follow the pupil's interests. 'I feel I can confidently say that a trademark of all PDAers is that, in order to learn, it is paramount that our freedom is not trampled on. At school this happens an awful lot, where teachers are constantly trying to make us learn things, not because we ask for it, but because they say so. It's not that we aren't academically inclined, it's that we are only inclined to learn something when we feel the time is right' (Thompson, 2019, p.48). The learning objective is more important than the planned activity. If the pupil completes the expected learning objective (even if it is outside through their own choice of activity, they have still met the objective), this is a win. The task is secondary; it is the learning that counts. Offer an element of control and choice allowing the pupil to suggest an alternative activity.

■ Using folders with different learning choices so pupils can choose from a range of activities increases feelings of control and can give pupils calming time participating in activities they enjoy. Multiple-choice questions, quizzes, true and false activities, games or puzzles, research projects and non-fiction writing have been observed to work well.

■ It is essential that the pupil feels an element of control to feel safe, lessen anxiety and therefore to learn. Offer positive choices (from a limited selection) such as the choice of two tasks with the same objective (one should be easier than the other), choices of equipment to use, adult to work with or where to sit to increase feelings of control.

■ Allow opportunities to return to tasks later.

■ Create a sense of mystery, excitement and suspense by using 'discovery boxes' or envelopes – put an activity in a box or envelope for the pupil to open and 'discover' for themselves, or hide clues or facts around for them to find, like a treasure hunt.

■ Offer alternative means of recording and give options; for example, draw up lists together, scribe at times, use the laptop, use sticky notes, record on a poster, write captions or video verbal responses to lower anxieties around tasks and prevent confrontations.

■ Correcting the teacher's mistakes is often easier than receiving feedback (criticism) around their own work.

■ Novelty and change can be effective, with staff reporting that a strategy may work one day and not the next. It is necessary to have a bank of strategies to return to time and again.

■ Be proactive in avoiding triggers and provide opportunities for demand-avoidant pupils to feel in control. For example, when planning a sports day, allow the pupil to research key information about the sports, use a map to plan the activities, design the posters or programmes, carry a clipboard with a checklist or map of activities or give the pupil the job of putting out all the blue cones.

■ Use drama, role play and fantasy based on individual interests; for example, be Cleopatra, a pilot or an astronaut to make the learning fun, enjoyable and memorable. If they complete their writing about Ancient Rome from the perspective of Dr Who, so be it (at least they are writing).

## Agree on priorities

■ In teaching a pupil with a demand-avoidant profile, it is essential to pick your battles and avoid confrontation. Fidler & Christie (2019, pp.40–45) have developed a **Priority Rating Scale** (see example on p.247) and it is highly recommended that school staff use one of these to unpick behaviours as a team. They enable all key adults (including caregivers) to work in collaboration to focus on what is currently achievable for the pupil, those behaviours which are preferable but flexible and those that are not priorities as yet. Adjust expectations around medium- and low-priority behaviours, until they become a priority or a pupil has the capacity to cope with them and deal with them in an alternative way, such as by diverting or distracting, tactically ignoring, negotiating, offering alternatives or addressing in a more playful manner. It is important to reflect and review these regularly.

---

**Case study:**

Angus was a Year 3 pupil with a diagnosis of ASD with a demand-avoidant profile. He had recently been given 2:1 support in school due to his behaviour. He was put on a part-time timetable. He needed to be in constant control of the adults, escalating to aggression and violence if they talked to other people or gave him instructions.

School tried making his learning tasks very accessible and achievable but he continued to display high levels of anxiety. He spent a considerable time out of the classroom. Angus had access to a safe space, which he refused to use when asked. Angus was at high risk of permanent exclusion and adults were increasingly wary of working with him.

*How could adults support Angus to feel safer in school?*

The school staff met with parents and outside agencies and were given training on PDA approaches. In collaboration with the parents, priorities were drawn up. Staff were supported to help Angus to reduce his stress levels and reduce and reframe demands that were placed upon him.

Staff changed their approach and started collaborating with Angus in his learning. He was the designated class expert for their 'Living Things' topic, based on his love of amphibians. He engaged in research, found useful websites and books in the library for other pupils to use. The teacher gave him the planning and he highlighted the parts that he felt he could help with. Angus was also given a 'My Time' folder, with activities that he and his adult had chosen together, so he had access to activities when he couldn't engage with the class learning. His self-esteem and confidence developed and his aggressive incidents, although still there, reduced.

Angus built up trust with his adults, and they moved up to Year 4 with him to consolidate the new approach and maintain the relationships. He is beginning to accept some support using calming strategies. Concerns remain about transition to Year 5, yet in collaboration the systems and structures which work well will be shared and replicated. School will continue to work in partnership with Angus and his parents to reduce expectations, as needed.

## Environmental considerations

- Be aware of sensory sensitivities and the effect that these have on anxiety levels. Plan regular sensory breaks throughout the day. Reduce or eliminate environmental distractions such as noises, flickering lights or smells (See the 'Self-regulation' and 'Sensory Processing Disorder (SPD)' chapters).

■ If there is a change in behaviour, it is useful to reflect on any changes in the environment. 'Autistic people can be like walking barometers, in that when we are upset, people assume there is something wrong with us when in reality something is wrong around us' (Thompson, 2019, p.171). Pupils tend to absorb the tensions of other people, so will quickly pick up if those around them are becoming dysregulated.

■ Offer choices in terms of seating, with an option of a quiet area or workspace, standing to work or sitting on a beanbag or lying on the floor using a clipboard.

## Unstructured times

■ Plan for and support during unstructured times and provide access to a safe, quiet place if the pupil is beginning to feel overwhelmed. Anxiety and confusion often increase in the playground and dining hall.

## Rewards and consequences

Standard behaviour systems tend to be ineffective and even detrimental for a pupil with PDA. They increase stress levels as they can feel unpredictable, unfair and out of their control. Pupils are expected to behave in a certain way, following a chain of demands, with sanctions when they don't (or can't).

■ Rewards can convey implicit expectations and increase stress. A trigger is often other children receiving a reward when they have not. Many observed pupils with a PDA profile are highly intelligent and love learning (on their terms and within their interests) and intrinsic motivation is often reward enough. Pupils with a PDA profile will usually need a separate, individualised reward system which is within their own control. Unexpected rewards can sometimes be effective as pupils don't have to contend with a fear of failure. Accumulative point systems can give pupils an element of control, particularly if they offer a flexible way of earning and 'spending' these. Hatton (2017) suggests implementing 'a token board system where students get their reward after completing so many good lessons. This way nothing is lost if things go wrong as tokens which have been earned can be carried over to the next week.'

■ Sanctions are usually ineffective and should be avoided. They punish a child for behaviours they have no control over since, at that moment in time, the pupil is in a state of 'can't' not 'won't'. Rather than help improve behaviour, they can intensify anxiety and the sense of losing control. It is more effective to teach the pupils the skills needed to avoid escalations and reflect on, manage and restore situations, once they are calm. 'In place of firm boundaries and the use of rewards, consequences and praise, individuals with a PDA profile respond better to an approach based on trust, negotiation, collaboration, flexibility and careful use of language' (PDA Society, 2020).

# Resources, further information and 'tool kits'

## Books

*Can I Tell You about PDA* by Phil Christie and Ruth Fidler – fabulous quick insight into PDA for adults and children

*Collaborative Approaches to Learning for Pupils with PDA: Strategies for Education Professionals* by Ruth Fidler and Phil Christie – a must-read for teachers of pupils with a demand-avoidant profile

*The Explosive Child* by Ross W. Greene – collaborative problem-solving approaches for home and school

*Life on an Alien Planet: Pathological Demand Avoidance: A PDA Boy and His Journey through the Education System* by Katie Stott – insight into the struggles which a child with PDA may have in the school system

*Pathological Demand Avoidance Syndrome: My Daughter Is Not Naughty* by Jane Sherwin – insight into a family's experience with PDA

*Understanding Pathological Demand Avoidance Syndrome in Children* by Phil Christie, Margaret Duncan, Ruth Fidler and Zara Healy – expert support, guidance and information

*The PDA Paradox* by Harry Thompson – entertaining and insightful look into the world of PDA

*PDA by PDAers: From Anxiety to Avoidance and Masking to Meltdowns* by Sally Cat – a range of insights and experiences of PDA

*Underdogs*, *Underdogs Tooth and Nail* and *Underdogs: Acceleration* by Chris Bonnello – fiction with neurodiverse protagonists for older children

## Websites

https://www.autismwestmidlands.org.uk/wp-content/uploads/2017/11/PDA-1.pdf Useful behaviour strategies for PDA

https://www.harryjackthompson.com/about Fabulous insights from Harry Thompson with links to his other work https://www.pdasociety.org.uk/ Invaluable information, advice and resources

https://lizonions.files.wordpress.com/2019/09/180515_edaq-en.pdf EDAQ questionnaire

https://limpsfieldgrange.co.uk/wp-content/uploads/2016/01/PDA-booklet.pdf Useful booklet on PDA

http://pdaresource.com/ Advice and support for teachers, caregivers and professionals

https://www.stephstwogirls.co.uk/2017/11/pathological-demand-avoidance.html A wealth of experience, resources, links and advice

## Podcasts

https://www.pdasociety.org.uk/resources/podcasts/ Links to useful PDA podcasts

**YouTube videos or TED Talks** with successful, positive role models such as Sally Cat, Mollie Sherwin and Harry Thompson for an insight into all things PDA (check the content is appropriate if considering watching with pupils).

# References

Andrews, J. (2017) *Autism and PDA: What Can People Bring to the Workplace?* [online] Available at: https://myplusstudentsclub.com/blog/autism-and-pda-what-can-people-bring-to-the-workplace/ [Accessed 5 January 2021]

Christie, P., Duncan, M., Fidler, R. & Healy, Z. (2012) *Understanding Pathological Demand Avoidance Syndrome in Children – a Guide for Parents, Teachers and Other Professionals* Jessica Kingsley Publishers, London

Greene, R. (2014) *The Explosive Child: A New Approach for Understanding and Parenting Easily Frustrated Chronically Inflexible Children* Harper Collins, London

Fidler, R. & Christie, P. (2019) *Collaborative Approaches to Learning for Pupils with PDA* Jessica Kingsley Publishers, London

Hatton, V. (2017) *Pathological Demand Avoidance: Strategies for Schools* [online] Stephstwogirls.co.uk. Available at: https://www.stephstwogirls.co.uk/2017/11/pathological-demand-avoidance.html [Accessed 4 January 2021]

Newson, E. (2016) *Educational and Handling Guidelines for Children with Pathological Demand Avoidance Syndrome (PDA)* Autismeastmidlands.org.uk [online] Available at: https://www.autismeastmidlands.org.uk/wp-content/uploads/2016/10/Educational-and-handling-Guidelines.pdf [Accessed 4 January 2021]

PDA Society (2020) [online] Available at: https://www.pdasociety.org.uk [Accessed 14 December 2020]

Syson, Z. & Gore Langton, E. (undated) *Simple Strategies for Supporting Children with Pathological Demand Avoidance at School* [online] Pdasociety.org.uk. Available at: https://www.pdasociety.org.uk/wp-content/uploads/2020/01/Positive-PDA-booklet.pdf [Accessed 13 November 2017]

Thompson, H. (2019) *The PDA Paradox: The Highs and Lows of My Life on a Little-Known Part of the Autism Spectrum* Jessica Kingsley Publishers, London

Thompson, H. (2020a) *Episode 191: A Conversation with Author and PDA Emissary Harry Thompson* [online] Tilt Parenting. Available at: https://tiltparenting.com/2020/01/14/episode-191-a-conversation-with-author-and-pda-emmisary-harry-thompson/ [Accessed 14 December 2020]

Thompson, H. (2020b) *Mind Matters Podcast Episode 54: Understanding Pathological Demand Avoidance* [online] Available at: https://www.mindmatterspodcast.com/home/2020/3/4/episode-54-understanding-pathological-demand-avoidance [Accessed 16 December 2020]

Wood, C. (2020) *Positive PDA Virtual Summit* [online] Positivepda.com. Available at: https://positivepda.com/corrina-wood/ [Accessed 14 December 2020]

## Checklist to support pupils with PDA

| SUPPORT | COMMENTS |
|---|---|
| **Please also refer to the 'Behaviour is communication', 'Self-regulation' and 'Sensory Processing Disorder (SPD)' chapters** | |
| **Strength-based approach** | |
| Reframe language – focus on strengths and successes | |
| **Relationships** | |
| Collaboration with caregivers and pupil | |
| Listen to parental concerns and lessen anxieties at school | |
| Self-reflection after an incident | |
| Repair and restore relationships | |
| **Reduce anxieties** | |
| Pre-empt and avoid or support with known triggers | |
| Lower demands and anxieties | |
| 'Meet and greet' – calm and settle before entering classroom | |
| Ensure all staff know how to communicate with the pupil successfully | |
| Trial and choose and rehearse calming strategies | |
| Safe space and calm tools | |
| **Communication** | |
| Use non-threatening, positive language, reduce demands and avoid confrontation | |
| Collaborate, treat as a colleague or equal | |
| Indirect praise | |
| Help cards or leave alone cards | |
| Complex language and appropriate humour | |
| Pre-planned responses to some avoidance | |
| Teach positive self-talk | |
| Depersonalise requests – use messages, emails, notes, timetables, timers, posters, role play and puppets | |

| SUPPORT | COMMENTS |
|---|---|
| Reframing of language – invitations, suggestions, wondering (see useful phrases p.195–6) | |
| Allow processing time | |
| **Teaching and learning** | |
| Adjust expectations and demands according to pupil's capacity to cope in that moment | |
| Foster love of learning and 'hook' interest | |
| Range of options to complete the same learning objective | |
| Folders with individual learning choices | |
| Positive choices | |
| Sense of mystery, suspense or excitement | |
| Offer alternative means of recording | |
| Correct teacher's work rather than own | |
| Novelty and change | |
| Provide opportunities for control | |
| Use role play and base work on their interests | |
| **Agree priorities** | |
| Priority Rating Scale (Fidler & Christie, 2019) (see p.247) | |
| Adjust demands in line with tolerance levels | |
| **Environmental adaptations** | |
| Awareness of sensory sensitivities with sensory and movement breaks | |
| Choice of seating | |
| **Unstructured times** | |
| Plan for and support during unstructured times | |
| **Rewards and consequences** | |
| Accumulative, personal reward system, if used, although be aware rewards can be a trigger | |
| Avoid sanctions for anxiety and behaviours pupils have no control over, teach skills and reduce demands | |

## Chapter 11

# Sensory Processing Disorder (SPD)

Sensory Processing Disorder (SPD) may also be referred to as Sensory Integration Difficulties, sensory sensitivities or Sensory Processing Difficulties. SPD is 'the inability to use information received through the senses in order to function smoothly in daily life' (Kranowitz, 2005). Sensory processing is the body's ability to process and respond to a variety of sensory information. A person with sensory processing difficulties has trouble responding to, making sense of and organising sensory stimuli received by the brain.

Children with sensory processing difficulties may be hyper- (over-) responsive to certain sensory stimuli (being over-stimulated or overwhelmed and therefore withdrawing from or avoiding the sensation). Alternatively, they may be hypo- (under-)responsive to sensory information (seemingly unaware of sensory stimuli). Or they may be sensory-craving or sensory-seeking (needing additional sensation such as movement or pressure) (Kranowitz, 2005; Stephens, 2018). Kranowitz (2017) explains that people with sensory processing difficulties may struggle in 'interpreting and managing ordinary sensations such as how things feel on your skin, how gravity affects balance and movement, where body parts are and what they're doing. So, SPD affects the biggies, touching and being touched, moving and being moved.'

SPD can present independently but are likely to co-exist with other conditions such as autism, ADHD, selective mutism, dyslexia, genetic syndromes and allergies (Kranowitz, 2005). They can also be linked to a child's experiences of early trauma or attachment disruptions and with Developmental Co-ordination Disorder (DCD) and developmental delay (Stephens, 2018) as well as FASD (Blackburn et al., 2012) and Tourette Syndrome (Tourettes Action, undated).

## The eight sensory systems

Sensory integration theory was initially developed in the 1960s by Jean Ayres, an occupational therapist and psychologist who linked sensory processing difficulties to problems with learning and engagement at school. Ayres discussed the eight senses – visual (sight), auditory (hearing), gustatory (taste), olfactory (smell) and tactile (touch) as well as proprioception (awareness of body position and movement), vestibular (balance) and interoception (internal state of the body) (Sensory-integration.org.uk, undated).

All of the senses help pupils to learn about the world around them, to regulate and socially engage. People may be over- or under-responsive in one or more sensory system.

The **visual** system is how the brain interprets, processes and makes sense of visual information (and differs from a visual impairment). Pupils may find it difficult to 'direct their visual attention because they are distracted by conflicting visual stimuli' (Biel & Peske, 2018). Pupils who are over-responsive to visual stimuli may be sensitive to bright light (such as sunlight or flickering lights) and may close or cover their eyes or may become overwhelmed quickly in a visually stimulating or busy classroom (Kranowitz, 2005 and Biel & Peske, 2018). Pupils who are under-sensitive to visual stimuli may not turn away from bright light or appear to look straight through faces (Kranowitz, 2005). Those seeking visual stimulation may be drawn to sparkling, spinning, bright and flickering objects (Kranowitz, 2005) or flap their hands in front of their eyes. For pupils who struggle with visual processing, words may blur on a page, or they may have difficulties reading, handwriting and copying. They may skip words or lose their place and use their finger as a marker when reading. They may confuse the symbols in Maths and struggle to remember sequences. Pupils may also suffer from headaches, rub their eyes and appear to lack focus and attention or seem distracted (Biel & Peske, 2018; Orthoptics.org.uk, undated).

The **auditory** system is how sound is processed, interpreted and made sense of. A pupil who is hypersensitive may hear noises others don't, cover their ears or aim to avoid certain sounds. They may have trouble filtering out sounds in the classroom or discriminating which sounds are important or may be over-sensitive to certain frequencies

(Biel & Peske, 2018). A pupil who is hypo-sensitive may ignore or not hear when you are talking to them or struggle to control their volume when talking. The auditory seeker may crave loud noises and crowds (Kranowitz, 2005). Pupils with auditory processing disorder may have 'difficulty in understanding speech especially in noisy environments, like a classroom … They may also have trouble concentrating and reading when background noise is present. These problems may lead to difficulty in understanding and remembering instructions, speaking clearly and development of reading skills' (GOSH NHS Foundation Trust, 2014).

The **gustatory** (taste) system is how taste and flavour are interpreted and processed. When someone has an over-responsive gustatory system, they may find certain flavours and foods overpowering and may avoid certain foods, only eat bland foods or gag whilst eating (Kranowitz, 2005). With an under-sensitive gustatory system, a person may eat very spicy or sour foods without reacting, the seeker may crave strong flavours such as spicy, salty or sour foods and eat lots of crunchy snacks. The need for adequate oral input may cause a pupil to constantly chew on clothing and lick or mouth inedible objects (pica).

The **olfactory** (smell) system is how we interpret and process smells. A person with an over-sensitive gustatory system may be repulsed by certain smells, which others don't notice, vomit or gag easily or hold their nose. A person with an under-responsive system may be unaware of strong or unpleasant smells. The seeker may crave certain smells and sniff people, clothes and objects (Kranowitz, 2005). 'Smell travels directly to our limbic system, which is the centre of our emotions, memory, pleasure and learning' (Biel & Peske, 2018). Taste and smell are closely connected.

The **tactile** system enables a child to develop a sense of themselves in relation to other people, objects and their surroundings. The pupil with an over-responsive tactile system may 'react with a fight-or-flight response to getting dirty, to certain textures of clothing and food, and to light, unexpected touch' (Kranowitz, 2005). They may become upset, be anxious or tiptoe when barefoot on grass, sand or carpet (Biel & Peske, 2018). Pupils who have an over-responsive tactile system may drop things, lack coordination and trip over regularly (Stephens, 2018), they may not notice when their hands are messy or when they have been touched. The tactile-seeking pupil may fidget or touch things constantly or frequently bump into people and things (Kranowitz, 2005).

The **proprioceptive** system processes feedback from muscles and joints. 'This system helps us to know where our limbs are and how hard we are pressing, pushing or pulling. For example, it helps us to move in a coordinated way, hold a pencil with just the right amount of force and helps us to judge how hard to throw a ball' (Stephens, 2018). Pupils with over-responsive proprioception systems may avoid strong sensory muscle input and be rigid and uncoordinated (Kranowitz, 2005), a pupil with an under-responsive system 'may be physically clumsy or move slowly to compensate ... may slide off a classroom chair, stumble on stairs, or fall when they run' (Biel & Peske, 2018, p.33). Pupils may have difficulty with fine motor skills and often drop things or may be unaware of where parts of their body are, look at their feet when walking or need to watch their hand when writing (Allen, 2016). Pupils may feel out of touch with their hands and feet and have trouble dressing or using pens, pencils and cutlery. Pupils who seek proprioceptive input may crave 'jumping, crashing, pushing, pulling, bouncing and hanging' (Biel & Peske, 2018), apply excess force, chew on everything and often bump or push into others.

The **vestibular** system tells us the direction we are moving in and helps us plan for movements, move in a coordinated way and maintain balance and stability. Receptors in small, fluid-filled canals within the inner ear pick up the direction of motion, so we know where our body is in relation to the world around us. The vestibular system is important for self-regulation. A pupil with an over-sensitive vestibular system may avoid certain movements, dislike their feet being off the floor, lack balance and coordination and fear falling over, get dizzy quickly and suffer from motion sickness (Biel & Peske, 2018; Kranowitz, 2005). A pupil with an under-responsive vestibular system may never feel dizzy and may not feel themselves falling so fail to protect themselves adequately. The seeker may crave or seek out movement and heights, be constantly spinning, fidgeting, moving and risk-taking (Kranowitz, 2005).

The **interoception** system is how the brain interprets and processes information from the internal organs and tells us what is happening inside our body. It enables us to know whether we feel hungry, thirsty, need the toilet, feel physically well, and whether we are at a comfortable temperature. It is essential for effective self-care and meeting our basic needs to remain safe (Stephens, 2018). A pupil with interoception processing difficulties may have a very low or high pain threshold and have difficulty knowing if they are hot or cold, if they need the toilet or are hungry or thirsty. 'When a person struggles to read their body's signals and doesn't quite know how to recognize and select the best strategies to make them feel better, the result may be anxiety, fear and a stress response' (Biel & Peske, 2018). Interoception is essential to self-regulation.

# SPD in the classroom

Each person's sensory processing is different and what feels 'just right' will vary from person to person (Stephens, 2018) and from day to day. Pupils may be over-sensitive to a range of sensory stimuli (uniforms, crowded corridors, smells, noisy playgrounds or busy classrooms), which can make aspects of school life an overwhelming, frightening or even painful experience. 'Consequently, children may appear disorganised, confused, emotionally upset, scared, shut down or become out of control. Frequently, caregivers and educators interpret this behaviour as hyperactive, defiant, resistant, avoidant or aggressive. In reality, their nervous systems are having difficulty making sense out of the world around them' (NHS Ayrshire & Arran, 2019).

We are usually unaware that we process things differently to others, particularly as children. Confusion and frustration may arise, as pupils may not be able to, or know how to, communicate their feelings of discomfort, resulting in a wide range of seemingly negative behaviours as they will often react with their threat response of fight, flight, freeze (running away, hitting out or isolating) in order to protect themselves. The body responds as if survival is at risk, out of proportion to everyday stressors but in proportion to the threat perceived by the brain. As stress and anxiety increase, the brain becomes less able to process sensory information. Allen (2016) explains: 'When too much sensation is coming into my brain I get cross. When I feel like that, it's difficult for me to stay in control; I feel like shouting, running away, hitting out or curling up into a ball. It's hard for me to tell people how I feel or to listen to what people are saying to me.'

> **Case study:**
>
> Arthur was sitting next to a key adult with whom he had a very positive and trusting relationship. He was working on some challenging Maths questions (his favourite subject). Suddenly, he turned and started swearing at his key adult; his work was thrown on the floor, the table was up-ended and he left the room. It appeared as if this outburst had arisen totally out of the blue.
>
> Once Arthur had calmed down, he was able to reflect on the incident: 'The room had been cleaned and smelled horrible and the projector was making that buzzing noise, that bulb hasn't been changed and is still flickering and then Mrs K started playing with

the zip on her fleece and I was trying to do my Maths and it was really hard and it was just too much, I lost it and couldn't cope anymore'.

The staff all thought that his behaviours had no trigger, whereas, in reality, they were an accumulation of sensory stimuli which created overload and overwhelm. Arthur's body reacted with its threat response as if his life were at risk.

By reflecting with Arthur, staff understood what went wrong and supported him to put a plan in place should a similar situation occur in the future. Arthur was given a 'too much' card and rehearsed putting it on his desk and leaving the room through the outside door to get fresh air. He agreed to wait by the tree until an adult came to him or he felt ready to return to class. He used this strategy regularly at first and then just knowing he could escape, if overwhelmed, seemed to be enough and he was able to regulate within the classroom.

If a pupil has sensory processing difficulties, they may:

■ Display heightened anxiety
■ Appear easily distracted
■ Struggle to focus on a task
■ Be impulsive and take risks
■ Run away
■ Regularly reach crisis point (meltdown or withdrawal)
■ Prefer predictable routines and need support with transitions or change
■ Feel intense emotions
■ Need support with social interactions, social skills and friendships
■ Display bursts of aggression
■ React in unexpected ways to touch, movement, light, smell, taste or noise (cover ears, cry or run away from hand dryers, sirens or the school bell), and may fear crowds or unexpected touch
■ Be under- or over-sensitive to pain
■ Have difficulty with fine and gross motor skills
■ Struggle with spatial awareness and balance or fall over frequently
■ Engage in repetitive behaviours
■ Be energetic
■ Need to move, fidget, pace or rock
■ Have difficulty with self-care such as dressing, eating, brushing teeth or sleeping

- Lack energy and be fearful of trying new things
- Be unable to eat certain foods due to texture, colour, taste or temperature
- Chew and mouth or lick inedible objects
- Only wear certain fabrics or prefer clothes without tags and seams or favour tight- or loose-fitting clothing
- Lack awareness of personal space, stand too close to others or bump others accidentally during play
- Struggle with listening, reading and writing

## Strategies to support pupils with SPD

Pupils will benefit from an Occupational Therapist assessment to support and address individual issues and implement a plan for calming or alerting strategies. However, there are certain tried and tested activities to try, which many pupils find supportive within the classroom. Sensory strategies can help pupils to organise their thoughts, concentrate and focus for longer and regulate behaviours and emotions. Sensory-aware systems which are put in for individual children can benefit the whole class.

By enhancing and modifying the sensory environment pupils are able to adapt and improve responses and processing and therefore better able to engage in learning, relationships and everyday life. Sensory integration is important for all aspects of school life, particularly participating, engaging and learning within a social, classroom environment.

Below is a range of suggestions that have been tried and tested and found to be supportive of pupils with SPD in school. There is a checklist at the end of this chapter.

### *A strength-based approach*

- Focus on what the pupil can do and draw attention to their achievements. Give roles and responsibilities based on their strengths and areas of interest. Report the successes home, rather than the challenges.
- When observing pupils, as well as looking for difficulties, patterns and triggers, look for times when the pupil is successful. Explore what has contributed to this success and what is working for the pupil. Aim to recreate these successes at other times of day and in different areas of the school.

## *Relationships*

- Work in collaboration with pupils, caregivers and outside agencies such as Occupational Therapists and Speech and Language Therapists, allowing for some trial and error to establish pupil's sensory needs and preferences.
- Pupils need supportive and thoughtful adults to help them towards greater self-awareness and to model and trial a range of strategies with the pupil. Understanding the pupil's strengths and struggles is key: 'The inability to function smoothly is not because the child won't but because he can't' (Kranowitz, 2005). Establish positive relationships based on the PACE approach (see p.65–6) and get to know the pupil as a person.

## *Environmental considerations*

Understanding the different sensory difficulties that pupils may have is essential. If a change in behaviour is observed, explore whether there has been a recent change within the environment. 'As the environmental stimulus increases or decreases, the person's behaviour also alters. The person can also react to stimulus differently depending on their stress levels, other demands on them and what has happened earlier ... Changing the environment can have a direct impact on how a person behaves and reacts' (Pennell, 2020).

- Completing an environmental checklist may help adults reduce triggers and make the environment more favourable for a pupil (such as autismeducationtrust.org.uk Tool 44).
- Reduce sensory overload, 'simplify, simplify, simplify' (Kranowitz, 2005). Have a low arousal environment and reduce distractions and stimulation. Keep wall displays clear and simple, with consistent borders. Avoid things hanging, twirling, and twinkling in the light. Keep whiteboards, surfaces and shelves tidy and free from clutter.
- 'A classroom's hard surfaces, such as desktops, linoleum tiles, and painted walls, reflect sound. Wherever possible, cover hard surfaces with carpet, cloth or corkboard' (Kranowitz, 2005) or place felt pads on furniture legs to minimise scraping noises and turn off unnecessary fans, air conditioning or projectors. Pupils with auditory processing difficulties may struggle to filter out or process different sounds, causing confusion or frustration. They may not identify the adult as the main sound that needs to be attuned to.

- Wearing ear defenders may be helpful for pupils with auditory sensitivities at certain trigger points in the school day, particularly if they are having difficulty concentrating or reading. Forewarn these pupils, where possible, of sudden noises such as the fire alarm, school bell or sports whistles. Listening to white noise or calming music through headphones can help. 'Sometimes our hearing is too sensitive and tells us there is danger when there is not. I hate really loud sounds like the school bell, hand dryers or people shouting. I feel sick inside and want to run away ... with ear defenders ... I can feel calmer and pay attention' (Allen, 2016, p.17).
- For pupils who need increased audio stimulation, go on listening walks, play listening games, play musical instruments, and use rhythm and beat to support learning tasks. 'Sometimes songs or clapping a rhythm help Anna to organise her movements. Sound helps her to know where she is and music with a good beat helps her to move better' (Allen, 2016, p.16).
- The visual sense is often the first to become over-stimulated. For pupils who are light-sensitive, ensure lights aren't flickering or eliminate fluorescent lighting (Learnfromautistics.com, 2015) and be aware of bright light from windows. Allow the pupil to wear sunglasses or a cap and adjust blinds in bright sunlight to help them feel more comfortable. Remove reflective, bright surfaces and reduce visual distractions.
- For those seeking visual stimuli, provide liquid motion timers, blow bubbles and pop them with different body parts, and watch and make shapes from cloud formations (Beck, 2016). Play visual memory games (see p.16–17), use light-up fiddle toys, kaleidoscopes, make glitter jars, complete visual tracking activities such as mazes, cut out shapes and dot-to-dots, highlight all the letter 'e's in a text or watch a marble in a marble run.
- Carpet time can be challenging. It may be helpful to outline an area to sit in or offer a carpet tile or spot. Be aware of sensory sensitivities and explore personal preferences. The carpet may be too prickly or itchy and a softer carpet spot may resolve these issues or a pupil may prefer the sensory feedback from a more textured surface. Some pupils will need to be towards the edge of the group rather than in proximity to others.
- Be aware of sensory sensitivities in terms of clothing, labels may need to be removed from clothes or pupils may need sensory-friendly clothing.
- Pupils will need access to a calm, safe space and a range of calming tools (see p.42).

- Smells may invoke (conscious or unconscious) memories, triggering the threat response. Certain smells, such as foods, art materials, pets or perfumes can be a trigger. Pupils may need to cover their nose with a tissue that smells nice to them or get some fresh air. 'Sometimes smells that other people think are OK are horrible for me. It can help me to suck on a straw or chew something' (Allen, 2016, p.18).
- Learnfromautistics.com (2015) suggest that teachers wear neutral colours (avoiding bright colours) and avoid strong perfume or after-shave.

**Case example:**

Mrs C was teaching her class, as usual, when Finn entered the classroom. Mrs C and Finn had a positive, trusting relationship. This particular morning, she greeted Finn as usual, only to be ignored. She gave him time and approached him once more, and again she was ignored. This behaviour went on for several days. Mrs C was baffled. She reflected on anything that had changed. There had been no changes to the school environment that she could think of, there had been no reported incidents in the classroom or playground. Mrs C called home and was surprised to hear that Finn had told his parents that his teacher hadn't been at school all week. She had been there every day. It took a few more days of reflection and she realised that the only difference was that she had changed her shampoo. As soon as she returned to her original shampoo, life with Finn returned to normal. It seems that he hadn't recognised his teacher because she smelt different.

## *Teaching and learning*

- Provide positive choices to give pupils a sense of control and allow for individual preferences, for example, choices over where to work or what type of seat to sit on, texture of paper, writing implement or pencil grip.
- Pupils who have difficulties in processing information can find it challenging to self-regulate. Teach self-regulation strategies to help them gain self-awareness and to relax and calm (see the 'Self-regulation' chapter).

- Using a ruler or bookmark or following the words with a finger can help pupils keep track when reading (Allen, 2016). Coloured overlays may help make the text clearer and reduce blur and have been reported to improve reading and reduce eye strain, discomfort and headaches for pupils with difficulties in visual processing.
- Ensure worksheets are clear and uncluttered, include minimal information and lots of white space. Pupils may respond better to being presented with one question. Alternatively, Kranowitz (2005, p.252) suggests framing each question with a cardboard template.
- Multi-sensory approaches support and integrate different ways of learning, improve memory and understanding and add interest. Where possible, reinforce verbal input with hands-on learning; use real items for the pupils to hold and explore, provide written copies of notes to highlight and encourage moving around, where possible.
- Support with transitions (see p.15). Pupils may need to be first or last when lining up or need to avoid busy corridors or cloakrooms by moving around slightly earlier or later than others. Visual cues are useful when a pupil needs to move from one place to another, for example, giving them a photograph of the next teacher or classroom as a visual reminder of where they need to go next. Having a job to do, such as a box to carry or equipment to tidy, can support pupils returning to class at the end of break times.

## *Sensory input*

Physical movement can improve focus and attention and help with self-regulation. Provide pupils with vestibular and proprioceptive input while working or listening, such as fiddle tools, resistance bands, weighted lap pads or wobble cushions (see p.42).

- Further **proprioceptive** or **heavy work** activities could include resistance band exercises, wall or chair pushes, drumming, climbing or hanging on bars.
- **Vestibular** input could include sliding, yoga, riding trikes, bikes or scooters, balancing on a wobble board or a therapy ball, going on the swing, spinning in an office chair, 'sit n spin' toys, a scooter board, running in circles, hanging upside down or doing cartwheels (Biel & Peske, 2018). Provide visual reminders of how and when to use these.
- Pupils who need further deep pressure may benefit from using a Lycra™ cape to wrap around themselves. An Occupational

Therapist may suggest a weighted vest, at times, for additional input. Wearing a compression T-shirt such as a tight sports vest under clothes can discreetly offer some needed sensory feedback, as can a weighted hoodie or sensory inflatable jacket. Allowing a pupil to keep their backpack on for the beginning part of the lesson also has a similar grounding and calming effect.

- **Tactile play** (activities such as playing with playdough, water, sand, rice, gloop, shaving foam or clay) helps pupils to integrate and process sensory information and can improve concentration and engagement over time.
- Allow pupils to complete their work in a variety of positions throughout the day. For example, standing up to work, lying on their stomachs or sitting on a beanbag and leaning on a clipboard to write, or using alternative seating such as a therapy ball chair or wobble stool for part of the lesson.
- An angled writing slope may help with arm positioning and make handwriting more comfortable. A **vibrating pen** provides tactile input and may be calming, during occasional writing tasks, particularly for reluctant writers. Sensory pencil grips come in a range of textures, colours and materials, providing sensory feedback whilst writing.
- Explore a range of sensory and regulating strategies and present these visually on a stress scale (see p.248).

---

**Case study:**

Ryan was in Year 2. He had started stroking and rubbing his key adults' arms and stomach when they wore the new staff fleeces. When asked to stop, he got very frustrated and said he couldn't help it.

*What strategies would you suggest to support Ryan to stop inappropriately touching the adults?*

Ryan was given his own fleece to wear, which reduced some of the touching, but did not eliminate it. He was then offered a hot water bottle with a fleece cover to hold. He was given a soft teddy and some similar fleece material to keep in his pocket and a larger piece was stapled onto the underside of his desk for him to stroke while he was listening. With all of the additional tactile input, Ryan stopped touching the adults.

## Unstructured times

Unstructured times must be managed carefully. The increased crowds, sounds and smells and needing to wear additional clothing layers along with difficulties processing body temperature can be overwhelming for those with sensory sensitivities.

- Offer a quieter area to eat in or allow the pupil to eat slightly earlier or later to avoid crowds, noises and smells. Similarly, offer a safe, quiet zone to access if the playground becomes overwhelming. Provide a range of activities and clubs such as running, climbing, sensory circuits, yoga, trampolining and gymnastics at break and lunchtimes.
- Provide access to a key adult and safe space at break and lunchtimes. Rehearse where and who to go to (when the pupil is calm). Provide a visual reminder such as a photograph.
- Provide support for wet break times, offering a list of activities to choose from and a quieter place to access. The noise and lack of clarity around expectations can be overwhelming and frustrating.
- Support may be required for PE lessons, such as preparing the pupil for going to the hall or field. Rehearse this beforehand and build up gradually (see step-by-step plans, pp.245, 246). The pupil may also need to be given an alternative place for changing. Sensory processing difficulties abound in PE lessons due to changes of clothing and footwear, loud instructions and poor acoustics, smells and textures of equipment, different speeds and ways of moving, change of space and changes in body temperature.

## Rewards and consequences

- If a pupil's sensory needs are not being met appropriately, it will manifest in more negative, sensory-seeking behaviour within the classroom (such as absconding, going under tables, rocking back on the chair, lack of engagement, walking around, touching other children or objects). Rather than implementing sanctions for behaviours that the pupil cannot control, children need to be taught the skills to understand and regulate their behaviour and emotions, with the support of an adult who understands and responds to their sensory needs.
- Observe pupils and spot sensory triggers and help students avoid them where necessary or support them in developing skills and strategies to manage them more effectively. Completing a sensory

checklist for pupils, such as in Biel and Peske (2018, pp.55–60) or Kranowitz (2005, pp.17–20 or pp.41–47) may help assess a pupil's individual sensory needs.

■ Avoid removing playtimes or sensory breaks as consequences. Sensory breaks are a necessity, not a reward.

## Resources, further information and 'tool kits'

### Books for adults

*Improving Sensory Processing in Traumatized Children* by Sarah Lloyd

*Living Sensationally: Understanding Your Senses* by Winnie Dunn

*The Out-of-Sync Child: Recognizing and Coping with Sensory Processing Disorder* by Carol Kranowitz – essential reading for all adults who would like to know more

*Raising Happy Children: The Key to a Calm, Composed Child* by Lizanne du Plessis

*Raising a Sensory Smart Child: The Definitive Handbook for Helping your Child with Sensory Processing Issues* by Lindsey Biel and Nancy Peske

*Sensational Kids: Hope and Help for Children with Sensory Processing Disorder* by Lucy Jane Miller

### Books to share with pupils

*Can I Tell You about Sensory Processing Difficulties? A Guide for Friends, Family and Professionals* by Sue Allen – easy, informative guide for adults and children

*The Kids' Guide to Staying Awesome and In Control: Simple Stuff to Help Children Regulate their Emotions and Senses* by Lauren Brukner – fantastic ideas to help children to understand and regulate their feelings

*Squirmy Wormy: How I Learned to Help Myself* by Lynda Farrington Wilson

### Websites

https://www.autismeducationtrust.org.uk/tools-for-teachers2/ Training and tools for teachers

https://www.aettraininghubs.org.uk/wp-content/uploads/2012/05/37.1-Sensory-audit-tool-for-environments.pdf Sensory audit

https://fascets.org/wp-content/uploads/2020/07/Sensory-Processing.pdf How heavy work can help

https://www.geteduca.com/blog/displays-in-early-childhood-settings/ Creating low arousal displays

https://www.gonoodle.com/ Whole class movement ideas

https://theinspiredtreehouse.com/23-ways-to-create-a-sensory-friendly-classroom/ Ideas for creating a sensory-friendly classroom

https://www.learnfromautistics.com/advocating-for-a-sensory-friendly-classroom/ Ideas for creating a sensory-friendly classroom

https://lemonlimeadventures.com/sensory-break-ideas-for-kids/ Sensory break ideas

https://www.relaxkids.com/ Relaxation products for children

https://www.spdstar.org/ Information, advice and resources

https://www.sensorydirect.com/ For a range of sensory tools, equipment and clothing

https://www.sensoryintegration.org.uk/ A wealth of information and training courses

https://sensoryprocessingchallenges.com/images/Sensorytoolschool.pdf Sensory screening tool

https://www.sensory-processing-disorder.com/heavy-work-activities.html Ideas for heavy work and sensory breaks

https://sensory-processing.middletownautism.com/sensory-strategies/strategies-according-to-sense/ Sensory processing information, case studies and strategies for pupils

https://tinyurl.com/GuernseyOTSensoryStrategies Sensory strategies for teachers and caregivers

https://www.understood.org/en/learning-thinking-differences/child-learning-disabilities/add-adhd/the-difference-between-sensory-processing-issues-and-adhd Explanation of the differences (and similarities) between ADHD and SPD

## Podcasts

https://www.thesendcast.com/sensory-issues-with-sara-jane-critchley-podcast/

https://tiltparenting.com/2017/09/26/episode-76-carol-kranowitz-talks-about-sensory-processing-disorder-and-the-out-of-sync-child/

# References

Allen, S. (2016) *Can I Tell You about Sensory Processing Difficulties? A Guide for Friends, Family and Professionals* Jessica Kingsley Publishers, London

Biel, L. & Peske, N. (2018) *Raising a Sensory Smart Child: The Definitive Handbook for Helping your Child with Sensory Processing Issues* Penguin, New York

Blackburn, C., Carpenter, B. & Egerton, J. (2012) *Educating Children and Young People with Fetal Alcohol Spectrum Disorders – Constructing Personalised Pathways to Learning* Routledge, Oxon

Beck, C. (2016) *Visual Sensory Processing Backyard Activities* [online] Available at: https://www.theottoolbox.com/visual-sensory-processing-backyard/ [Accessed 26 January 2021]

Brukner, L. (2014) *The Kids' Guide to Staying Awesome and In Control: Simple Stuff to Help Children Regulate their Emotions and Senses* Jessica Kingsley Publishers, London

GOSH NHS Foundation Trust (2014) *Information for Families: Auditory Processing Disorder* [online] Available at: https://www.gosh.nhs.uk/medical-in formation/auditory-processing-disorder [Accessed 20 January 2021]

Kranowitz, C. (2005) *The Out-of-Sync Child: Recognizing and Coping with Sensory Processing Disorder* Tarcher Perigee Books, New York

Kranowitz, C. (2017) *Carol Kranowitz Talks about Sensory Processing Disorder* [online] Available at: https://tiltparenting.com/2017/09/26/episode-76-carol-kranowitz-talks-about-sensory-processing-disorder-and-the-out-of-sync-child/ [Accessed 17 January 2021]

Learnfromautistics.com (2015) *Advocating for a Sensory Friendly Classroom* [online] Learn From Autistics, 30 June. Available at: https://www.learn fromautistics.com/advocating-for-a-sensory-friendly-classroom/ [Accessed 12 January 2021]

NHS Ayrshire & Arran (2019) *Understanding Fetal Alcohol Spectrum Disorder (FASD) What Educators Need to Know – for Education Staff Working with Children and Young People with FASD* [online] Available at: https://www. nhsaaa.net/media/8391/fasd_whateducatorsneedtoknow.pdf [Accessed 12 January 2021]

Nixon, G. (2017) *New Thinking on Wall Displays in Early Childhood Settings* https://www.geteduca.com/blog/displays-in-early-childhood-settings/ [Accessed 8 January 2021]

Orthoptics.org.uk (undated) *Visual Processing Difficulties (VPD)* [online] Ortho-ptic Clinical Advisory Group. Available at: https://www.orthoptics.org.uk/ resources/clinical-advisory-group/visual-processing-difficulties-clini cal-advisory-group/ [Accessed 20 January 2021]

Pennell, J. (2020) *FASD in Focus – Sensory Integration* [online] The National Organisation for FASD. Available at: https://nationalfasd.org.uk/docu ments/FASD%20in%20Focus%20EducationProfile.pdf [Accessed 12 Jan uary 2021]

Sensoryintegration.org.uk (undated) *What is SI?* [online] Available at: https:// www.sensoryintegration.org.uk/What-is-SI#:~:text=Jean%20Ayres%20 was%20particularly%20interested,self%2Dcontrol%20and%20aca demic%20skills [Accessed 19 January 2021]

Stephens, R. (2018) *Sensory Processing, Coordination and Attachment* [online] Beacon House. Information courtesy of Beacon House Therapeutic Ser vices and Trauma Team, www.beaconhouse.org.uk. Available at: https:// beaconhouse.org.uk/wp-content/uploads/2019/09/Sensory-process ing-coordination-and-attachment-Article-min.pdf [Accessed 31 October 2018]

Tourettes Action (undated) *Co-occurring Features and Conditions* [online] Avail able at: https://www.tourettes-action.org.uk/74-managing-ts—associat ed-conditions.html [Accessed 20 July 2021]

## Checklist to support pupils with SPD

| STRATEGY | COMMENTS |
|---|---|
| **Please also refer to the 'Behaviour is communication' and 'Self-regulation' chapters** | |
| **A strength-based approach** | |
| Focus on and communicate achievements and give responsibilities based on strengths | |
| Observe strengths and successes as well as triggers, to establish patterns | |
| **Relationships** | |
| Collaborate with caregivers, pupil and outside agencies | |
| Be supportive and understanding and help them towards self-awareness, use the PACE approach (see p.65–6) | |
| **Environmental considerations** | |
| Environmental checklist | |
| Reduce distractions and sensory overload | |
| Reduce sound by covering hard surfaces or putting felt pads on furniture legs, turn off unused appliances | |
| Audio-sensitive – provide ear defenders, pre-warn of noises, listen to music or white noise | |
| Audio-seeking or under-responsive – listening walks, listening games, musical instruments, use rhythm and beat | |
| Visual-sensitive – eliminate flickering/ fluorescent lights, bright surfaces and visual distractions | |
| Visual-seeking – liquid motion timers, blow and pop bubbles, play visual memory games, make shapes from the clouds, visual tracking | |
| Carpet spot (explore appropriate texture) | |
| Be aware of sensitivities to clothing – labels may need removing, sensory-friendly clothing | |
| Access to a calm, safe space with calming tools | |

*(Continued)*

## Continued

| STRATEGY | COMMENTS |
|---|---|
| Awareness that smells can be a trigger – may need fresh air, to cover nose or smell something nice or comforting | |
| Wear neutral colours and avoid strong perfumes | |
| **Teaching and learning** | |
| Offer positive choices to allow for individual preferences | |
| Teach self-regulation strategies | |
| Follow text with finger or use a ruler or bookmark under words and offer coloured overlays | |
| Clear, uncluttered handouts or present one question at a time | |
| Multi-sensory approaches | |
| Support to manage transitions | |
| **Sensory input** | |
| Proprioceptive (resistance bands, wall/chair pushes, climbing) and vestibular input (yoga, balancing, riding, spinning) | |
| Lycra™ cape, sports vest, heavy Jacket/backpack | |
| Tactile play | |
| Allow a range of seating or working positions | |
| Angled writing slope, vibrating pen, a range of sensory pencil grips | |
| Explore sensory and calming strategies and complete stress scale | |
| **Unstructured times** | |
| Quieter place to eat, safe, quiet zones and access to a range of clubs | |
| Key adult and safe space | |
| Support for wet break times and PE lessons | |
| **Rewards and consequences** | |
| Teach skills and strategies for self-regulation and respond appropriately to sensory sensitivities rather than impose sanctions | |

| STRATEGY | COMMENTS |
|---|---|
| Observe to spot sensory triggers and avoid or support with these, complete a sensory assessment | |
| Avoid removing break times and sensory breaks as consequences | |

*Chapter 12*

# Tourette Syndrome (TS) and tic disorders

Tourette Syndrome (TS) is a genetic, neurological condition that causes a person to make involuntary movements or sounds called tics.

TS is estimated to affect about 1 per cent of school children in the UK and is more common in boys than girls (Tourettes Action, 2017). It is a spectrum condition ranging from mild to severe and usually starts in childhood. Each pupil is an individual and symptoms will differ for each child.

Over 85 per cent of people with TS have comorbidities (co-existing conditions) (Tourettes Action, undated) , including Obsessive Compulsive Disorder (OCD), autism, Attention Deficit Hyperactivity Disorder (ADHD), Sensory Processing Disorder (SPD), anxiety or learning difficulties.

## Tics

Tics are involuntary and caused by a chemical imbalance in the brain and 'can be "simple" involving one muscle or one simple sound, or "complex" involving a coordinated movement of a number of muscles or an utterance of a meaningful phrase' (GOSH NHS Foundation Trust, 2016). A tic is described by Chowdhury (2004, p.19) as 'an involuntary, rapid, recurrent, non-rhythmic vocal action. It is sudden and purposeless. Tics consist of simple or co-ordinated, repetitive

DOI: 10.4324/9781003146292-13

or sequential, movements, gestures and utterances that mimic frag-
ments of normal behaviour.'

Tics usually start during early childhood and increase in intensity
during adolescence. The number and severity of tics can fluctuate over
time or change unpredictably (referred to as the waxing and waning of
tics). People might experience a reduction in tics by the age of 18, when
they may disappear altogether (Chowdhury, 2004).

Tics tend to increase during times of stress, anxiety and excitement
and can change depending on the people around them. (For example,
they may lessen around supportive, understanding friends, family and
staff, as anxiety is reduced. Alternatively, they may worsen, as the person feels comfortable and no longer feels the need to suppress.) Tics
can also decrease in severity if the individual is engrossed in something they enjoy (such as playing video games) or absorbed in a task
such as music or sport (Ball & Box, 2008).

Every child with TS has tics; however, a person can have tics (or a
tic disorder) without having TS. For a diagnosis of TS, multiple motor
tics (movement tics) and one or more vocal tics (noise tics) need to
be present, multiple times each day, for at least 12 months, with the
onset of symptoms in childhood or adolescence. Tics must also not be
explainable by any other medical conditions.

## Motor (movement) tics

Initially, tics tend to develop around the head or face area. Simple
motor tics are usually rapid and meaningless, such as blinking, twitch-
ing, eye-rolling, grimacing, abdominal tensing, shrugging or jerking
(Chowdhury, 2004; Tourettes Action 2017).

Complex motor tics are slower and may appear more controlled, such
as head banging, jumping, twirling, licking, gyrating or touching objects
or people. A person may have compulsive tics, for example, the urge to
do something or touch something a fixed number of times. Tics may
also present as an involuntary repetition or imitation of the actions or
movement of others (echopraxia or echokinesis) or the involuntary performance of obscene gestures or inappropriate touching (copropraxia),
which is a rarer symptom (Chowdhury, 2004; Tourettes Action, 2017).

## Vocal (noise) tics

Vocal tics result from a neurochemical imbalance and are involuntary;
they are not the person's thoughts.

Vocal tics are tics that make a sound and often occur at inappropriate times. Simple vocal tics are noises such as whistling, sniffing, throat clearing, snorting, squeaking, barking, humming, tongue-clicking or coughing (Chowdhury, 2004; Conners, 2012; Tourettes Action, 2017).

Complex vocal tics may involve the repetition or change in articulation of specific words or phrases, name-calling, animal noises, muttering, involuntary repetition of sounds and language (echolalia) or involuntary swearing, aggressive and racial remarks or other socially inappropriate comments (coprolalia, which many people and the media often associate with TS, but only about 10 per cent of people with TS have this) (Chowdhury, 2004; Tourettes Action, 2017).

Non-Obscene Socially Inappropriate (NOSI) behaviour is the term used when a person is compelled to say or do something socially unacceptable (commenting on or touching someone or something inappropriately).

## Suppression of tics

Individuals can, at times, suppress or camouflage their tics for a short period of time. However, suppressing tics is exhausting and unsustainable. Many pupils who suppress their tics at school cannot focus on a task or listen attentively, as suppression requires much energy and attention. Parents have reported an increase in the intensity of tics at home if pupils have suppressed them during the day and have linked this to subsequent outbursts of aggression and difficulties sleeping.

The more a student is asked not to tic, the more difficult it is to suppress them and can make them worse in the long run (Conners, 2012). It is also incredibly damaging to self-esteem, mental health and wellbeing.

## Tourette Syndrome in the classroom

Pupils with TS often have delayed executive functions such as working memory, flexible thinking, self-regulation, impulsivity, concentration (particularly on tasks that are not perceived as interesting), starting and completing new tasks, shifting focus from one activity to another and with organisational and planning skills (Matthews, 2020). 'They may have a poor attention span, fail to complete tasks, be easily distracted, unable to listen, fidgety and impulsive. However, TS is not an indicator of low IQ and, given the right support and encouragement, students can reach their full potential' (Toghill, 2020).

Adults need to understand the pupil and the reason behind the behaviours. Pupils may seem task-avoidant and disruptive to lessons. 'Having TS means I find it hard to concentrate on things I'm not interested in. Sometimes at school, when my tics are jerking me about, it's like they use up all my concentration and all my energy' (Leicester, 2014, p.16). Tics themselves or the suppression of tics is exhausting and make concentrating on a task, or sitting still and listening, very uncomfortable and difficult. Neck and facial tics can make reading problematic or painful, and pupils may lose their place due to eye tics or might be embarrassed reading aloud due to vocal tics. Motor tics may affect fine and gross motor skills and coordination, causing difficulties with handwriting and in PE activities. Social situations may also increase anxieties.

Pupils with TS often have difficulties regulating their emotions and behaviours. They may also suffer from low self-esteem.

If staff are empathic and understanding that the difficulties the pupil is experiencing are caused by a neurological condition rather than deliberate actions, they are better able to support effectively. 'When the student is not misperceived as intentionally causing a problem, educators are more likely to consider what they can do *for* a student, rather than *to* a student, paving the way for supportive, empathic, proactive, and creative strategies which more effectively address the behaviors in the classroom' (Deibler, 2020).

## Strategies to support pupils with TS to thrive

All staff need to be aware and understand the difficulties experienced by a pupil with TS to support them effectively, increase engagement in learning and develop wellbeing and self-esteem while focusing on their strengths and successes. 'Essentially, it is important to understand that the student is not *giving* the educator a hard time, the student is having a hard time' (Deibler, 2020). Every pupil is different and tics wax and wane so strategies need to be 'individualized and flexible' (Deibler, 2020).

Below is a range of strategies that have been tried and tested and found to support pupils with TS in school. There is a checklist at the end of this chapter.

### A strength-based approach

Adult responses strongly influence pupils' behaviour and attitudes towards difference. Therefore, it is essential that adults in school model tolerance, acceptance and patience and view the condition as a 'difference' rather than a 'deficit'.

■ Reframe communication around TS and focus on each individual's strengths and achievements. People with TS are often very good at sport and tend to be creative, energetic, successful in tasks they enjoy and have a good sense of humour (Simpson, 2020, referencing www.cpri.ca – *Leaky Brakes Toolbox*). People with TS are often very musical and show good empathy skills (Leicester, 2014, p.17). They are often high achievers and successful in many different professions (CDC, undated). Give roles and responsibilities based on interests and strengths.
■ Work with pupils to research successful people and positive role models with TS.
■ Encourage participation in a range of clubs and extra-curricular activities to harness strengths and interests outside of the classroom. 'Having TS means I am really good at some things, but I find other things hard. I am so good at concentrating on things I like doing, such as drumming and karting, my brain can forget to make me tic' (Leicester, 2014, p.16)

## Relationships and communication

■ It is essential that all staff, peers and the pupils themselves understand TS to ensure empathy, acceptance and to provide support and reduce pupil anxiety. Tourettes Action has advice and resources for this (see 'tool kit'). The book *Can I Tell You about Tourette Syndrome?* by Mal Leicester is also a good starting point and, as he states, 'It's great when people accept me as I am' (Leicester, 2014, p.20). Conners (2012) reiterated the importance of educating those around the pupil, 'Once classmates understand TS and why the student is doing what he/she is doing, the tics usually calm down naturally because the stress is lessened. Kids can be very understanding when we just tell them the truth. The world is filled with differences and the sooner all students realize this the more tolerant and empathetic they become. They will make fun of and even fear what they don't understand.'
■ Form positive relationships with caregivers, the pupil and involved agencies to work collaboratively, share strategies and concerns, and listen to the caregivers and pupil about what works well for them. 'Having open channels of communication between the child's parents, treating professionals, colleagues and the child about what might be helpful for the child can considerably reduce

some of the frustrations associated with Tourette syndrome. Recognition and acknowledgement of the student's struggle with their condition and encouraging him/her to discuss with you the support and help that is needed to work around the tics will make a world of a difference to the student' (GOSH NHS Foundation Trust, 2016).

■ Regular, positive communication between home and school is essential in order to work together to help pupils explore possible solutions for certain tics or compulsions which may be causing problems, embarrassment or be inappropriate. For example, if the tic is spitting, offer a cold drink or suitable oral chew tool or encourage spitting discreetly into a tissue or going to the bathroom to spit. If a pupil uses inappropriate language, it may be possible to teach them an alternative but similar-sounding word or phrase to use instead. Be aware that symptoms may fluctuate and change over time, so plans need reviewing regularly and adjusting to meet the pupil's current needs.

---

**Case study:**

Terry was in Year 5 and had a diagnosis of TS and ADHD. At the end of break time, he kept pushing people in the line. He would only line up next to one female pupil and would rub the end of her plait on his face and repeatedly shout 'fish fingers'.

*What strategies would you suggest to support Terry at the end of break times?*

Terry was given the job of collecting all the equipment up at the end of break time. He then needed to take the box to the PE cupboard next to his classroom. This gave him some 'heavy work' at the end of break time, as well as a job to do so he could avoid lining up. He also was given some embroidery threads, plaited together, and tied at either end, to use instead of rubbing the girl's hair on his face. The shouting out was completely ignored (and pupils were asked to ignore this too).

---

■ Symptoms often appear, to others, as if they are within the pupil's control. However, the most essential step towards acceptance is understanding vocal and motor tics as being completely involuntary, then reasonable and supportive adjustments can be made. Adults need to model an accepting and understanding attitude towards tics. 'It is first and foremost your understanding of and secondly your attitude towards vocal tics that will make or break your success of having a child in your class with TS … You can escalate or deescalate a situation simply by your reaction to it. You can allow a child to thrive and be accepted or you can role model for the other students that being different is indeed not to be tolerated. What will you do?' (Conners, 2012).

■ Where possible, ignore tics to avoid drawing attention to them and never ask a pupil to stop ticcing. 'Ignoring tics can help someone with TS feel comfortable, as this avoids drawing any unnecessary attention towards them … you might feel the need to talk to a person about a particular tic if it seems to be causing them distress or harm. This is OK to do, as long as it is done in a sensitive way. This is very different to highlighting a tic for no apparent reason or asking a person to simply stop' (Tourettes Action, 2017). Ask the pupil what will support them to feel comfortable.

■ Ensure a consistent approach from all staff. A pupil profile is helpful to highlight strengths and strategies (see 'tool kit').

■ Encourage positive behaviours by stating the expected behaviour rather than drawing attention to the negative behaviours. Reframe language into positives. Avoid 'don't' and 'no', where possible (and safe); for example, 'don't wander around the room' becomes 'sit down in your seat'.

■ Reduce stress and anxiety, which tends to exacerbate symptoms. Identify triggers and support pupils to manage these and make them less stressful (see the 'Anxiety' chapter). Be proactive and plan for times that the pupil finds difficult. For example, during assemblies encourage the pupil to sit at the end of the row, near a key adult and an exit, so they can leave as necessary, or take a fiddle tool or ear defenders. If a pupil struggles at transition times, they may be more successful at the front or end of the line or given a job to do. They may fare better by avoiding busy corridors and the dining hall and accessing them at quieter times.

■ Catch pupils being good and praise small steps towards success. Provide specific praise for effort, attitude and behaviours for learning rather than correct answers, completed work or neat presentation. Aim for ten positive comments for each perceived negative.

■ Use 'when–then' commands (Chowdhury, 2004 p.83) such as '*when* you have put your books away, *then* you can play with your play dough'.

■ Due to the uncontrollable nature of the tics, increase feelings of control for pupils in other areas by offering (limited) positive choices, where possible; for example, 'Where are you going to work today? Next to me, at your work station or with your group? You choose.' Or 'What are you going to use to do your writing task, your favourite handwriting pencil, my special pen or the laptop?'

## Teaching and learning

- Practical, hands-on tasks are often effective. Where possible, include a multi-sensory element to lessons, such as a phonic or number treasure hunt, matching a sentence, topic word or number sentence with someone else in the room or activities which involve movement and concrete items to hold and explore.
- Pupils with TS often have sensory processing difficulties which can make tics worse and increase anxiety. Be aware of sensory sensitivities and support the pupil by exploring preferences. Provide regular movement and sensory breaks in the form of heavy jobs (watering the plants, pushing the lunch trolley or taking a message to another room) to give proprioceptive and vestibular input (see the 'Sensory Processing Disorder (SPD)' and 'Self-regulation' chapters).
- Writing can often be difficult and uncomfortable and even painful. Alleviate anxieties and pressure over written tasks by reducing the amount of writing and offering alternative means of recording, at times by providing a scribe, dictation software or typing. Reduce the number of questions or offer more time to complete tasks.
- Be aware that copying (from the board or paper) can be time-consuming, challenging and even painful for a pupil with TS. Limit this and avoid where possible. Instead, give printed notes to annotate or highlight. Print or scribe dates, learning objectives and questions, so that the pupil can focus their energy and time on the learning task rather than copying text.
- Teach and model self-regulation (see the 'Self-regulation' chapter).
- Provide fiddle tools or a doodle pad or provide the pupil with a copy of the notes to annotate and highlight whilst sitting and listening.
- Pupils with TS often find transitions and changes to routine difficult to manage, leading to increased tics and anxiety. Forewarn of change and transitions and provide visual supports, such as timers and a *Now and Then* board (see p.15). Pupils will need an enhanced transition plan when changing year group, adult and particularly when moving school.

- Pupils with TS often find homework very difficult. Caregivers have reported outbursts of aggression at home after school and pupils often need calming time and physical activities. An increase in motor tics often makes homework more difficult and time-consuming. Some pupils may take an excessive amount of time to complete an assignment, feeling compelled to make it perfect (Robertson & Baron-Cohen, 1998, p.73). Make reasonable adjustments around homework and, where possible, set practical, hands-on learning tasks, or reduce writing by giving cloze procedures or allow typing or an adult to scribe. Reduce the amount of work expected and break it down into achievable chunks (Chowdhury, 2004). Avoid copying homework tasks from the board and email instructions, post them on a virtual platform or write in their diary for them.

## *Environmental considerations*

- Provide pupils with an exit strategy, such as a legitimate break outside of the classroom (for example, running an errand) or an exit card to leave when needed. Provide a safe, private space out of the classroom to access if they need to release tics or if they feel anxious or overwhelmed. Ensure that this is seen as a supportive measure (not used as a sanction). Avoid suggesting or demanding that the pupil leaves the room, as this can increase anxiety.
- Plan the seating carefully. Pupils may need to be near an exit if they feel overwhelmed or need to leave the room. Alternatively, they may prefer to sit at the back or side of the class to minimise drawing attention. Some pupils may need more space around them. 'Allow larger "personal space" if student has touching tics or large motor tics involving limbs. Let the student work in the position that he/she feels comfortable with' (GOSH NHS Foundation Trust, 2016). Discuss with the pupil where in the classroom feels the most comfortable and supportive, and be flexible, as the pupil's needs may change over time. Offer movement whilst working, such as standing, sitting or lying with a clipboard. Place a resistance band on the chair legs, or use a wobble cushion at times.
- The choice of a quiet work station with minimal distractions may be a supportive choice at times.
- Implement reasonable adjustments around tests and exams. Test pupils in a separate room to avoid increased anxiety around tics and apply for extra time for exams.

**Case study:**

Cora was a Year 8 pupil with a diagnosis of TS. She was coughing excessively in school and through her attempts to hide her tics she developed a persistent, very sore throat. She also flicked her arms out to the side periodically and bounced her legs. Cora was feeling very self-conscious, which made her tics worse and she started to avoid lessons.

*What could staff do to support Cora?*

School sought advice from outside agencies and staff had a training session on TS. Following this, key staff worked with Cora and her parents, discussing the strategies they all thought would best support her. They all agreed on strategies which staff would consistently apply. Regular movement breaks were incorporated into every lesson for the whole class. It was agreed that Cora would be allowed to leave the classroom to release her tics if required. She was given an exit card (she chose to have a photo of her dog on this, as she felt it would calm her). She was given a safe space with a trusted adult (she chose the Deputy Head's office, as she had a positive relationship with him). If the Deputy Head was busy, Cora would leave a 'calling card' and he would check in with her later. When he was busy, she was permitted to go for a five-minute walk around the building or courtyard. She rehearsed the strategy with the Deputy Head, every day, until she felt confident.

Staff talked to all the Year 8 pupils about TS and Cora, although not confident to stand up in assembly and present to her peers, produced a video about what she found difficult in school and how this made her feel. She also talked about what she liked doing and what she was good at, and finished by playing a short piece on her flute, having just passed her Grade 5 exam. Her peers were encouraged to ask her questions and state positive comments about Cora or could write these down, if preferred. Cora reported feeling more confident and her peers felt that they knew and understood her more. Staff had more empathy for Cora and were better attuned to her needs.

## Unstructured times

■ Unstructured times can cause anxiety. Ensure a key adult's support to help with making and maintaining positive friendships,

teaching structured games and turn-taking and be a point of contact at break times.
■ Provide access to a safe space and quieter zones or areas to avoid feeling overwhelmed. Offer clubs and activities of interest as an alternative to a busy playground.

## *Rewards and consequences*

■ 'Neither rewards nor punishment will enable a student to control tics' (Toghill, 2020). Tics are involuntary. Do not sanction pupils for an action that they have no control over. 'This may negatively impact the student psychologically and socially. Moreover, drawing attention to the tics and the tension this may create, has the potential to increase the tics and other related behaviors' (Deibler, 2020).
■ Rather than imposing sanctions, teach self-regulation and offer exit strategies.
■ Rewards and praise are more effective when they are immediate. Reward for things the pupil has control over, such as good manners, being kind, effort to a task, contribution to lessons, or engagement in learning. Never reward or praise for tic suppression.

# Resources, further information and 'tool kits'

## *Books*

*Can I Tell You about Tourette Syndrome? A Guide for Friends, Family and Professionals* by Mal Leicester
*Welcome to Biscuit Land: A Year in the Life of Tourettes Hero* by Jess Thom
*Why Do You Do That? A Book about Tourette Syndrome for Children and Young People* by Uttom Chowdhury, Mary Robertson and Liz Whallett
*Tics and Tourette Syndrome: A Handbook for Parents and Professionals* by Uttom Chowdhury

## *Websites*

https://www.gosh.nhs.uk/medical-information/search-medical-conditions/tourette-syndrome/tourette-syndrome-information-pack Resources for families and young people
https://movementdisorders.ufhealth.org/category/treatment/tourette-updates/ Links to stories and updates

https://www.tourettes-action.org.uk/62-teachers.html A whole host of invaluable advice, information, resources, facts sheets, links to presentations and webinars

https://www.tourettes-action.org.uk/storage/downloads/1399472453_TS-Passport-Final.pdf Useful example of a pupil passport

https://www.tourettes-action.org.uk/storage/downloads/1598276310_TS-Social-Story-A4-v4.pdf Social story about TS

https://tourette.org/about-us/diversity-inclusion/ Videos and stories from people with TS

https://tourette.org/about-tourette/overview/living-tourette-syndrome/children-with-tourette-0-12/ Tourette Association of America, links to information, advice and resources

## Podcasts

https://www.nccd.edu.au/professional-learning/classroom-adjustments-tourette-syndrome

https://soundcloud.com/user-664361280/education-and-educating-about-tourettes-lucy-toghill-in-conversation-tourettes-syndrome-ep-3

# References

Ball, C. & Box, H. (Eds) (2008) *Education Issues and Tourette Syndrome – an Introduction for Parents & Schools* [online] Tourettes Action. Available at: https://www.tourettes-action.org.uk/5.6-Education-Issues-and-Tourette-Syndrome [Accessed 1 February 2017]

CDC (Centers for Disease Control and Prevention) (undated) *Five Things You May Not Know About Tourette Syndrome* [online] Available at: https://www.cdc.gov/ncbddd/tourette/features/tourette-five-things.html#:~:text=%232%20Just%20having%20a%20tic,is%20more%20to%20the%20story [Accessed 26 April 2021]

Chowdhury, U. (2004) *Tics and Tourette Syndrome: A Handbook for Parents and Professionals* Jessica Kingsley Publishers, London

Conners, S. (2012) *Understanding and Dealing with Vocal Tics in the Classroom* [online] Tourette Syndrome Association of Greater New York State, 4 February. Available at: http://tsa-gnys.org/understanding-and-dealing-with-vocal-tics-in-the-classroom/ [Accessed 5 January 2017]

Deibler, M. (2020) *Creating a Supportive Learning Environment for Students with Tourette Syndrome and Related Disorders* [online] NJCTS. Available at: https://njcts.org/resources/supportive-learning-environment/ [Accessed 2 February 2021]

GOSH NHS Foundation Trust (2016) *Information for Teachers: Tourette syndrome and managing tics in the classroom* [online] Available at: https://media.gosh.nhs.uk/documents/Tourette_and_managing_tics_F0798_A4_bw_FINAL_Oct16_1.pdf [Accessed 3 February 2021]

Leicester, M. (2014) *Can I Tell You about Tourette Syndrome? A Guide for Friends, Family and Professionals* Jessica Kingsley Publishers, London

Matthews, P. (2020) *Tourettes Action Factsheet: Executive Functioning* [online] Available at: https://www.tourettes-action.org.uk/storage/downloads/160 5794292_Factsheet—-Executive-Funtioning.pdf [Accessed 29 January 2021]

Roberson, M. & Baron-Cohen, S. (1998) *Tourette Syndrome: The Facts* Oxford University Press, New York

Simpson, H. (2020) *Strengths of Tourette Syndrome* [online] Available at: https:// movementdisorders.ufhealth.org/2020/01/31/strengths-of-tourette-syndrome/ [Accessed 1 February 2021]

Toghill, L. (2020) *Key Facts for Teachers* [online] Tourettes Action. Available at: https://www.tourettes-action.org.uk/storage/downloads/1583409432_ tourettes-action-key-facts-for-teachers_Feb2020.pdf [Accessed 29 January 2021]

Tourettes Action (2017) *What Makes Us Tic* [online] Available at: https://www. tourettes-action.org.uk/storage/downloads/1499766563_TA-What-Makes-Us-Tic-Brochure-2017.pdf [Accessed 28 January 2021]

Tourettes Action (undated) *Co-occurring Features and Conditions* [online] Available at: https://www.tourettes-action.org.uk/74-managing-ts—associat ed-conditions.html [Accessed 20 July 2021]

## Checklist to support pupils with Tourette Syndrome

| STRATEGY | COMMENTS |
|---|---|
| **A strength-based approach** | |
| Reframe language to focus on and celebrate positives, strengths and successes | |
| Research successful people and positive role models with TS | |
| Encourage participation in clubs and extra-curricular activities | |
| **Relationships and communication** | |
| Educate staff and pupils about TS | |
| Positive relationship and collaborative approach with caregivers, pupil and outside agencies | |
| Regular positive communication between home and school | |
| Understand that tics are completely involuntary, model acceptance, empathy and understanding | |
| Ignore tics, where possible, and avoid drawing attention to them | |
| Consistent approach from all staff – use a pupil profile or similar | |
| State expected behaviour and focus on moving the pupil on | |
| Reduce anxiety, spot triggers and support pupils to manage and reduce these | |
| Catch pupil being good and praise small steps to success | |
| Use 'when–then' commands | |
| Increase feelings of control by offering positive choices | |
| **Teaching and learning** | |
| Practical, hands-on, multi-sensory tasks, where possible | |
| Regular movement and sensory breaks | |
| Alleviate pressure and anxiety over writing tasks | |
| Limit copying and avoid where possible | |
| Teach and model self-regulation strategies | |

| STRATEGY | COMMENTS |
|---|---|
| Provide fiddle tool | |
| Give warnings and support around change and transitions | |
| Reasonable adjustments around homework | |
| **Environmental considerations** | |
| Exit strategy and safe space | |
| Careful seating plan and offer movement whilst working | |
| Option of a quiet work station, at times | |
| Reasonable adjustments around exams and tests | |
| **Unstructured times** | |
| Key adult support | |
| Access to safe space | |
| **Rewards and consequences** | |
| Never sanction pupils for tics | |
| Teach self-regulation and offer exit strategies | |
| Immediate praise and rewards, never reward for tic suppression | |

# Appendices

# Example of step-by-step plan to support school attendance

| | _____'s step-by-step plan |
|---|---|
| **1** | Walk into school with (key adult's name), say hello to the office staff and walk out again<br>**Positive self-talk:** I can do this; the office staff are friendly<br>**Support:** (Key adult's name) will be with me |
| **2** | Walk into school with (key adult's name), play a game in a quiet place, walk out again<br>**Positive self-talk:** I can do this, I like playing in the quiet area<br>**Support:** (Key adult's name) will be with me |
| **3** | Walk into school with (key adult's name), do a fun activity of my choosing, walk out again<br>**Positive self-talk:** I can do this, the activity will be fun<br>**Support:** (Key adult's name) will be with me |
| **4** | Walk to my classroom with (key adult's name), say hello to my teacher, walk out again<br>**Positive self-talk:** I can do this, my teacher will be pleased to see me<br>**Support:** (Key adult's name) will be with me |
| **5** | Walk into my classroom with (key adult's name) and do a fun activity with my friend, walk out again<br>**Positive self-talk:** I can do this, I am looking forward to the fun activity<br>**Support:** (Key adult's name) will be with me |
| **6** | Engage in some work in my classroom, with (key adult's name)<br>**Positive self-talk:** I can do this, look how well I have done so far<br>**Support:** (Key adult's name) will be with me |
| ☆ | **Ultimate goal:** To enter the school with confidence<br>**Positive self-talk:** I can do this, I have done so well so far<br>**Support:** (Key adult's name) will be with me |

NB: Depending on the pupil, an appropriate reward may be added to each step. Only move on to the next step as the pupil becomes fully comfortable with the present one.

Based on the Stepladder Approach: https://raisingchildren.net.au/toddlers/health-daily-care/mental-health/anxiety-stepladder-approach

## Example of step-by-step plan to increase confidence talking in class

| | _____'s step-by-step plan |
|---|---|
| **1** | Say hello to the teacher as I enter the classroom<br>**Positive self-talk:** I can do this, it is just hello, and I practised at home, I might even smile |
| **2** | Ask the teacher a question when they come over<br>**Positive self-talk:** I can do this, I have planned the question in advance |
| **3** | Go up to the teacher and ask a question<br>**Positive self-talk:** I can do this, I have planned the question in advance |
| **4** | Answer a (pre-planned) question that the teacher asks me (1:1)<br>**Positive self-talk:** I can do this, I have planned the answer |
| **5** | Ask and answer a question in a small group<br>**Positive self-talk:** I can do this, I am getting much more confident |
| **6** | Answer a question in front of the class<br>**Positive self-talk:** I can do this, I have practised the question |
| ☆ | **Ultimate goal:** To present my work in front of the class<br>**Positive self-talk:** I have practised this in front of my family and know I can do it |

NB: Depending on the pupil, an appropriate reward may be added to each step. Only move on to the next step as the pupil becomes fully comfortable with the present one.

Based on the Stepladder Approach: https://raisingchildren.net.au/toddlers/health-daily-care/mental-health/anxiety-stepladder-approach

# Priority rating chart

**Name:**                                                                 **Date:**

| Prioritising behaviour – how important is it that this pupil …? | Priority rating | Comments and plan |
|---|---|---|
| Remains on a chair during lessons | | |
| Wears uniform | | |
| Does not damage property | | |
| Arrives at lessons on time | | |
| Does not hurt other people | | |
| Completes homework tasks | | |
| Completes all tasks in lessons | | |
| Does not hurt self | | |
| Answers when register is called | | |
| Enters lessons quietly | | |
| Joins in class-based group activities | | |
| Records all work in own handwriting | | |
| Feels positive in school and develops emotional wellbeing | | |
| Goes home feeling as calm and settled as possible | | |
| Takes coat/bag off in class | | |
| Sits in seat | | |

**Priority level:**

**High** = high priority at all times

**Medium** = highly desirable but not essential

**Low** = low priority – we need to work around this another way

Adapted from: Fidler, R. & Christie, P. (2019, pp.40–45) *Collaborative Approaches to Learning for Pupils with PDA* Jessica Kingsley Publishers, London

## ___'s Calm Down Scale

| Level | Person, place or thing | Makes me feel: | | I can: | | |
|---|---|---|---|---|---|---|
| **3** | | I am feeling out of control | | Go to my safe place | Squeeze a cushion | Have a drink |
| **2** | | I am getting stressed | | Go for a walk | Squeeze my calm toy | |
| **1** | | I feel calm and happy | | Carry on with my task | | |

Adapted from: Dunn Buron, K. & Curtis, M. (2012) *The Incredible 5-Point Scale – the Significantly Improved and Expanded Second Edition: Assisting Students in Understanding Social Interactions and Controlling Their Emotional Responses* AAPC Publishing

# _____'s Task Checklist

**Task:** To complete my English work

**Equipment Needed:** Pencil, English book and work, word mat, glue, pencil sharpener, playdough

**1** Paste LO and date in my book ☐

**2** Use sentence starter to complete sentence 1 in book ☐

**Quick movement break:** Sharpen 3 pencils ☐

**3** Complete sentence 2 in book ☐

**4** Label the picture ☐

**5** Check my work and show Mr Smith ☐

**Sensory Break:** Play dough (use 5-minute timer) ☐

# Task Checklist

| Task: | Equipment Needed: |
|-------|-------------------|

**1** ⬜

**2** ⬜

**Quick movement break:** ⬜

**3** ⬜

**4** ⬜

**5** ⬜

**Sensory Break:** ⬜

# Worry Box

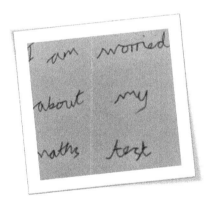

# Index

Page numbers in **bold** refer to tables and page numbers in *italics* refer to figures

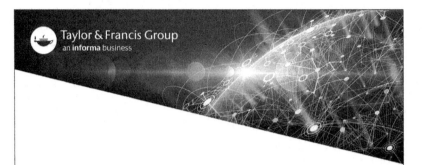

Printed in the United States
by Baker & Taylor Publisher Services